I0799844

IMAGES
of America

OSBORNE COUNTY KANSAS

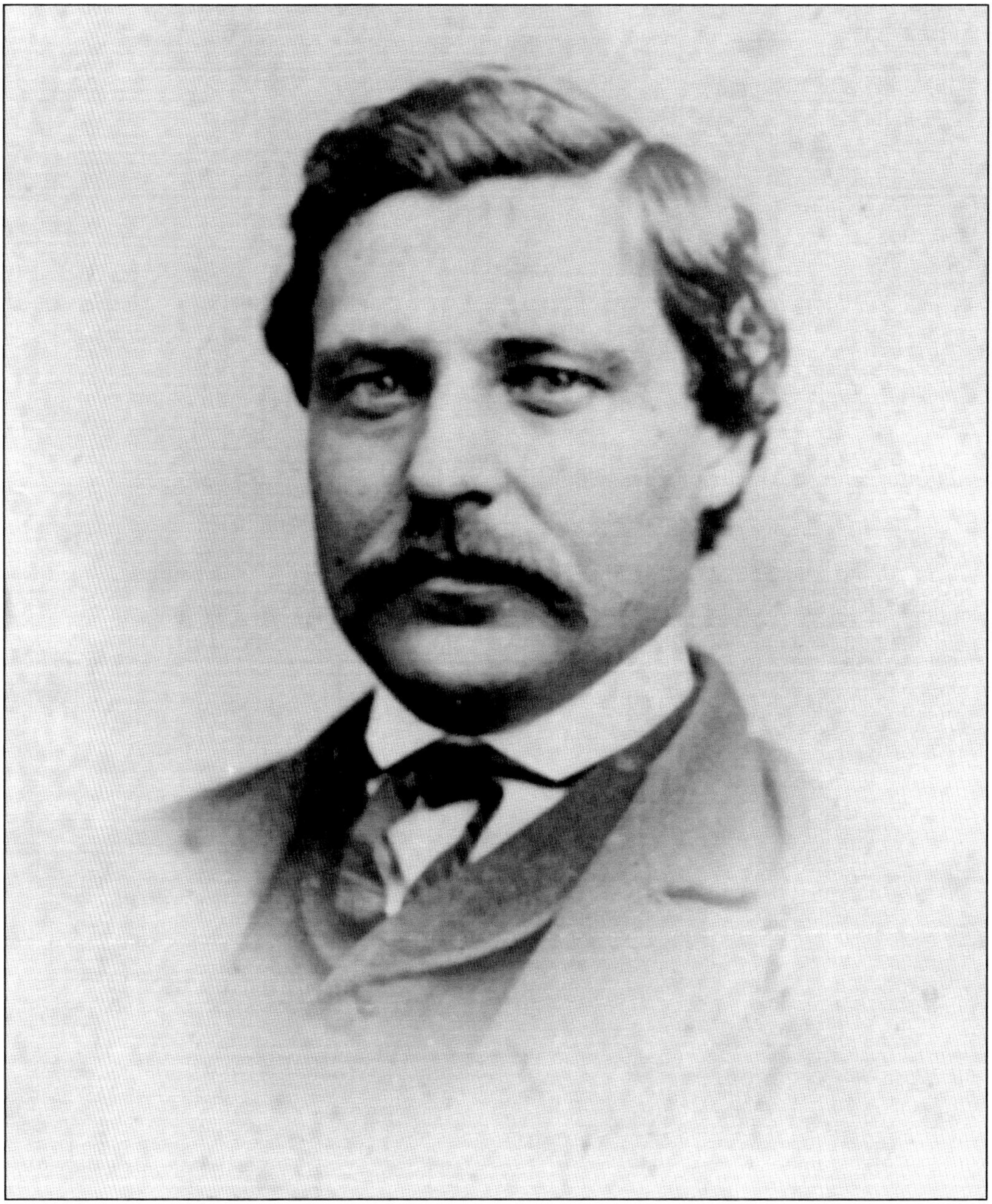

Pictured here is Vincent B. Osborne, for whom Osborne County was named. Osborne was born in Hampden County, Massachusetts, in 1839. With the start of the Civil War he enlisted in the Second Kansas Cavalry and served under Capt. Samuel Crawford. He was one of the soldiers who captured the notorious guerrilla leader William Quantrill. By war's end Osborne was a decorated veteran who had been wounded several times, even losing a leg in 1865 in Arkansas. When he was 27 years old he was appointed to a civilian position at Fort Harker in Ellsworth County, Kansas, by now-governor Crawford but soon resigned to live in the town of Ellsworth. There he became a justice of the peace and was elected Ellsworth County Probate Judge in 1873. Osborne died after a short illness on December 1, 1879, at the age of 40 years. He never set foot in the county named for him.

IMAGES
of America

OSBORNE COUNTY KANSAS

Von Rothenberger

ARCADIA PUBLISHING

ISBN 978-0-7385-0164-2

Published by Arcadia Publishing

Printed in the United States of America

Library of Congress Catalog Card Number: 99-63438

For all general information contact Arcadia Publishing at:
Telephone 843-853-2070
Fax 843-853-0044
E-mail arcadia@charleston.net
For customer service and orders:
Toll-Free 1-888-313-BOOK

Visit us on the Internet at www.arcadpublishing.com

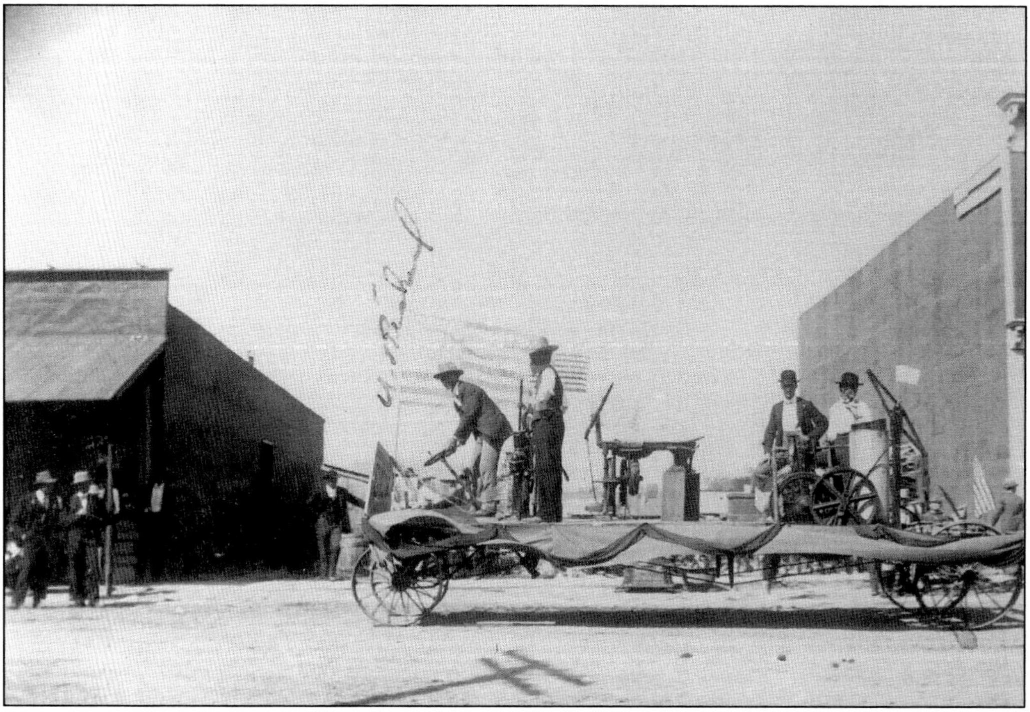

What is considered to be the first self-driving vehicle ever built in Kansas is shown here cruising down South First Street in Osborne, possibly on July 4, 1887. Holding the wheel is 17-year-old Richard Ruth Jr., and behind him stands the vehicle's inventor, local blacksmith Frank Hatch. A four-cylinder vapor engine propelled it, together with some parts of a still lying around the smithy and a spare wagon. During the spring and summer of 1887 Hatch drove his creation through the streets of Osborne and the surrounding countryside, scaring people and animals alike before dismantling it.

Contents

ACKNOWLEDGMENTS

Over the years a large number of people have worked hard to gather and preserve the history of Osborne County through both documents and photographs. We are all indebted to them for their hard work and sacrifice that has so often gone unnoticed. Several of them have contributed information to this book and to them I express my gratitude for their belief and patience in this project.

While space does not allow for the exact notation of each picture's origin, the following is a list of the people and institutions whose photographs appear in this book: Kenneth Bartholomew, Alton; Janet Brooks, Portis; Doug Brush, Downs; Bill Cady, Osborne; Velma Cone, Portis; Carla Davis, Portis; Irene Fisk, Osborne; Karen Foster, Bloomington; the Natoma Publishing Company, Natoma; Jan Paquoette, Downs; Deanna Roach, Alton; Delana Rothenberger, Osborne; and Beth Sharp, Downs. Special thanks must go to both the members of the Downs Historical Society and to the librarians at the Osborne Public Library. Most of the photographs shown here came from the pictorial collections of these two institutions and without access to their resources I could not have composed this book. A final thanks should go to David Readio for scanning and sorting the historical images on computer, thus making the photographic selection and organization far easier than if I had done the job alone.

INTRODUCTION

The 191 photographs presented in this book are intended to give a general pictorial overview of what the past was like in the region of Kansas known as Osborne County. They cover the crucial 70 years between 1876 and 1946 that shaped and defined the county, showing old street scenes, businesses, special buildings, bands, homes, and the people as they looked, played, prayed, learned, and worked both in the city and on the farm during those times. Descriptive captions have been added to each photographic scene in order to help understand and to give historical meaning to the images.

This book is not intended to give a complete detailed history of Osborne County but rather to present visual scenes that will often instruct the reader on the county's history far better than a thousand pages of text could hope to convey. History presented in this form has the added advantage of saving a bit of the past to endlessly teach those later generations, as a book is more likely to be kept and taken care of for many years to come.

A book like this one is timely in that as we now near the end of the twentieth century we are inclined to look back on those distant times presented here and ask ourselves how they have affected us in the present day. Viewing the changing styles of dress, architecture, and transportation that these images have captured forever helps us to understand how far we have progressed and yet how much we are still the same after all these years. *To know where you are going you must know where you have been* is an old proverb one should keep in mind while reading this book, for in understanding our past we can better serve ourselves in understanding how to shape our future for the betterment of everyone.

While perusing this book the reader may find difficulty in keeping track of the change in town names over the years. And along with that change the city of Osborne also added another in 1917 when it renamed all of its streets. Therefore several of the photographs were taken when Penn Street (now Main Street), East Street (now First), Arch Street (now Second), and South Street (now New Hampshire) were the names known. The captions have tried to explain this discrepancy and where possible all street names are given by the modern term.

As the state of Kansas grew after achieving statehood in 1861 the white man began to move into the area along the tributaries of the Solomon and Saline Rivers in north-central Kansas. For generations this portion of the Great Plains had been a prime hunting ground for various Indian tribes—the Pawnee, Cheyenne, Sioux—and also later for those Indian tribes moved onto reservations in eastern Kansas—the Delaware, Pottawatomie, Kickapoo, Omaha, and many more. The first recorded movements of the white man into this area in the 1860s are those of hunters seeking buffalo. More often than not their expeditions would end in altercations with bands of Native Americans. But the frontier between Indian-held and white-held territory moved swiftly west, and in 1866 the governor of Kansas ordered this area to be surveyed and divided into counties. Osborne County was formally declared a political entity in 1867 but it was not until June 1871 that the county was officially organized. Native Americans staged a last raid into the county in 1870 and then moved west, surrendering the area to the white man.

The nearly 900 square miles of Osborne County encompasses portions of the valleys of the North and South Forks of the Solomon River in the north, and several of the tributaries of the Saline River in the south, the principal one being Paradise Creek. It is a region dominated by the Blue Hills, by farms and ranches, and remains true to the agricultural roots laid down by the early white settlers, with small intrusions by primarily agricultural-based industries.

The people who settled the county were from every imaginable country and religion and this is often reflected in the images found in the book. The first town in the county was Bull City, known today as Alton and founded in the fall of 1870. In 1871 others swiftly followed—Osborne City, Arlington, and Bethany, known today as Portis. The next year saw Tilden, or what is now Bloomington, arise, and in 1879 Downs was started as a railroad division point. In 1880 Covert was established and in 1888 Cressen, now Natoma, was settled. In the early 1900s an attempt to promote the town of Academy failed. Osborne City, now known as Osborne, was named the permanent county seat in 1872 to the demise of Arlington, which then became the county's first ghost town. The county's population grew from just 33 in 1870 to over 12,000 by 1880, with the figure peaking in 1910 and slowly descending since.

The appearance of the county's first railroad in 1879 finalized the end of the frontier period. Into the next century the appearance of state and federal highways also marked the end of the old days and the start of what is considered the modern era in the county.

Hopefully this book will serve to introduce the early history of Osborne County to readers and as a convenient primary reference source for the twenty-first century. =

One

STREET SCENES

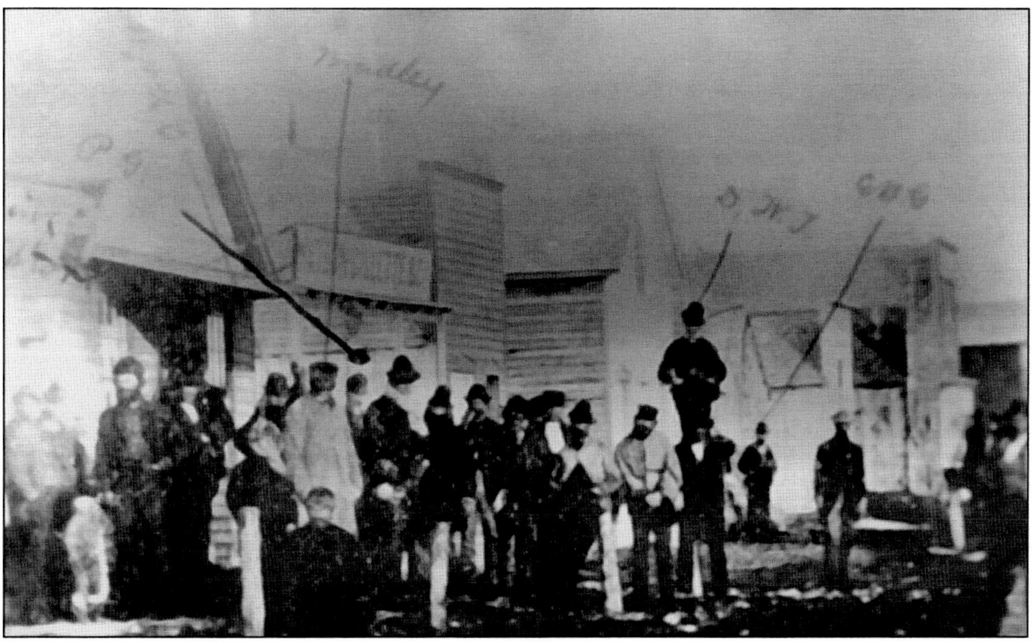

This 1876 photograph by an unknown photographer is believed to be the first of Osborne ever taken. The view is of the north side of downtown along West Main Street in front of the Watson, Gillette & Company store located center left. The names and initials given for members of the whiskered crowd, from left to right, are as follows: P.G., unknown, A. Nolan, Mr. Bradley, D.W.T. (David W. Tindal), and E.B.G. (Edward B. Garrigues).

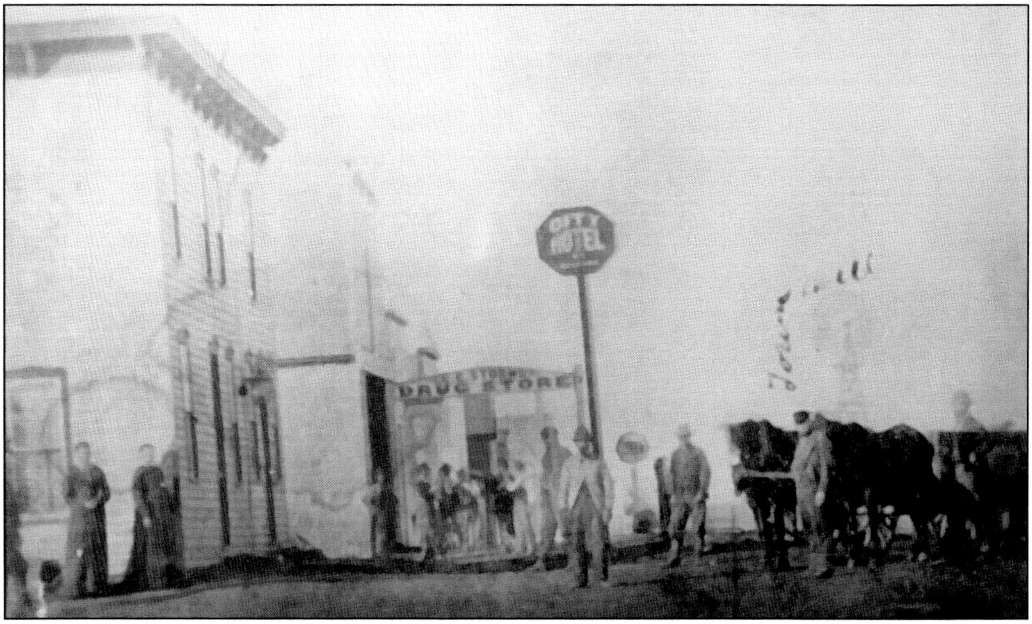

This picture looks west from the corner of First and Main Streets, along the south side of West Penn Street in Osborne in 1876. On the left is the City Hotel, operated by Emanuel Keever. Behind are signs for C.C. Storm's Drug Store and the Solomon Valley House Hostelry. On the right can be seen the Eclipse Windmill, the town's well in the 1870s.

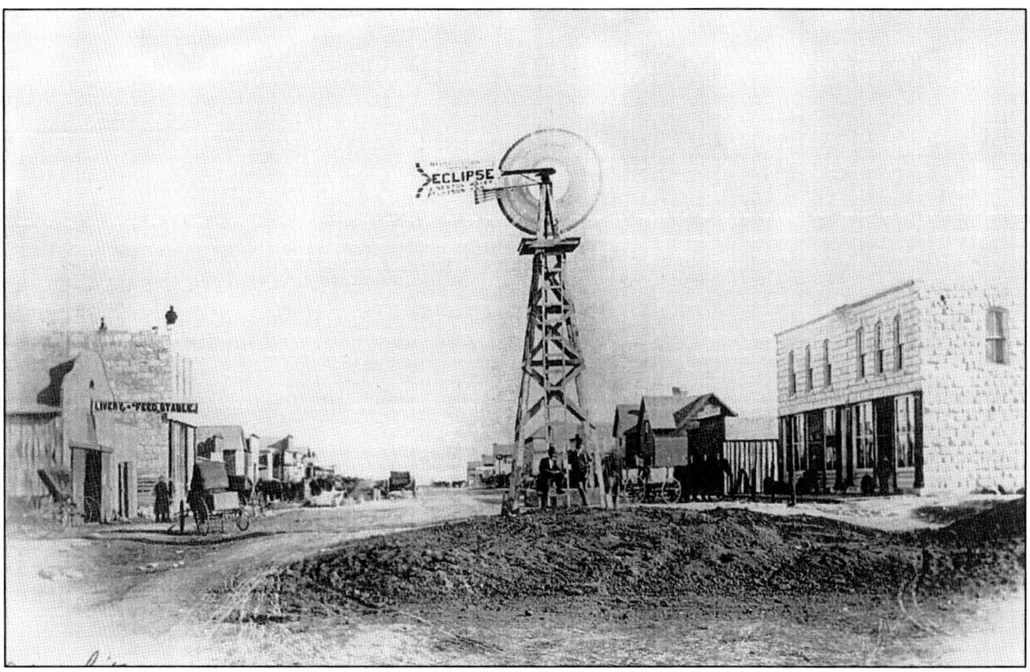

This 1878 photograph by Kleckner and Perkins shows Penn Street in Osborne, looking east. At center is the Eclipse Windmill, the town well, at the intersection of Second and Main Streets. The Harvey & Fargo Livery and Feed Stable is at the extreme left with the Watson, Gillette & Company store just behind. The windmill was removed later that year and the well filled in.

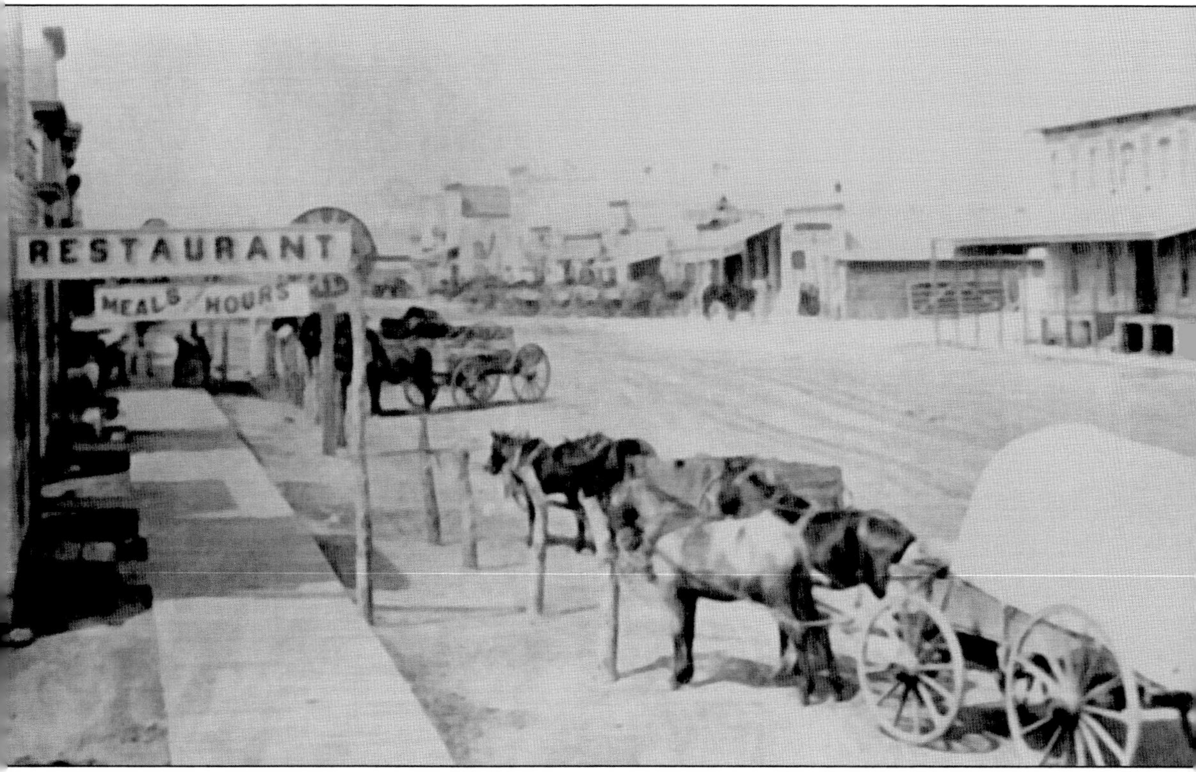

This 1878 photograph shows Main Street in Osborne looking to the west. Taken from the front door of the Kleckner and Perkins Photography Studio, the picture captures the city's frontier flavor of those early years. Notice the false fronts on the store buildings, the rough hitching posts, and the settler's wagon at the right. The Lipton House Hotel can be seen in the upper right. On the restaurant sign is the slogan "Meals At All Hours 25 Cents."

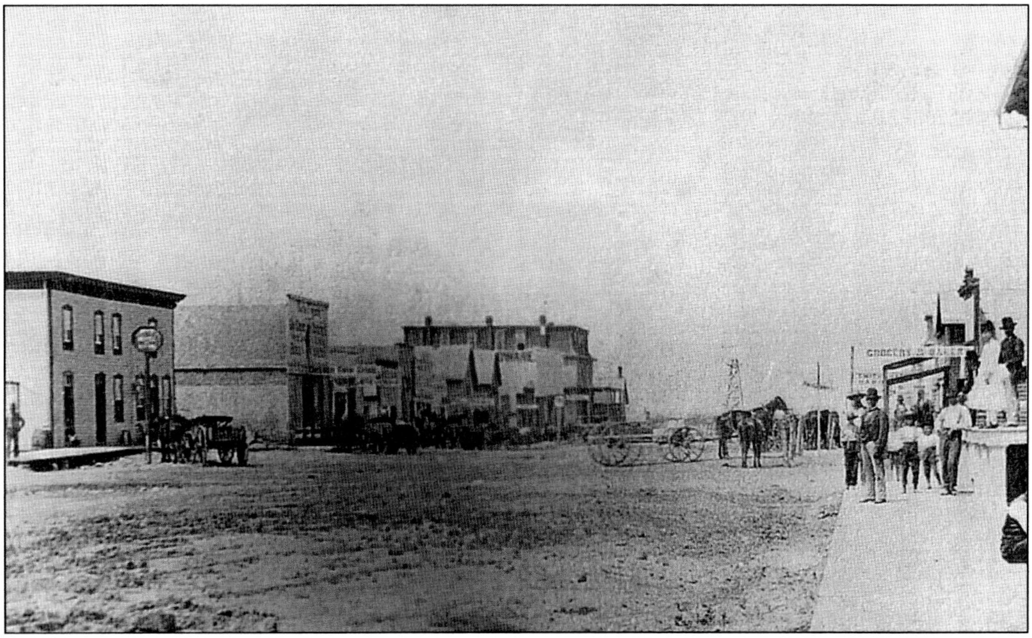

This 1879 photograph shows the south side of Main Street in Osborne looking west towards the Key West Hotel in the center background. On the extreme right is the Lipton Hotel, while in the right center background is the windmill over the town well. The sidewalks are wooden and greatly improved the business district, while the dirt street remained that way for another 30 years.

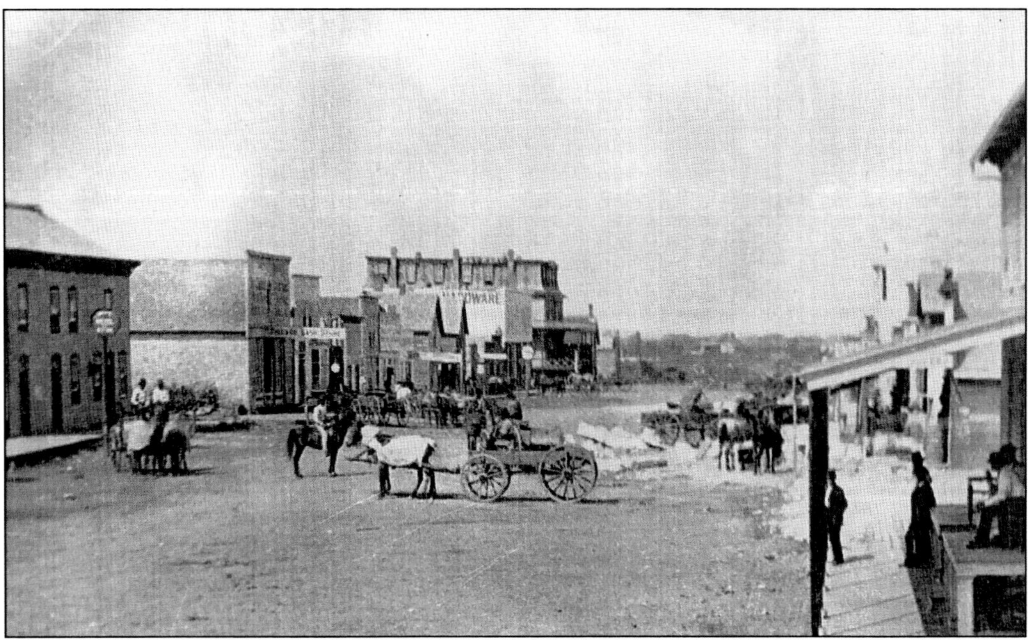

Here is another photograph of Main Street similar to the one shown above. But now the new porch of the Lipton House can be seen on the right, while in the distance the windmill is gone. The broken rock in the street is from the construction of a new building. On the left in both pictures is Emanuel Keever's City Hotel.

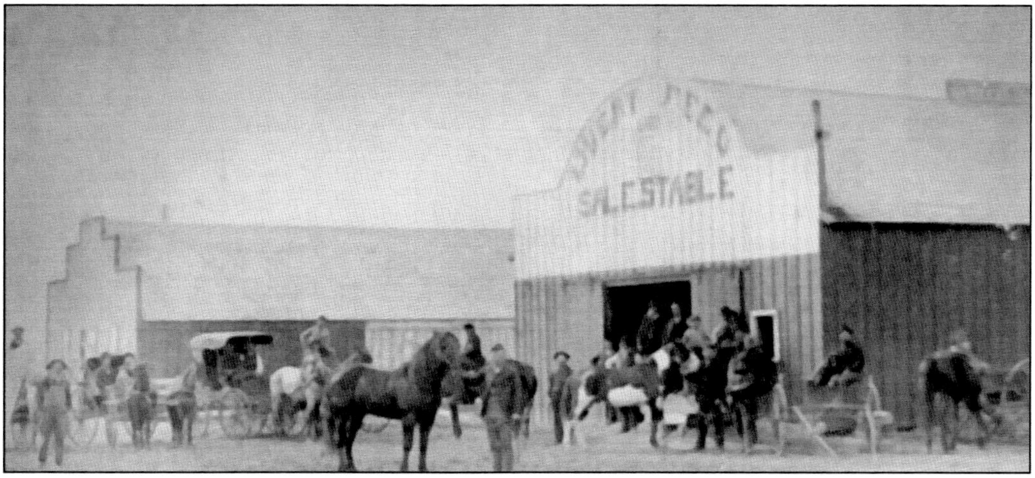

This 1887 photograph shows the Northway & Shaw Livery Barn on South Market Street in Portis. On the left is the Powell Brothers Lumberyard, the first such yard opened in the city. The two horses displayed for sale have drawn a large number of interested onlookers.

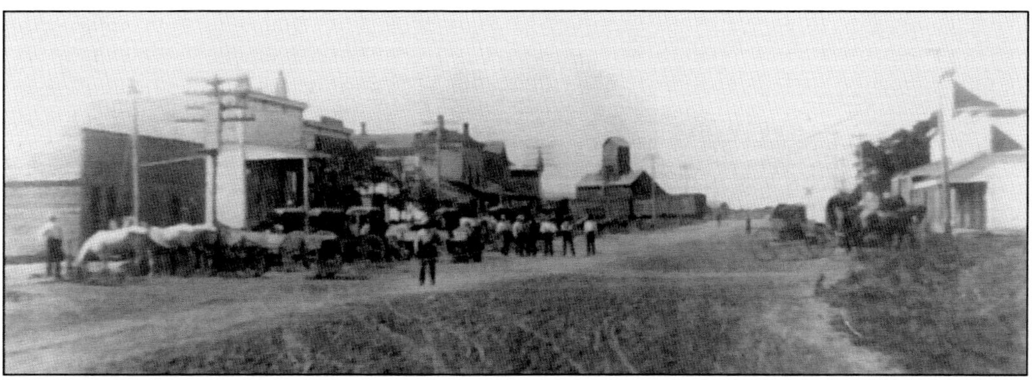

This view looks north along Market Street in Portis around 1900. This is a good representative view of how the business district appeared at the time. In the distance are railcars belonging to the Missouri Pacific Railroad. At first Portis was called Bethany until the railroad was built through it in 1879. The town was then platted and renamed for Thomas Portis, a railroad executive.

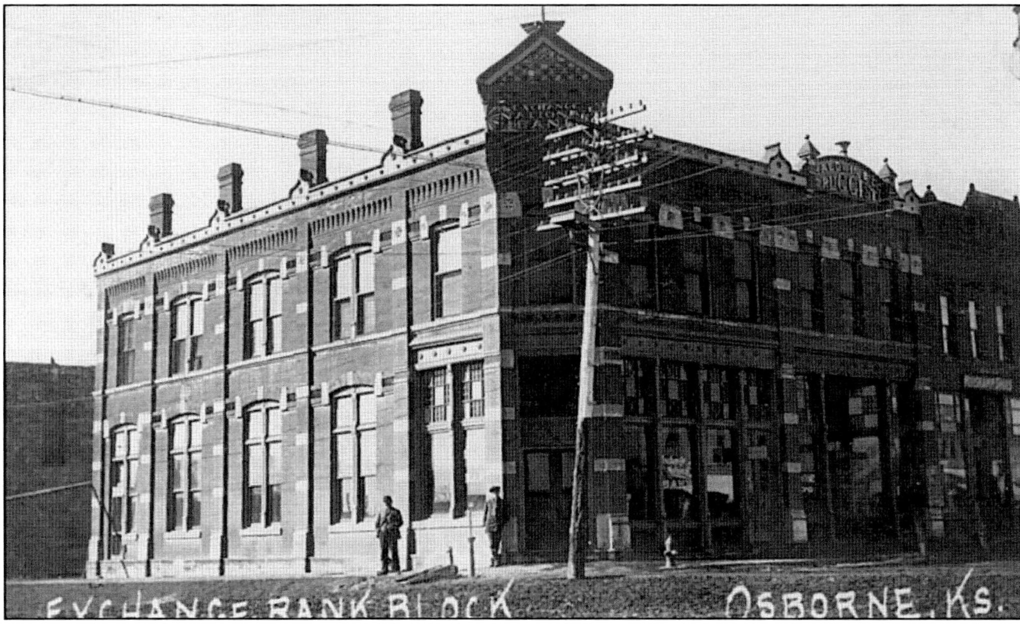

Taken about 1910, this photograph is of the Exchange National Bank block at the corner of First and Main Streets in Osborne with the Baldwin Drugstore on the right. The bank's east side and ornate brick and rock work is clearly shown here. The bare bulb that illuminated the intersection of First and Main Streets can be seen in the extreme upper right of the picture.

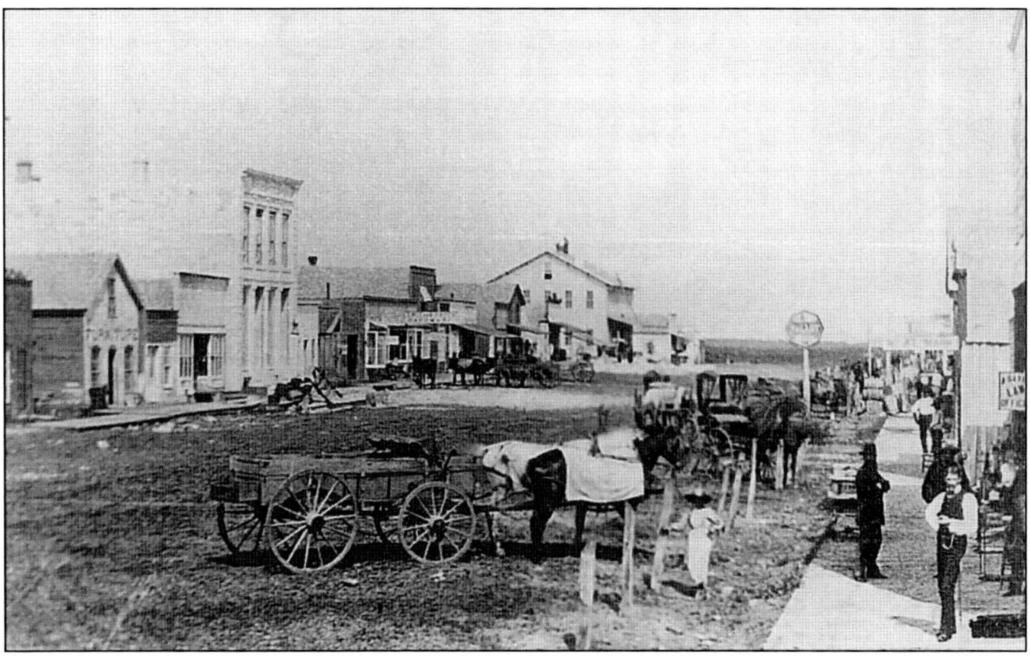

This photograph of Main Street in Osborne looks east from the Key West Hotel towards the Lipton House, which is in the center background. Another 1879 photograph by Moulton Kleckner, it shows the beginning of the transition in the city from the quickly erected, one-story frame buildings to more permanent two-story stone structures. Chan Baldwin, an early business leader, is seen standing in a vest to the right next to Albert Saxey's law office.

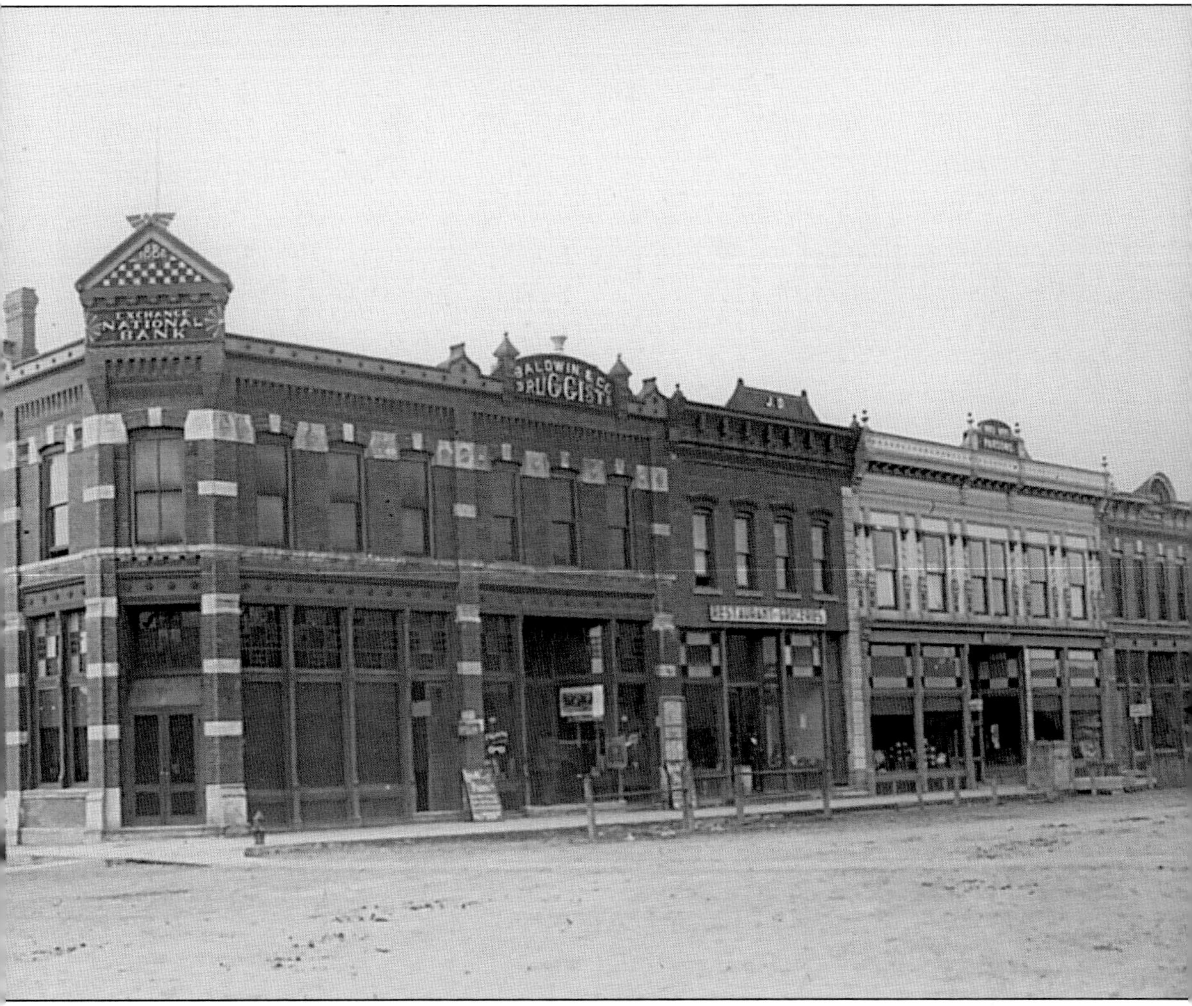

Taken in 1895 by photographer Charles W. Buell, this view shows the southwest corner of First and Main Streets in Osborne. The era's ornate brick fronts can be clearly seen on the Exchange National Bank, Chan Baldwin's Drugstore, and the Parsons Mercantile Company, all of which were important early businesses. Baldwin was Osborne's first pharmacist when he opened his store in 1874. The store trades currently as Ridgway Drug.

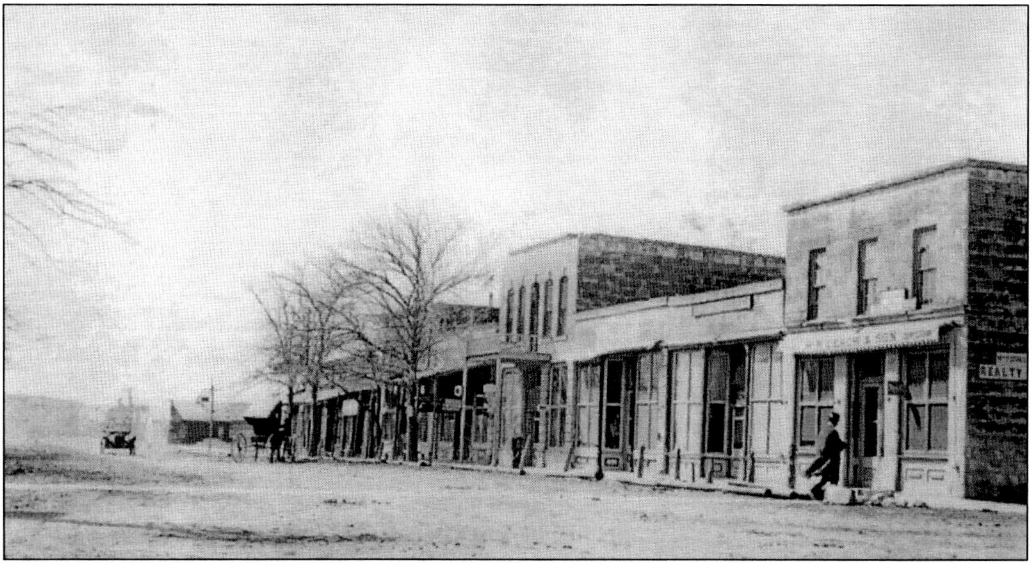

This 1905 photograph looks south along the west side of Mill Street from its intersection with Nicholas Avenue. On the left is a car and a buggy with the Alton Bluffs in the far distance. On the right is the H.B. Leach & Son Drugstore with Will Forman's real estate firm on the second floor. Homer Leach bought the drugstore in 1887 and operated it until 1921.

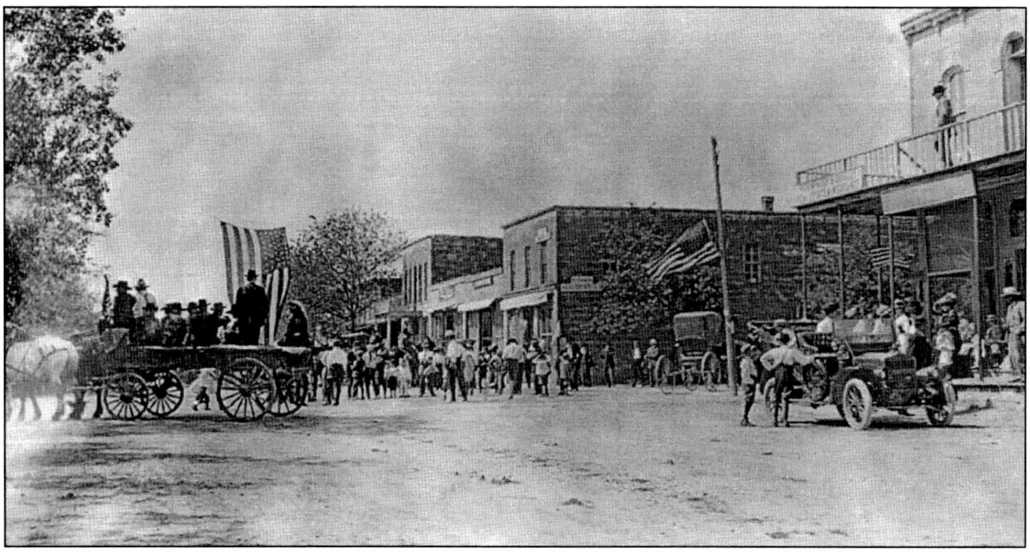

Pictured here is the view to the south of the crowd awaiting the Decoration Day festivities at the intersection of Mill Street and Nicholas Avenue in Alton around 1910. On the right is the Stephenson Store with the Pickinpaugh & Quigley Real Estate Insurance on the top floor. In the center background is the H.B. Leach & Son Drugstore.

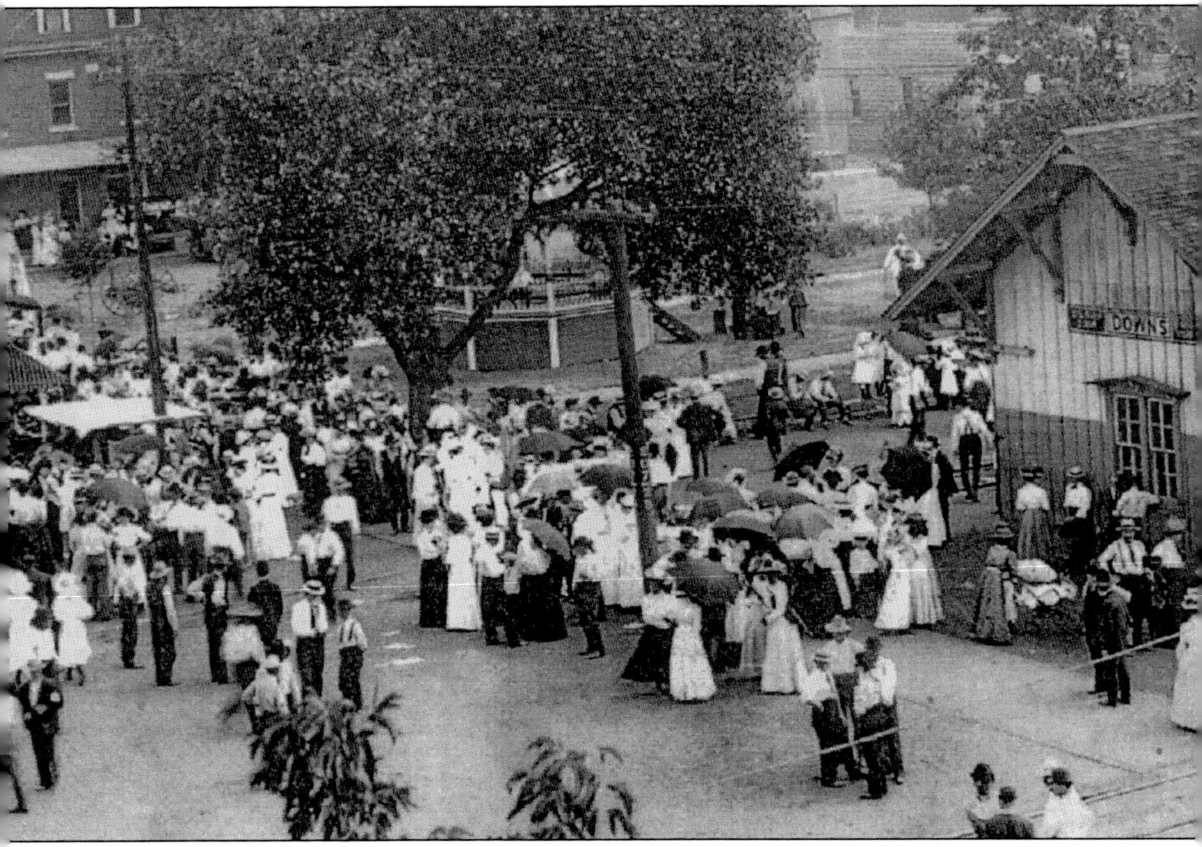

This early 1900s photograph shows a crowd of celebrants that one of the Missouri Pacific Railroad's special Downs Celebration trains has just deposited in Railroad Park on Morgan Avenue in Downs. In the upper left background, food tents can be seen as well as part of the Lipton Hotel. Under the trees at top center, city band members mill about the gazebo while to the right stands the Missouri Pacific depot, later destroyed by fire in 1916. Commemorating the town's birth in 1879, the Celebration once drew thousands of people for the annual event, which continues today.

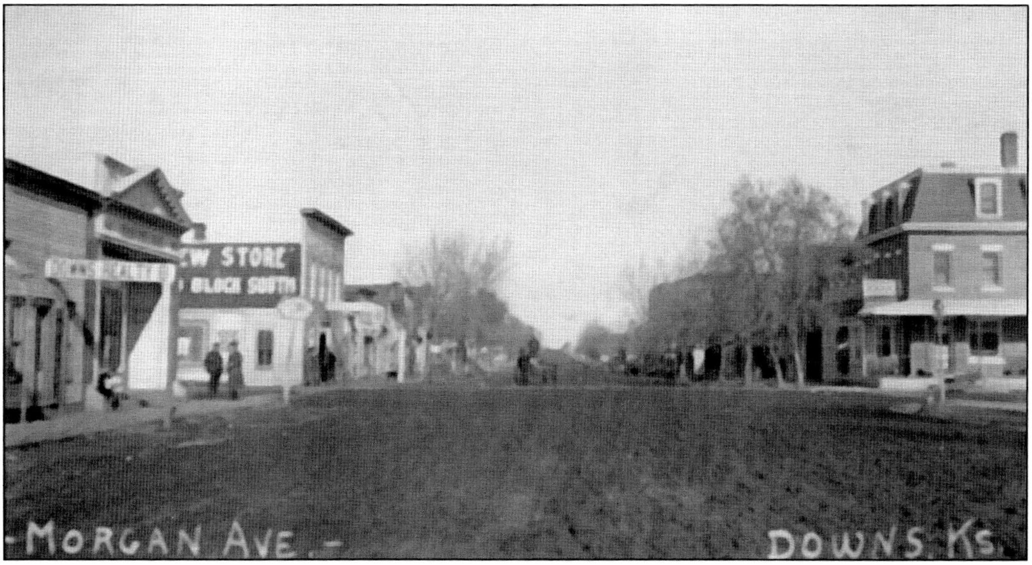

Taken in 1907 this view looks north from the Missouri Pacific Railroad tracks toward the corner of Railroad Street and Morgan Avenue in Downs. The Union State Bank is on the left next to the Downs Realty Company. Across the street to the right is the Lipton Hotel.

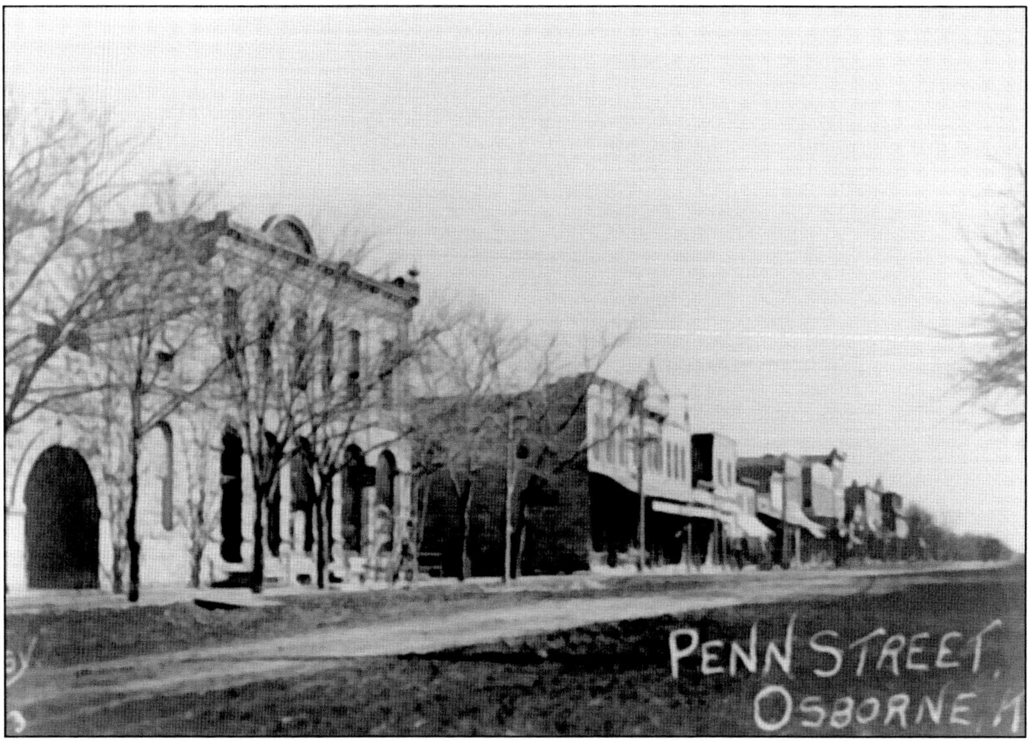

This 1908 photograph looks east along the north side of Penn Street in Osborne. At the extreme left is the Cunningham Auditorium, which was built in 1903 of native stone and seated 1,000 people. The building also housed Max Koesling's motor company and Stewart Lightle's car repair shop. In 1959 it was torn down. Notice the light bulb that illuminated the street corner at center right. In 1917 Penn Street was renamed Main Street.

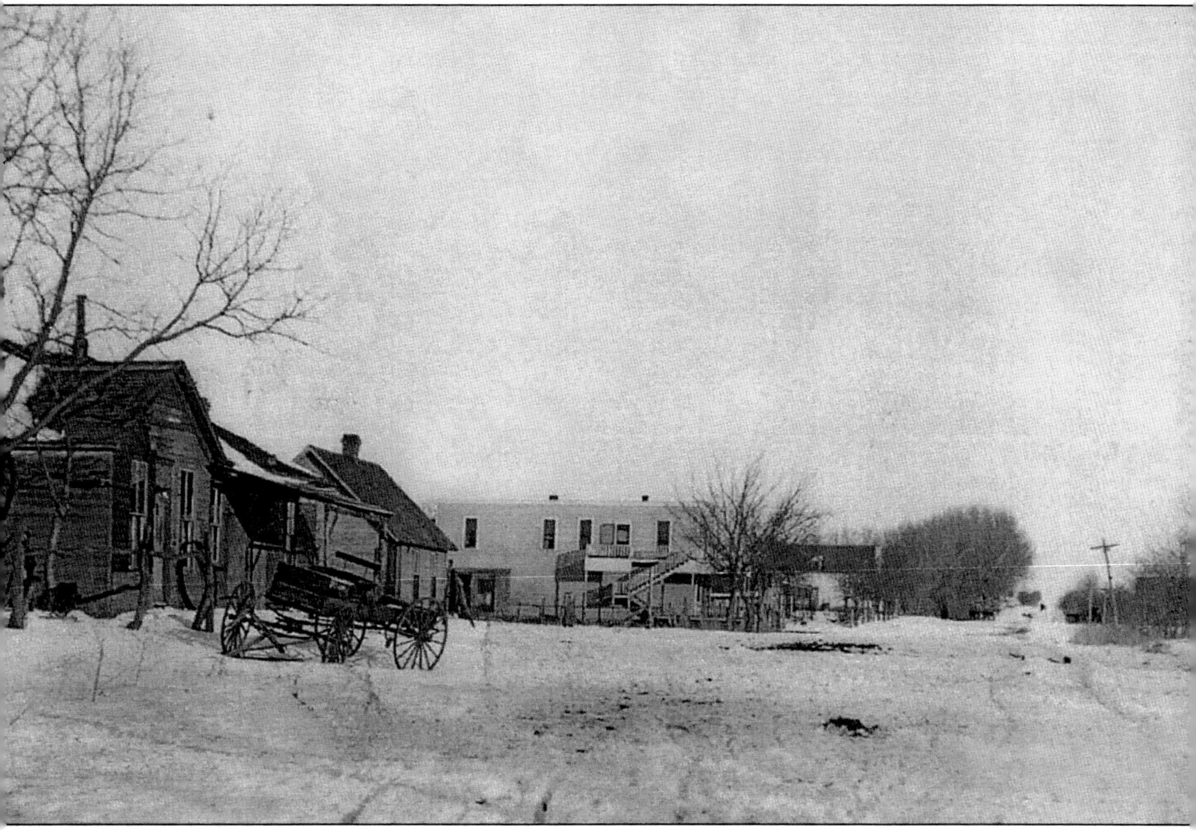

Believed to be taken about 1910 this photograph looks north into Covert from the south end of East Street. In the background center can be seen Hodges Merchandise Store, while behind it is the Van Pelt General Store. An abandoned wagon on the left awaits a more hospitable day.

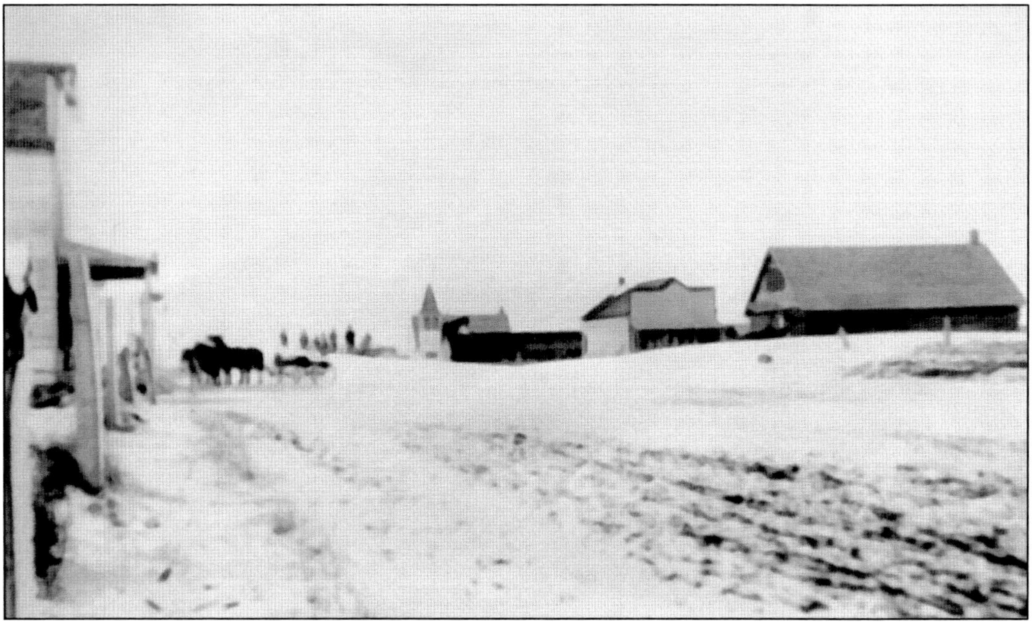

This photograph was taken looking to the west along Main Street in Bloomington around 1910. On the left is the Bloomington Store, while in the center background is the Union Congregational Baptist Church. To its right is the Hardman Lumber Yard and the Hahn Garage. First known as Tilden, Bloomington began in 1872. At its peak the village was home to over 70 people but it was never incorporated.

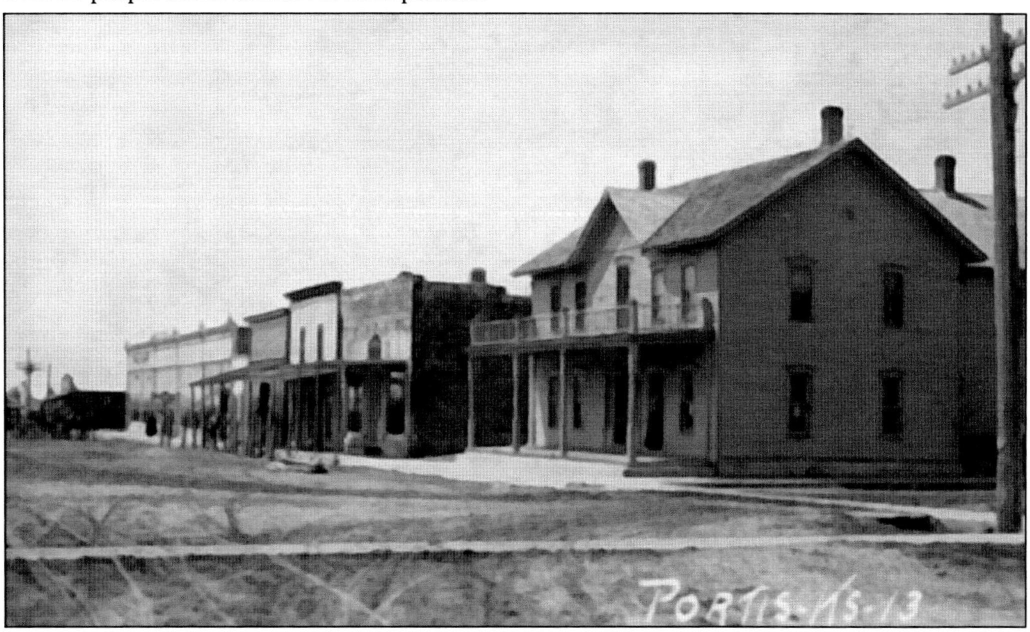

This 1913 shot of the west side of Market Street looks south from Fourth Street in Portis. On the right is the Northway Hotel, built in 1879 and torn down in 1927. The stone building to its left housed the Portis Post Office, while on the end of the business row the McGee & Sons store can be seen. The business district sported new concrete sidewalks but the dirt streets were still a nuisance in wet weather.

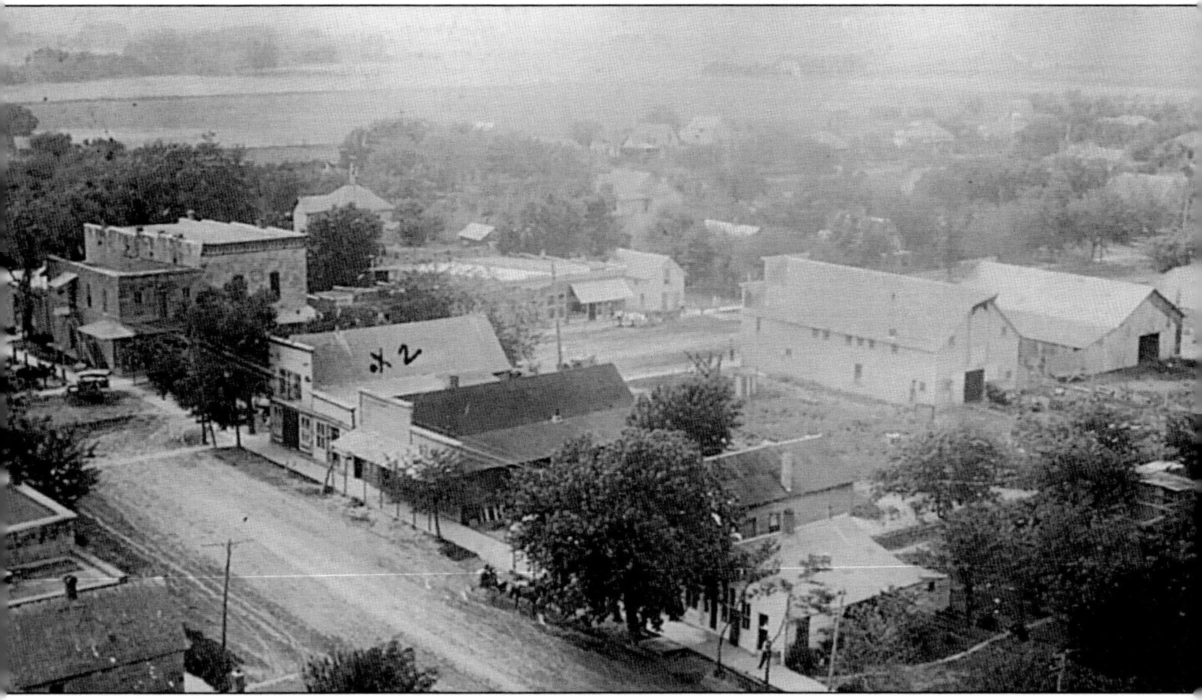

This view was taken in the late 1910s looking northwest over downtown Alton from the city water tower. Running across the center of the picture is Mill Street with Nicholas Avenue in the lower left. Almost all the buildings seen along Nicholas Avenue are now gone. In the upper left is the native stone Stephenson Store building, while next to it on the right is the Odd Fellows Hall.

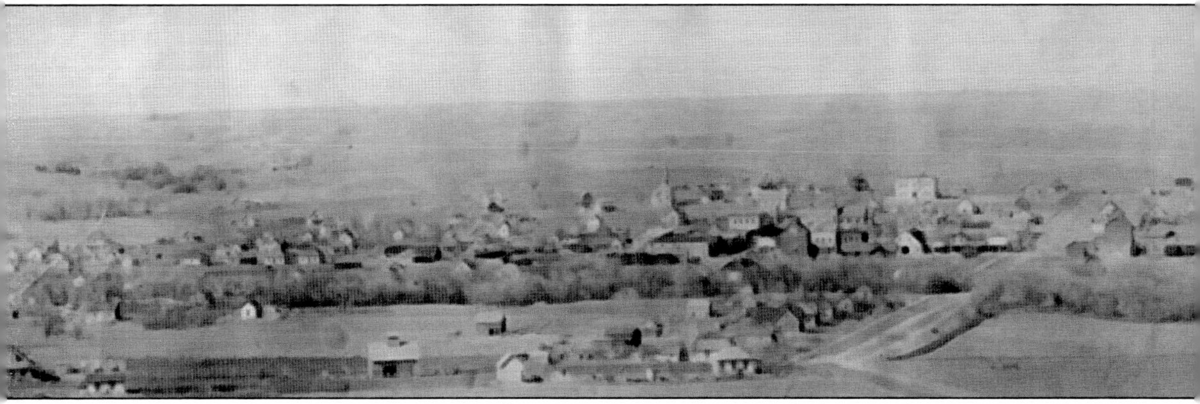

This view from the top of Craig Hill north across Natoma and the Paradise Creek Valley was taken in 1910. The city was founded at a shipping point on the Lincoln Branch of the Union Pacific Railroad in 1888 and was first called Cressen. The name Natoma is believed to be a Native American word meaning *new born*.

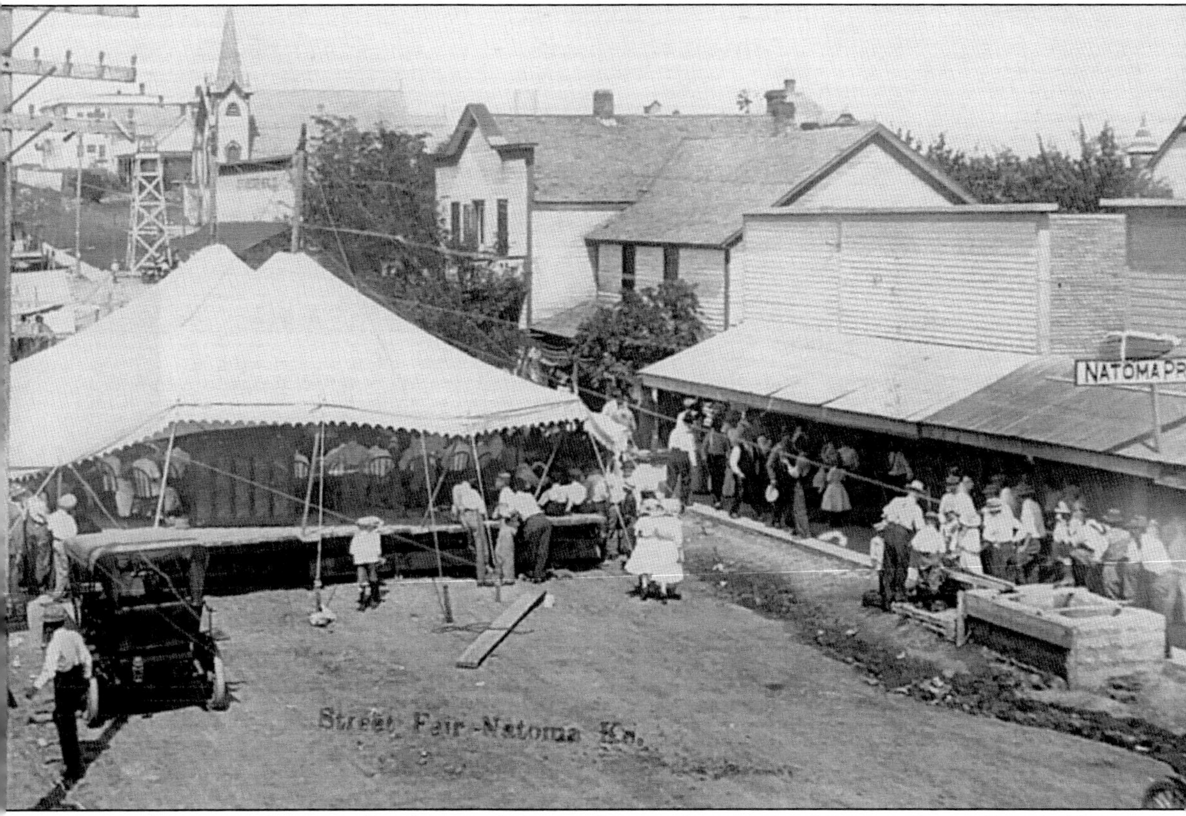

Shown here is a photograph of Second Street during the popular Natoma Street Fair held August 23–24, 1912. The Presbyterian Church, built in 1898, can be seen in the upper left portion of the photograph. The church is famous for its Gothic architecture and has since become the most sketched and photographed structure in Osborne County.

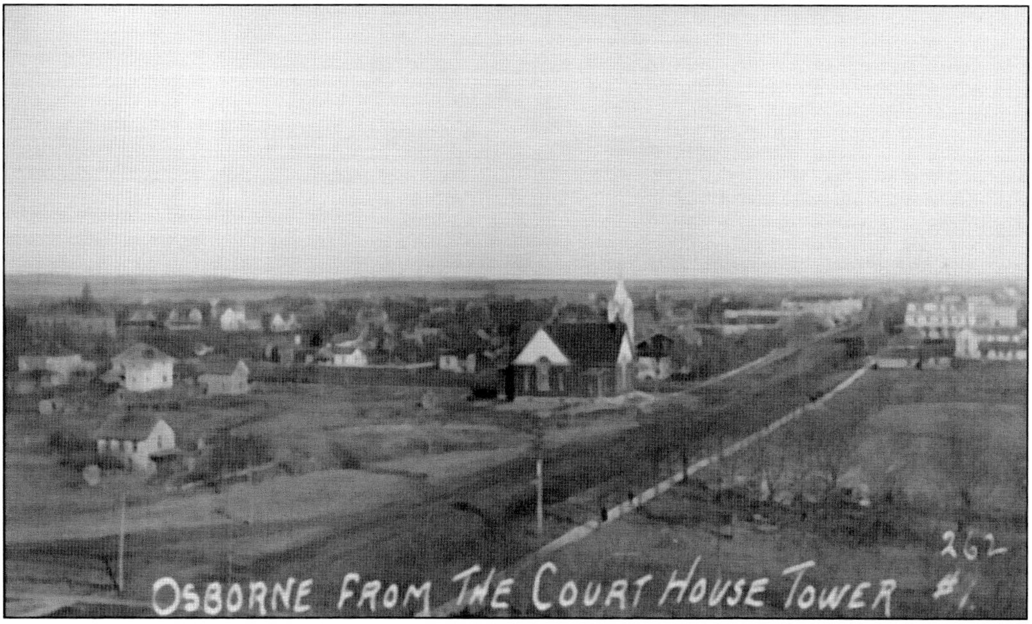

Taken from the courthouse clock tower in 1917 this view shows Osborne to the east along Main Street. Landmarks seen from left to right are: the Osborne Schoolhouse, the Christian Church, the Methodist Church, and the old hotel standing at the extreme right on the edge of the downtown district. At lower right in the City Park are the remains of the old city water tower, which had recently been replaced.

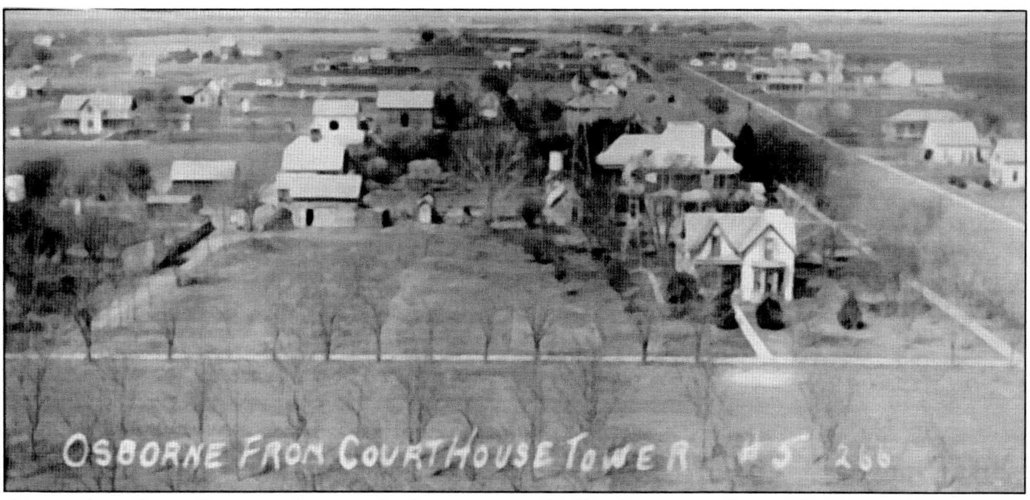

Also taken from the courthouse clock tower in 1917, this view shows Osborne to the west along Main Street, with South Fifth Street running across the bottom of the picture. Notice the windmills, water towers, and outhouses seen in several backyards.

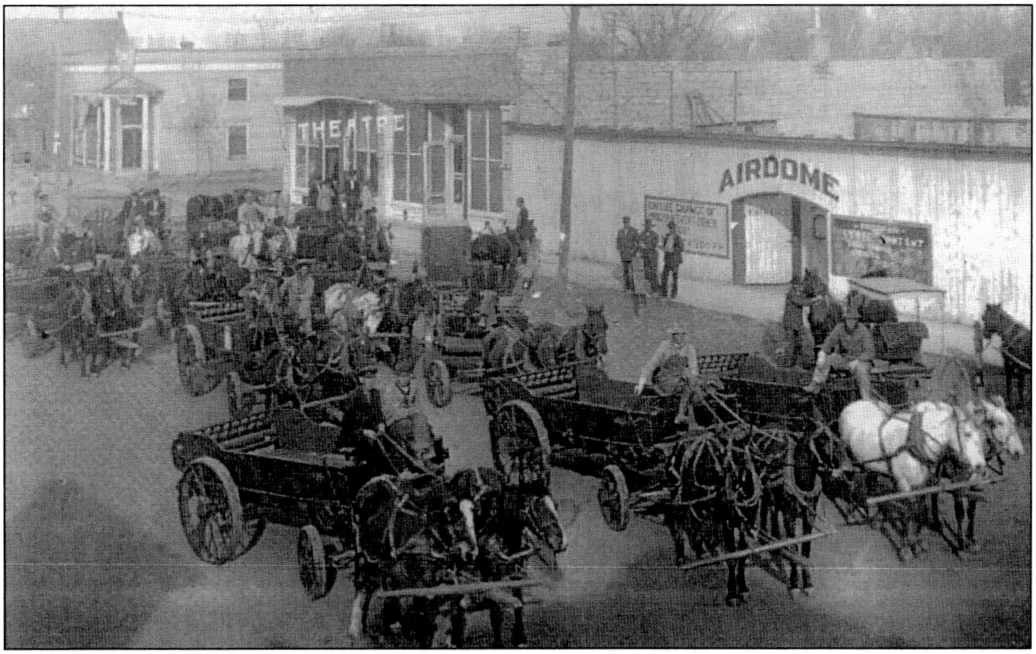

Manure and the Arts are the two subjects of this photograph taken around 1910 on North Morgan Avenue in Downs. Although it was supposed to be displaying the new manure spreaders recently received by the Washburn Implement Company, the Airdome, Downs' then outdoor theater, can be seen in the background "boasting a change of program every other night." In the upper left is the Turtle Photography Studio.

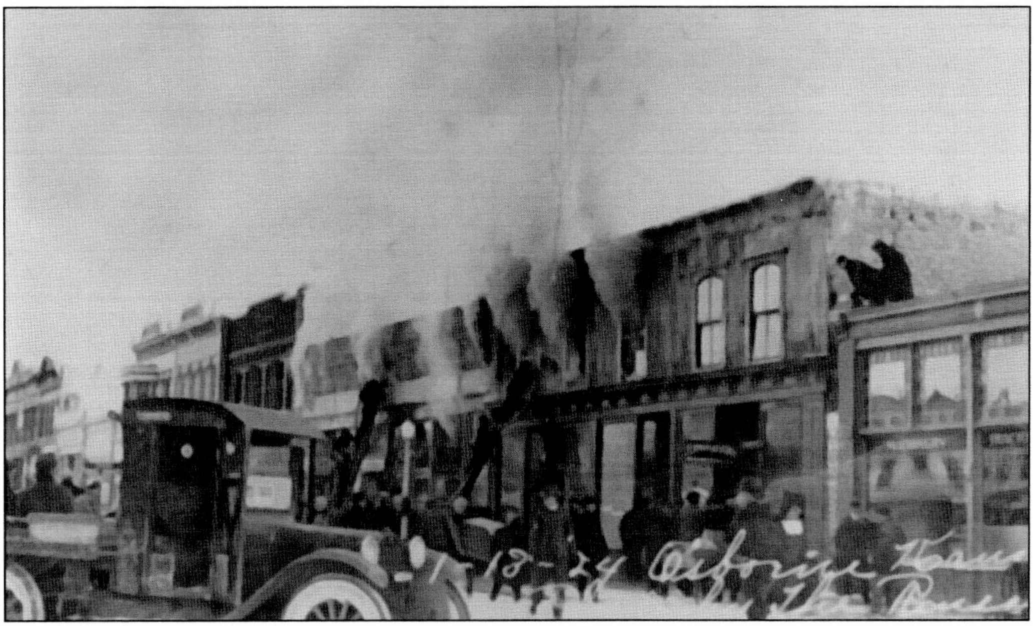

A devastating fire on the south side of Main Street in Osborne's downtown area occurred on January 13, 1924. The fire started in the Jones Café at center left and also engulfed the Osborne Post Office. Losses were estimated to be $20,000. A line of citizens can be seen desperately passing along items being saved from the inside of the burning buildings.

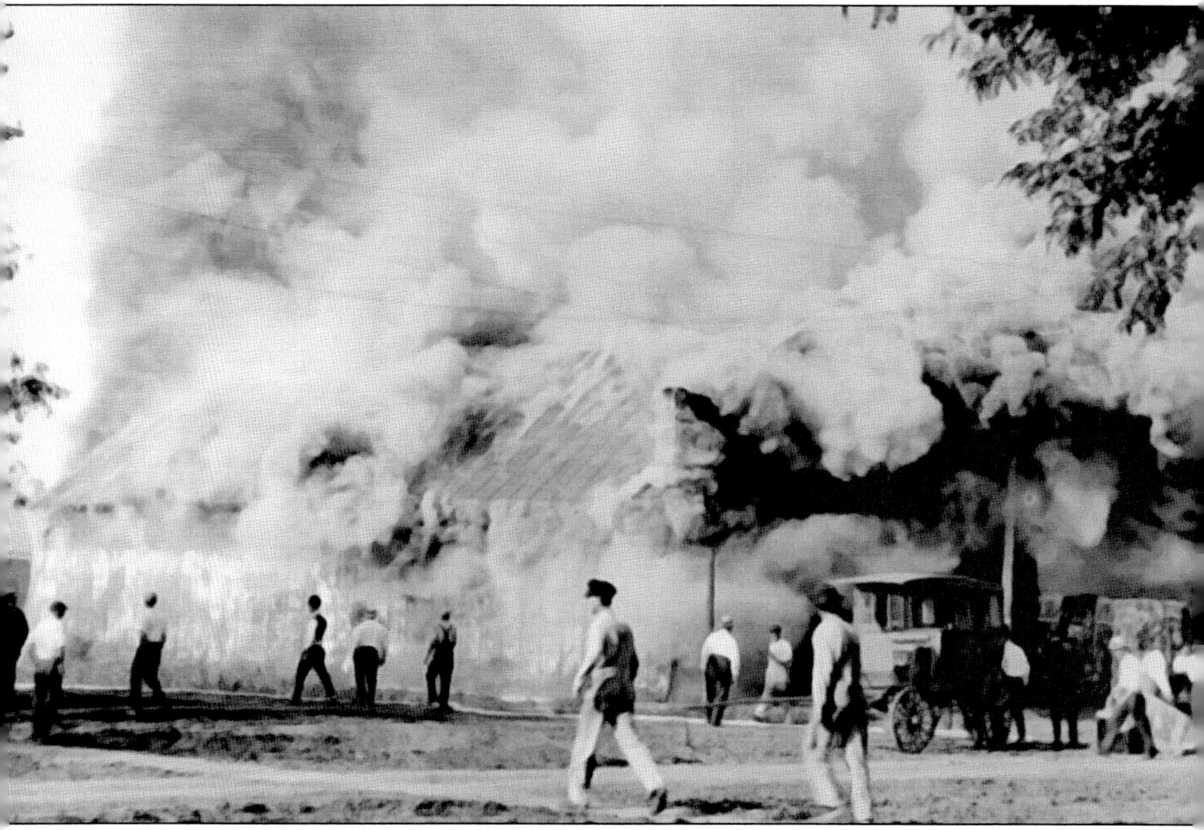

Pictured here is the Gilson Livery Barn in Osborne going up in flames on September 2, 1916. It was built around 1900 by William Riley on the southwest corner of Main and Elm Streets. The fire was too far gone by the time it was discovered and the building was allowed to burn to the ground. The wagon and a few other items saved are at the right.

Two

BUSINESSES AND SPECIAL BUILDINGS

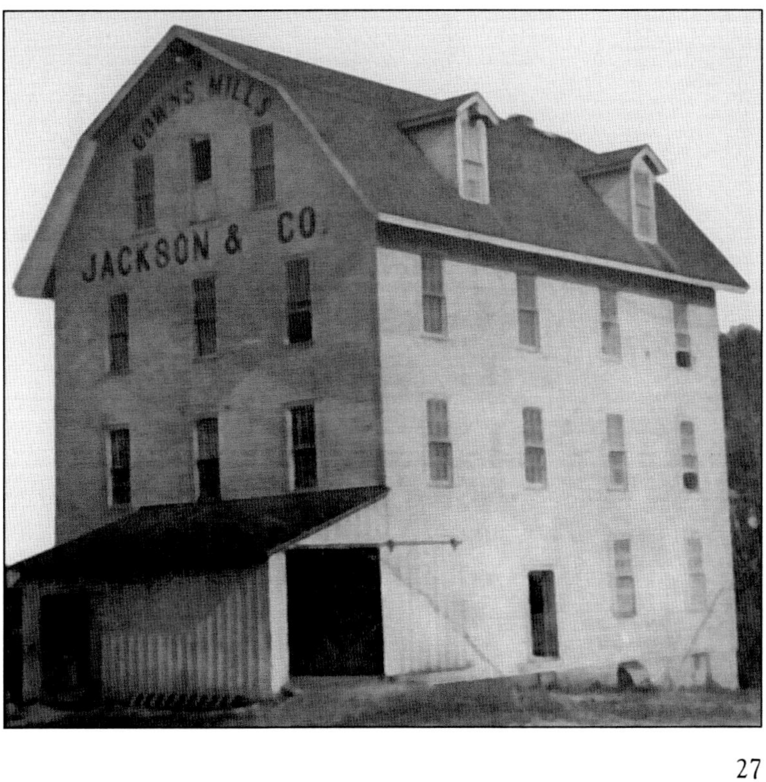

This view shows the Jackson Mill at the end of South Third Street on the North Fork Solomon River at Downs around 1901. Built in 1881 by the Jackson brothers for $25,000–$30,000, the mill was four stories high with the running machinery bought from the Richmond City Mill Works in Indiana. Flour brands produced included Champion, Farmer's Choice, and White Rose. The mill was a Downs landmark until it burned in the 1930s.

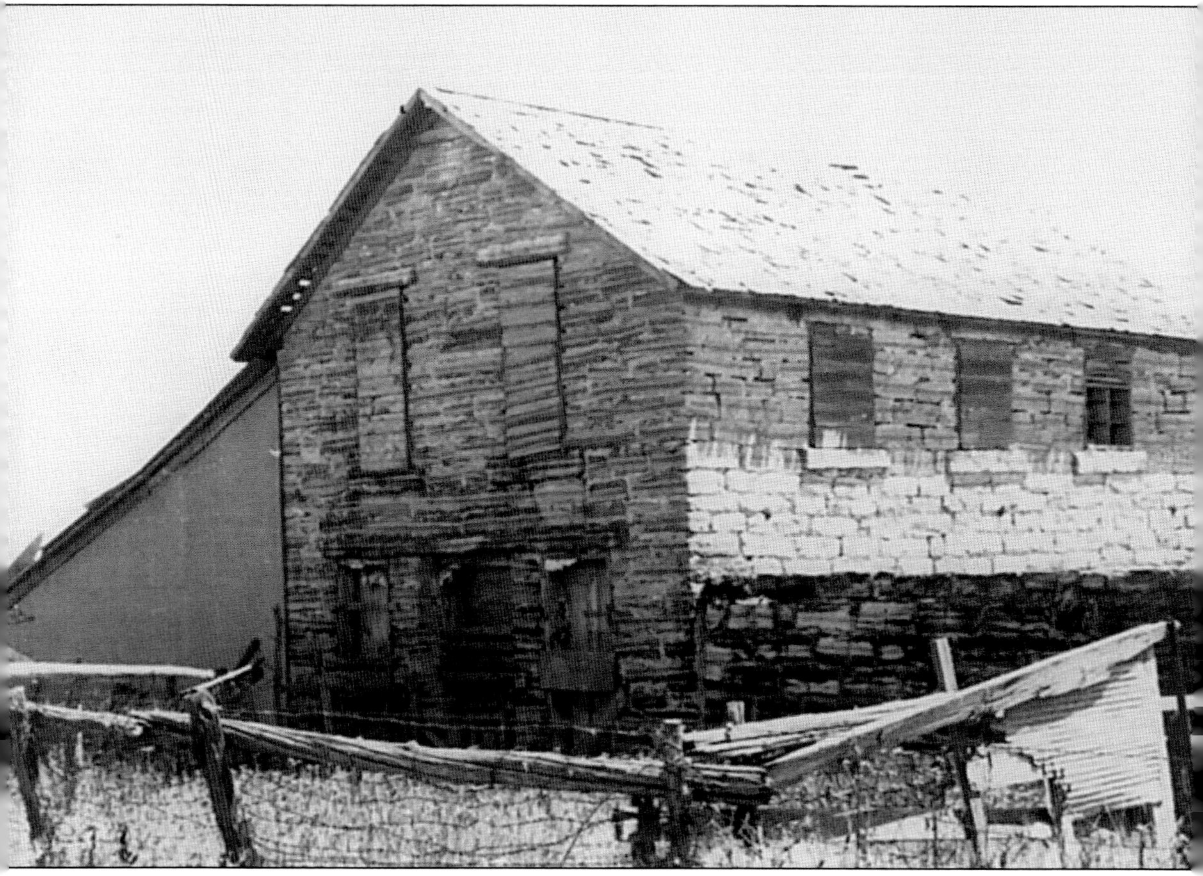

This photograph is of a two-story fencepost limestone structure built by Samuel McGee in 1878. The McGee Store intersection was the center of the community of Delhi, which flourished from the mid-1870s to the early 1890s in the southeastern part of Osborne County. It served as a mercantile store and livery stable, and in the large room on the top floor the Blue Hills Masonic Lodge, Number 198, was first organized in 1877. It later moved to Lucas, Kansas. The Delhi Post Office was organized here in 1875 and was discontinued in 1894. A tornado completely destroyed the building in 1993 and with it the last vestiges of the Delhi community.

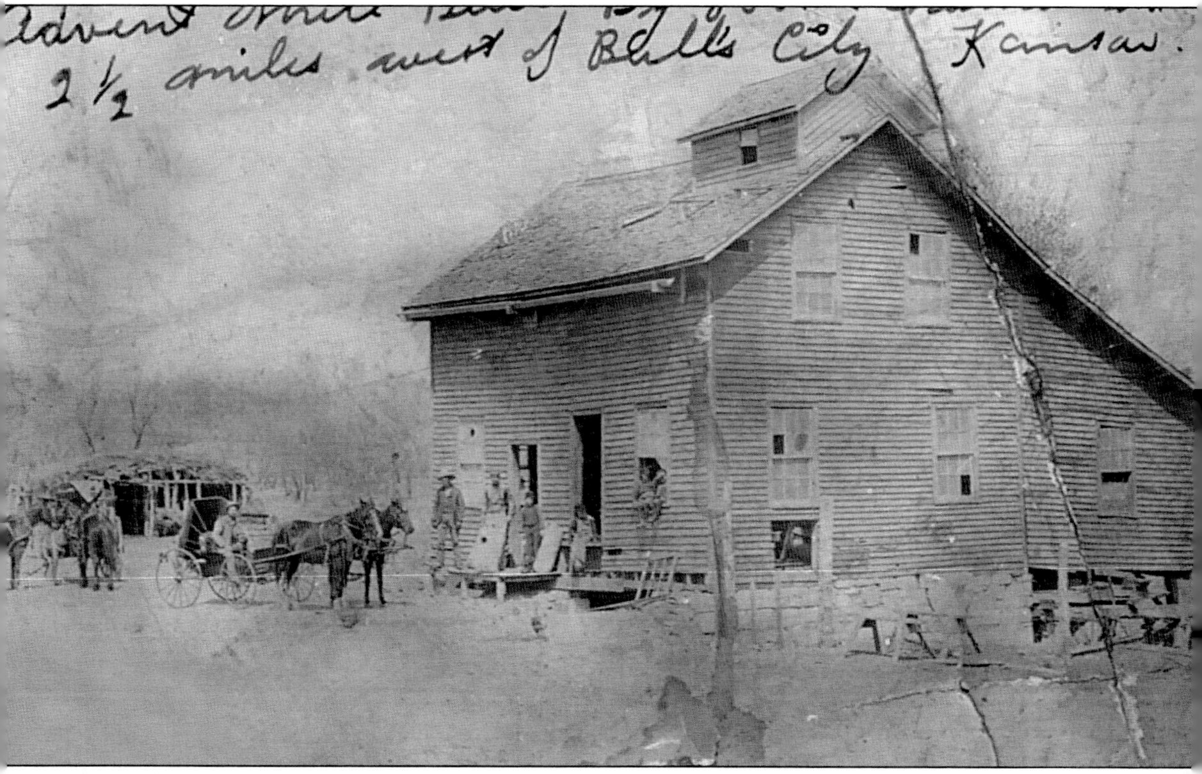

This is the only known scene ever taken of the Seventh-Day Adventist Colony's sawmill that was once located 2 miles west of Alton. Between 1871 and 1875 several families of this religious group came from Iowa and settled along Little Medicine Creek and in the South Solomon River Valley. They bought this mill and the firm of Chamberlain and Post ran it until Johnathan Post's death in 1885. His wife Sarah then went back to their former home in Battle Creek, Michigan, where she invented a drink she called Postum. Her nephew, C.W. Post, marketed the drink to great profit and went on to found the Post Cereals Company. The mill operated for several years until the dam washed out and it closed.

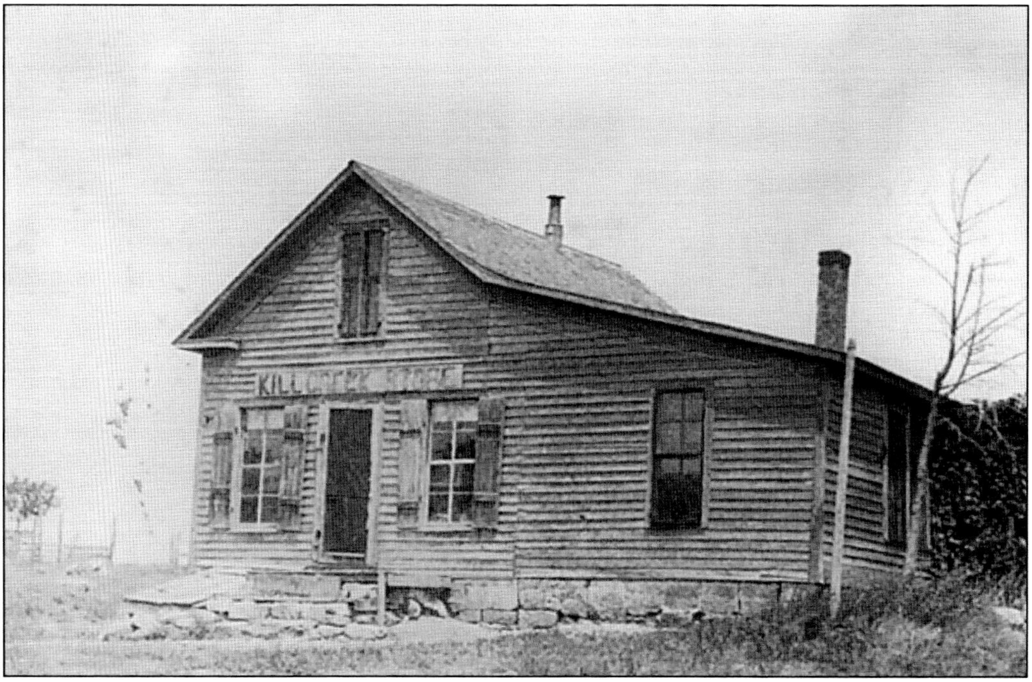

This photograph of the Kill Creek General Store in west-central Osborne County was taken shortly before it was torn down in the 1930s. The store was built in 1879 and was both the longtime home of the Richard Benwell family and the Kill Creek Post Office, which operated from 1872 to 1904. The Kill Creek community was made famous in *Sod-House Days*, Howard Ruede's classic 1937 book on the homesteaders.

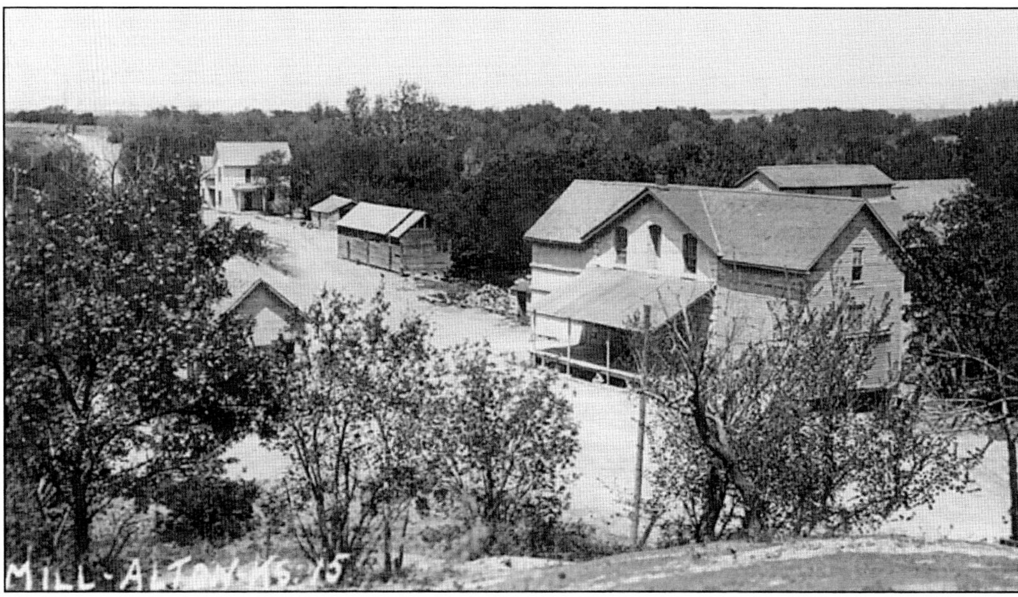

Pictured here is the Bush Mill as it appeared in 1915. Located on the South Fork Solomon River a mile south of Alton, it was built in 1872–73 and was operated by a number of owners before it burned to the ground in October 1915. Some of the flour brands from the mill included Big B, Tip Top, O.K., and Best Patent.

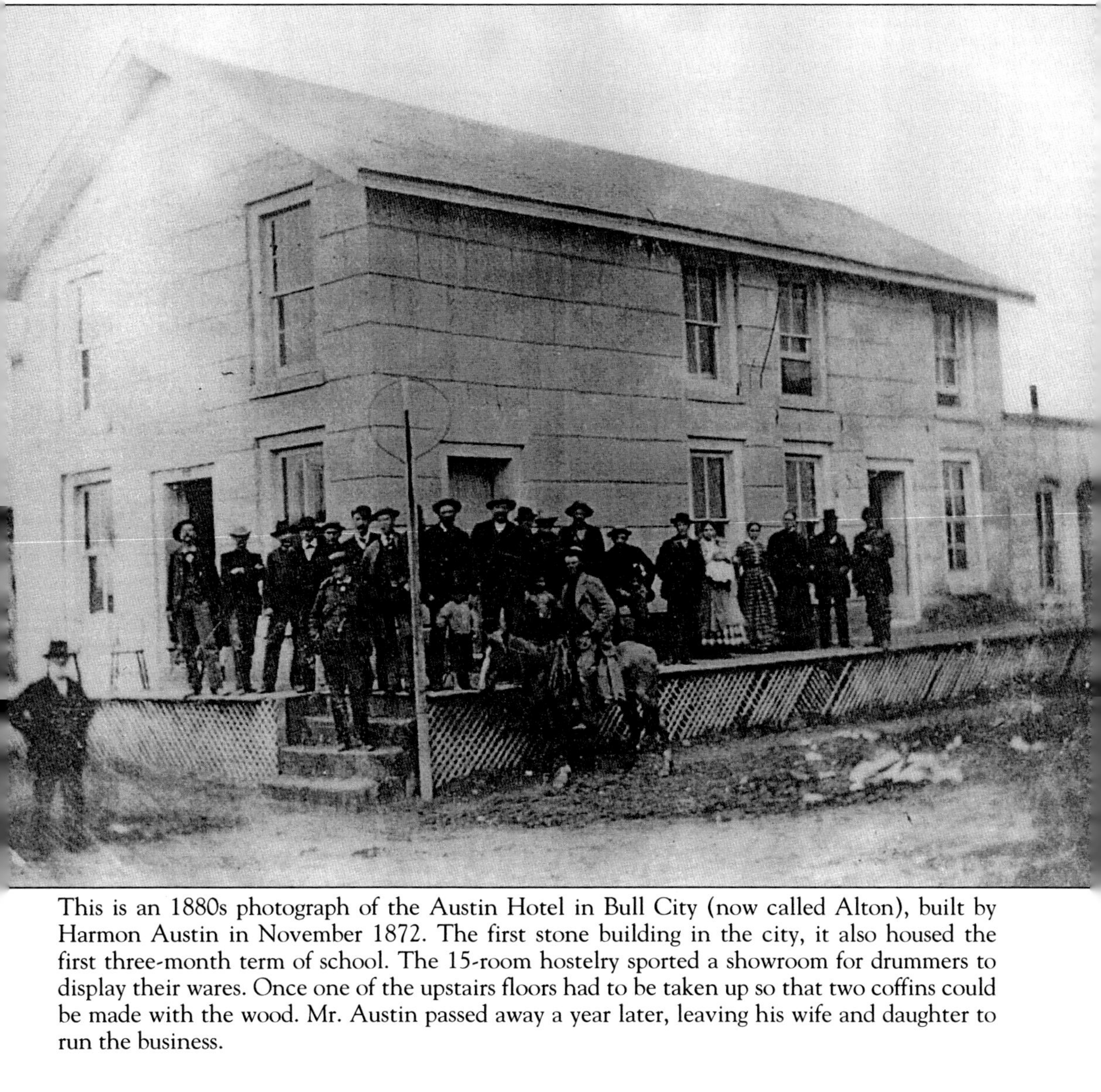

This is an 1880s photograph of the Austin Hotel in Bull City (now called Alton), built by Harmon Austin in November 1872. The first stone building in the city, it also housed the first three-month term of school. The 15-room hostelry sported a showroom for drummers to display their wares. Once one of the upstairs floors had to be taken up so that two coffins could be made with the wood. Mr. Austin passed away a year later, leaving his wife and daughter to run the business.

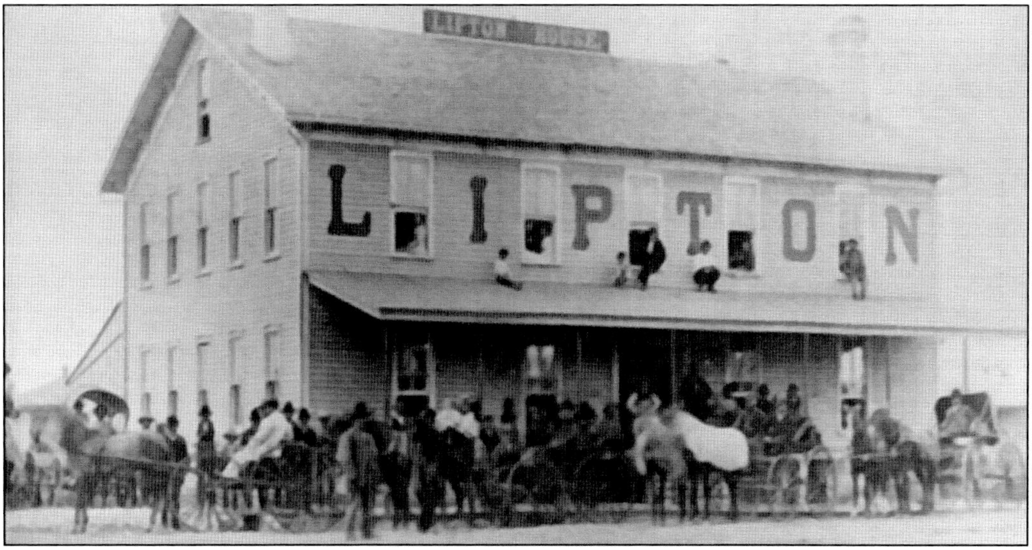

In 1878 James H. Lipton came to Osborne and built the Lipton House, a two-story frame building on the northeast corner of First and Main Streets. It is seen here in a photograph by Kleckner and Perkins taken the same year. Lipton owned it a year before selling out, and over the succeeding years the hostelry operated as the Maxwell House, the Osborne House, the Hotel McGuire, and the McGuire House.

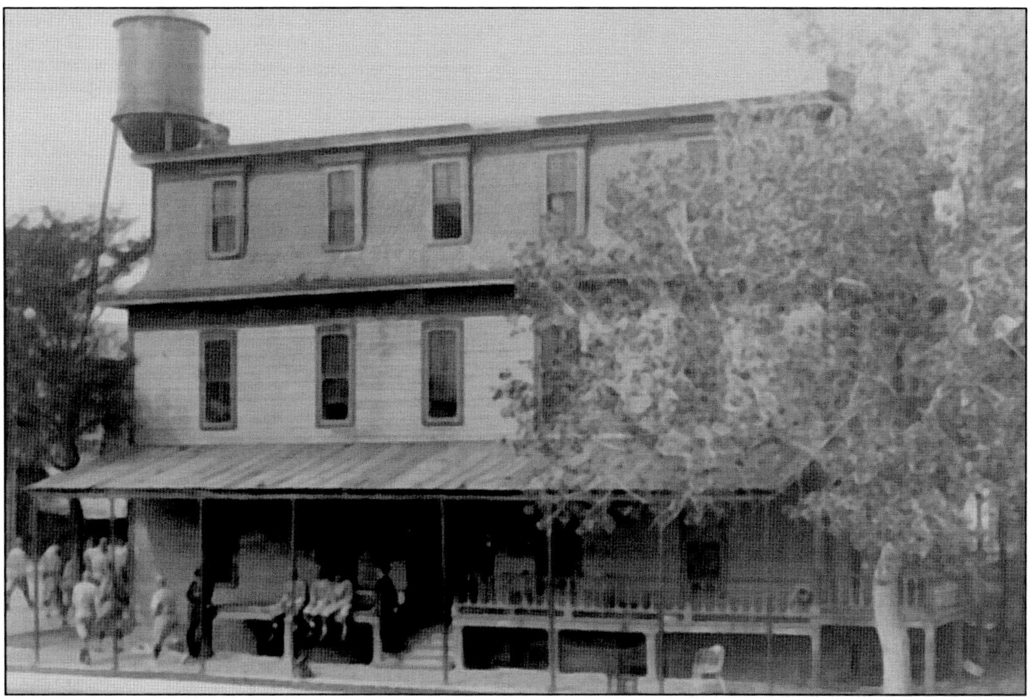

Shown here in the late 1910s the McGuire House stood on the northeast corner of First and Main Streets in Osborne. A third floor added in 1879 changed the hotel to a Second Empire architectural style. In May 1920 it was torn down to make way for the new Crystal Theater. At upper left is the east town water tower, erected in 1917. Notice the baseball team leaving in the lower left-hand corner.

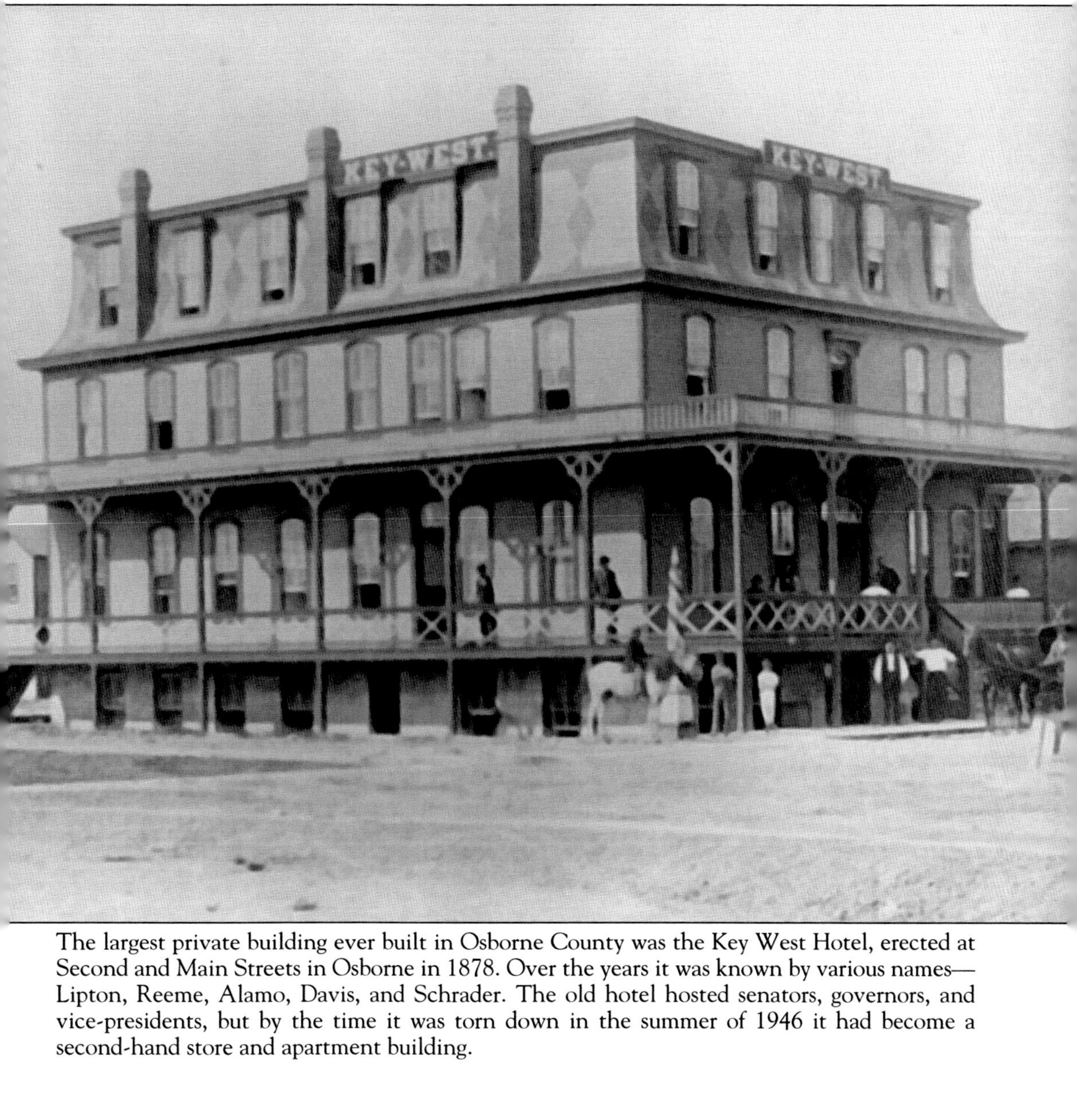

The largest private building ever built in Osborne County was the Key West Hotel, erected at Second and Main Streets in Osborne in 1878. Over the years it was known by various names—Lipton, Reeme, Alamo, Davis, and Schrader. The old hotel hosted senators, governors, and vice-presidents, but by the time it was torn down in the summer of 1946 it had become a second-hand store and apartment building.

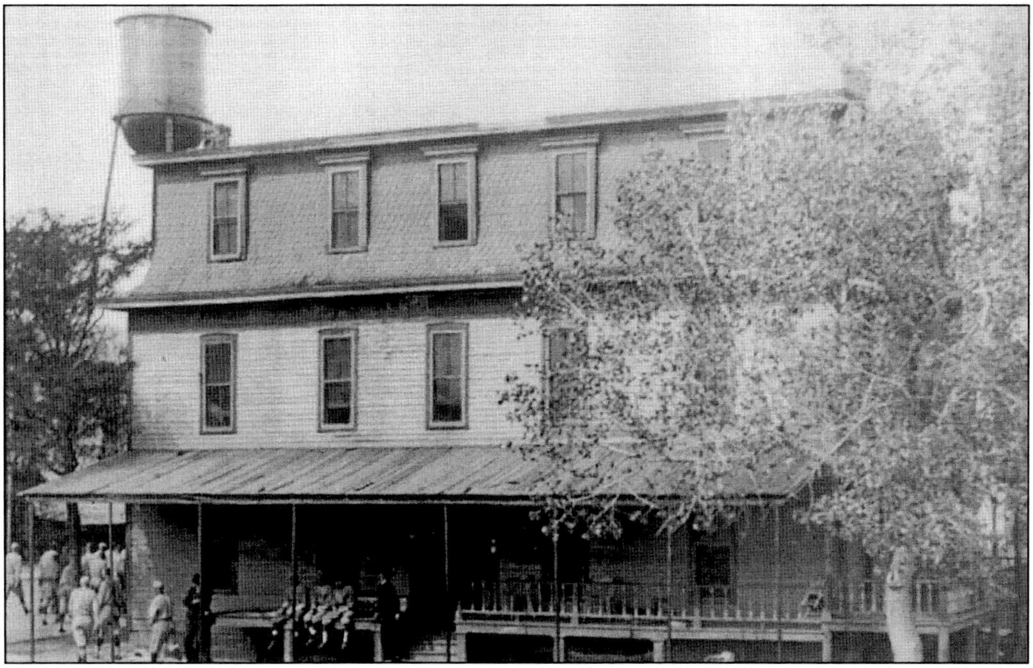

Taken about 1879, this photograph shows the Watson, Gillette & Company General Store on West Main Street in Osborne. The store opened in 1871 only a few months after the founding of Osborne in May 1871, and closed in 1949 after 78 years in business. Notice the hitching posts and board sidewalks. Charles J. Gillette can be seen holding the hands of his two children, Will and Millie Gillette.

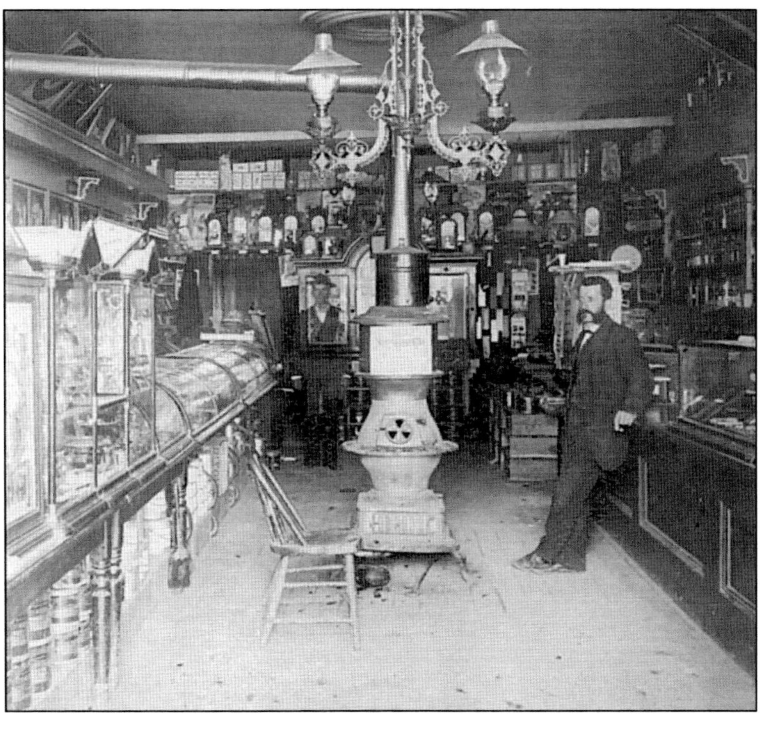

This is a view inside Chan Baldwin's Drug Store in about 1890 in Osborne. On the right is Francis Gruger, the store pharmacist and one of the founders of Osborne. When Baldwin first opened, his customers were Native Americans, buffalo hunters, and green settlers fresh from the East. Notice the ornate gas ceiling lamps and pictures along the ceiling. Baldwin operated the store for 66 years, a Kansas record for a pharmacist.

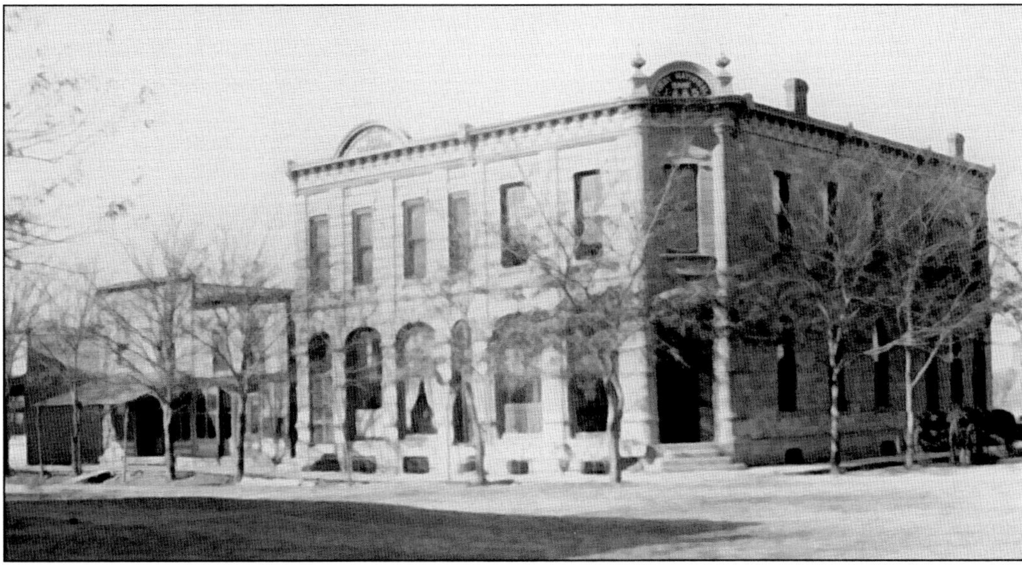

This photograph, taken in 1895 by Charles W. Buell, is of the First National Bank and the Walrond, Mitchell, and Heren Law Office buildings at Second and Main Streets in Osborne. They were built in 1885 and 1886 of native limestone. Several businesses were housed in these imposing structures in later decades until they were bought by Cecil Bloomer in the 1950s to house his family's law office and abstract business.

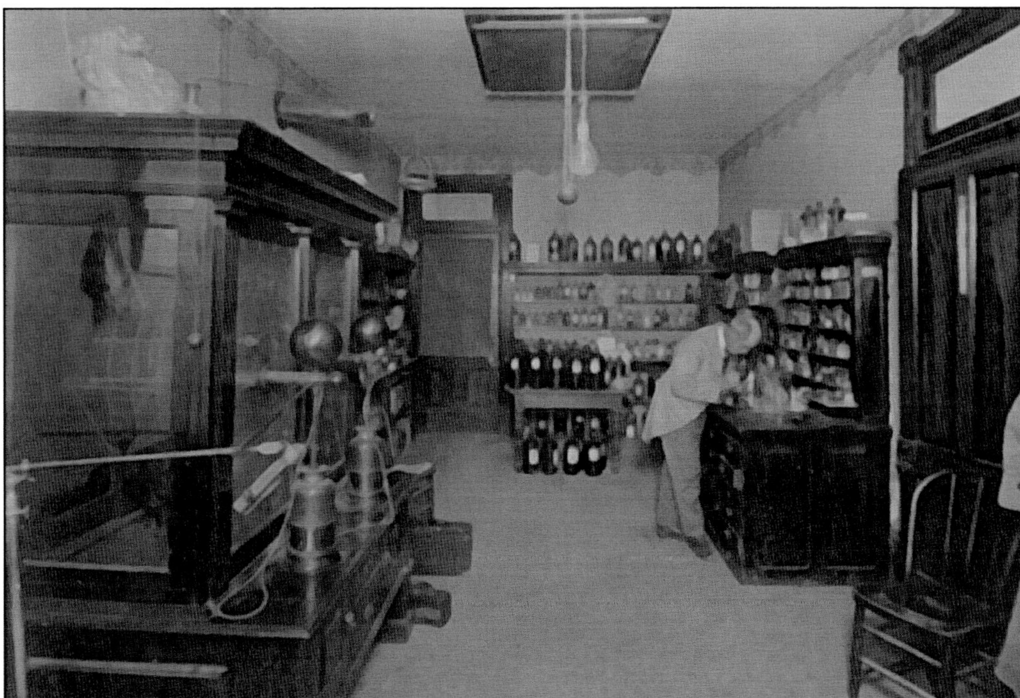

This photograph of Dr. Tasso O. Felix's office in Downs was taken about 1920. Dr. Felix started his medical practice in Downs in 1899 and served the area for over 40 years. The shelves are well stocked with medicines, compounds, alcohol, and bottles of ether. The large box-like cabinet on the left is an X-ray machine.

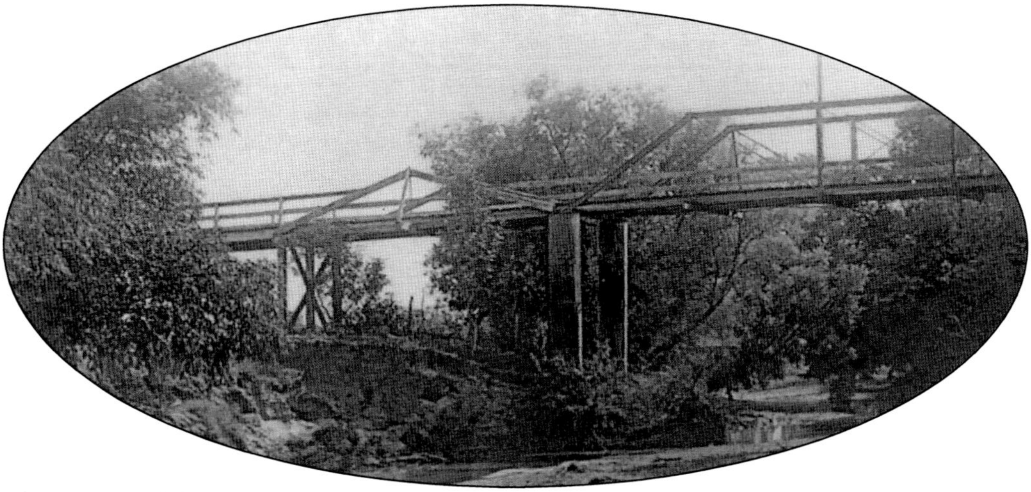

This view is of the iron bridge that spanned the South Fork Solomon River at the south edge of Osborne. Erected in 1887, the bridge served for nearly 50 years until it was replaced by a new concrete structure in 1936.

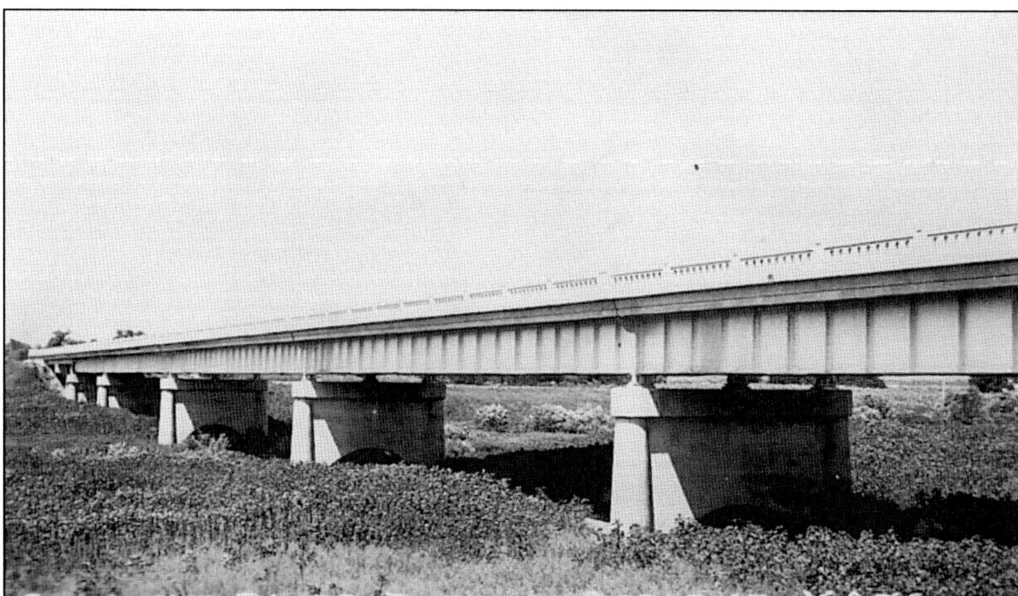

Taken in 1936, this picture is of the new concrete highway bridge over the South Fork Solomon River at the south edge of Osborne. It replaced the old iron bridge and was dedicated by Harry Darby, director of the Kansas Highway Commission, before a crowd of 7,000 people. The bridge is still in use.

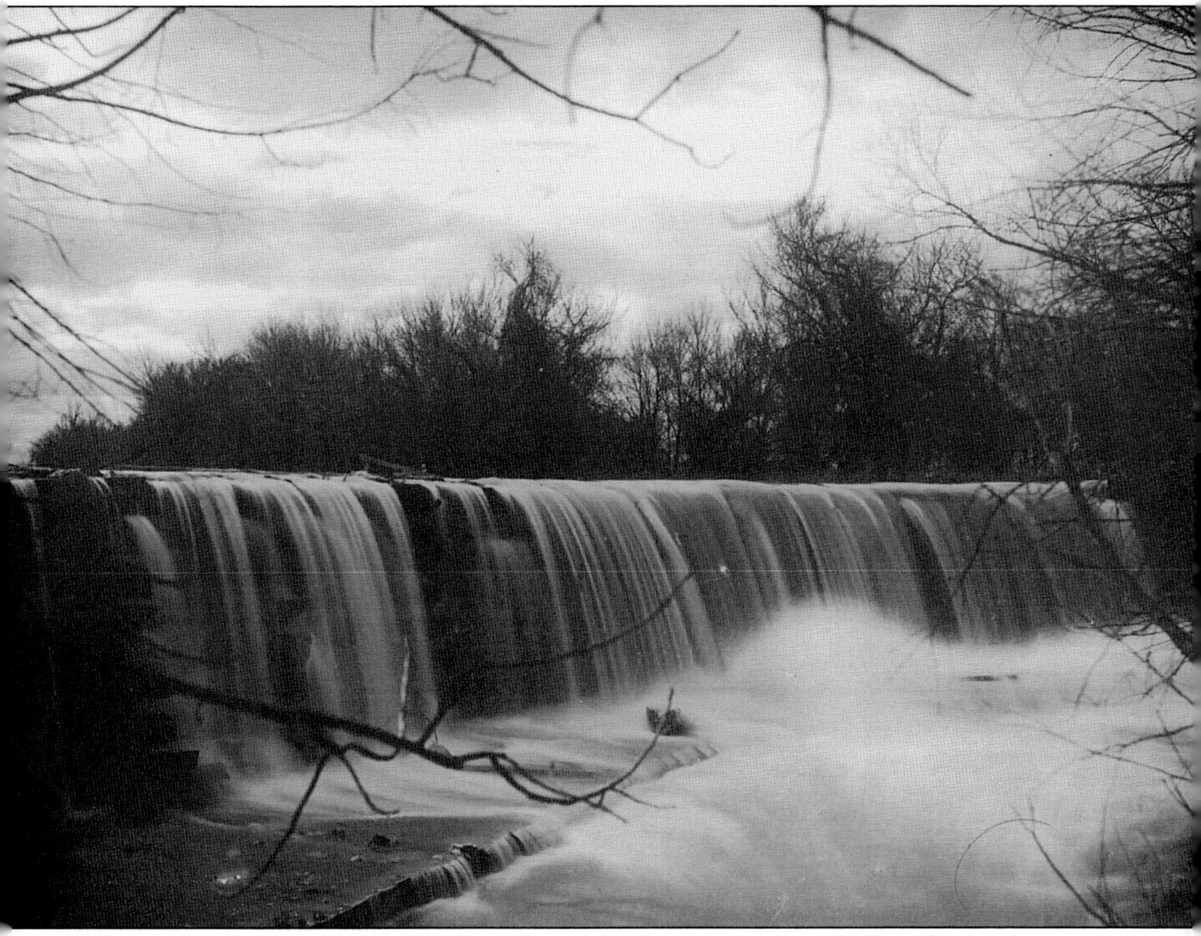

This is a remarkable photograph of the Jackson Mill dam on the North Fork Solomon River at Downs by the Turtle Art Studio. It is unknown whether or not it was taken on a cloudy day or by moonlight. The special white water effect of the water as it flows over the wooden beams of the 164-foot-long dam was a photographer's time-exposure trick.

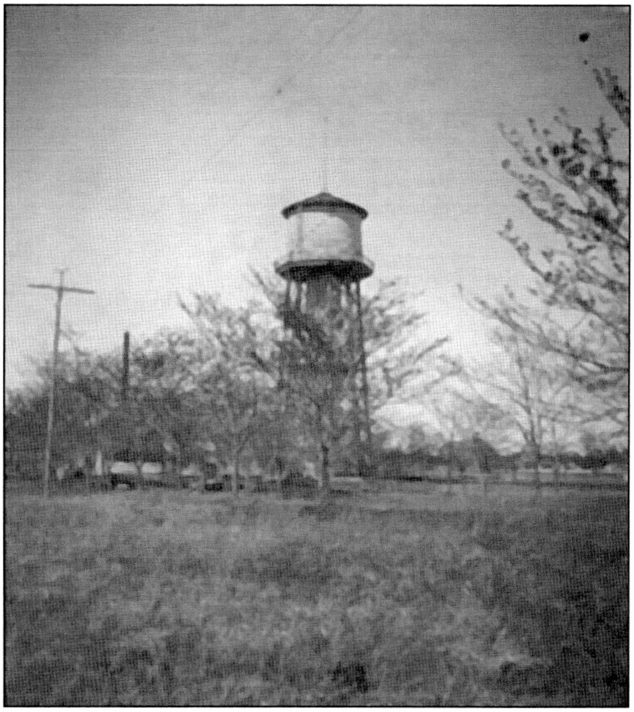

Taken in 1910, this view is of the water tower that was once situated in the northwest corner of Osborne's city park. The tower replaced the town well around 1880 and was torn down when the city's two current water towers were constructed in 1917.

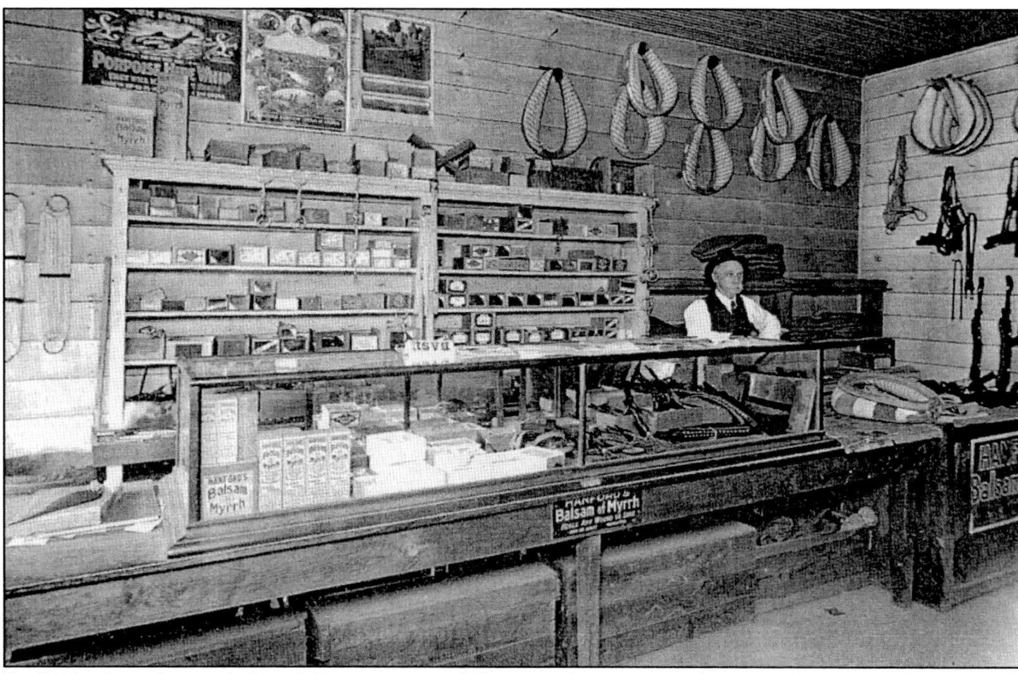

Earl Marsh is shown behind the counter of the Marsh Harness Shop on the west side of South Morgan Avenue in Downs. Located where the Senior Center now stands, the shop's wares hark back to a time when the horse was still the primary form of transportation around town.

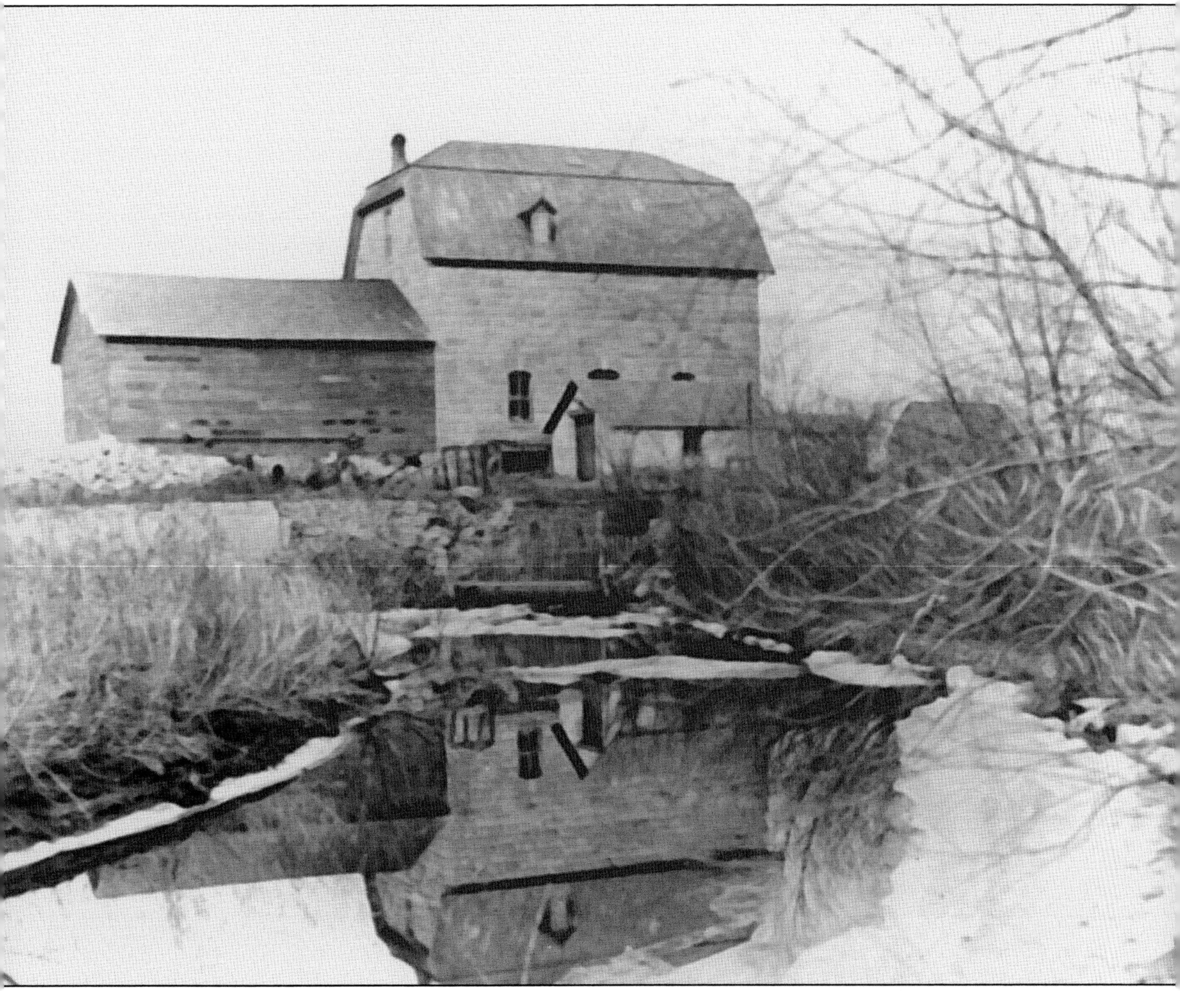

Shown here is a nice view of the Jackson Mill and its reflection, taken about 1910. The native stone mill stood at the end of South Seventh Street on the South Fork Solomon River at the edge of Osborne. The mill was built in 1883 as the Beach Mill and was later operated as the Osborne City Mills. The Jackson Milling Company owned it until it was torn down *c.* 1915.

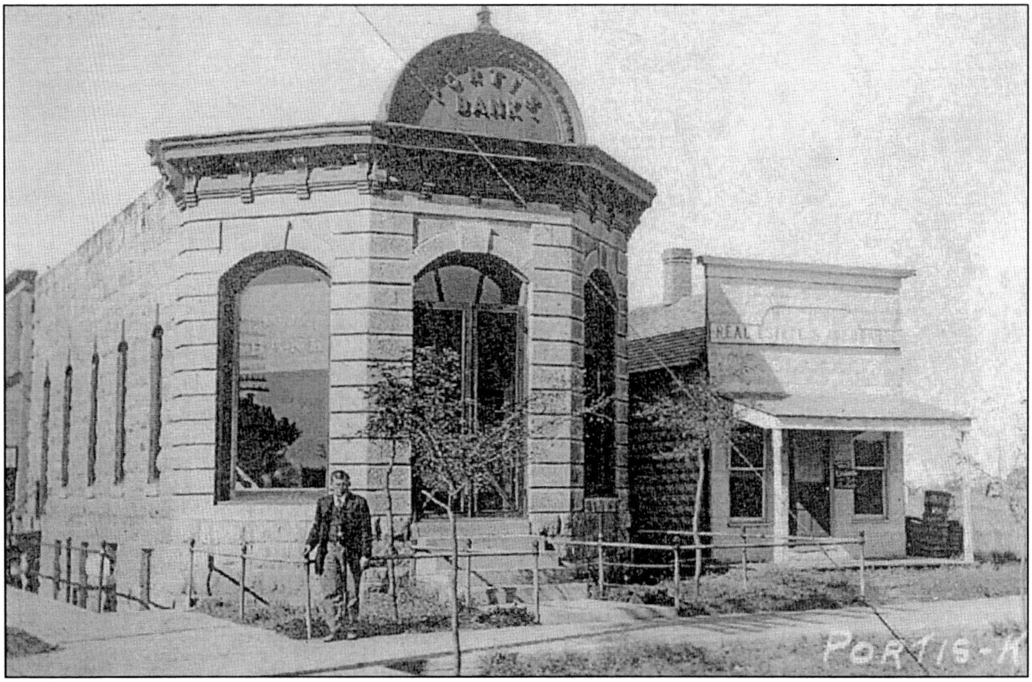

This is a 1910 look at the northwest corner of Market and Fourth Streets in Portis. The rock building on the left is the First State Bank of Portis while on the right is Hudson A. Turner's Real Estate & Insurance Company. The bank was established in 1885 with this native stone structure being erected two years later. Over the years there were five robbery attempts before the bank closed in 1992.

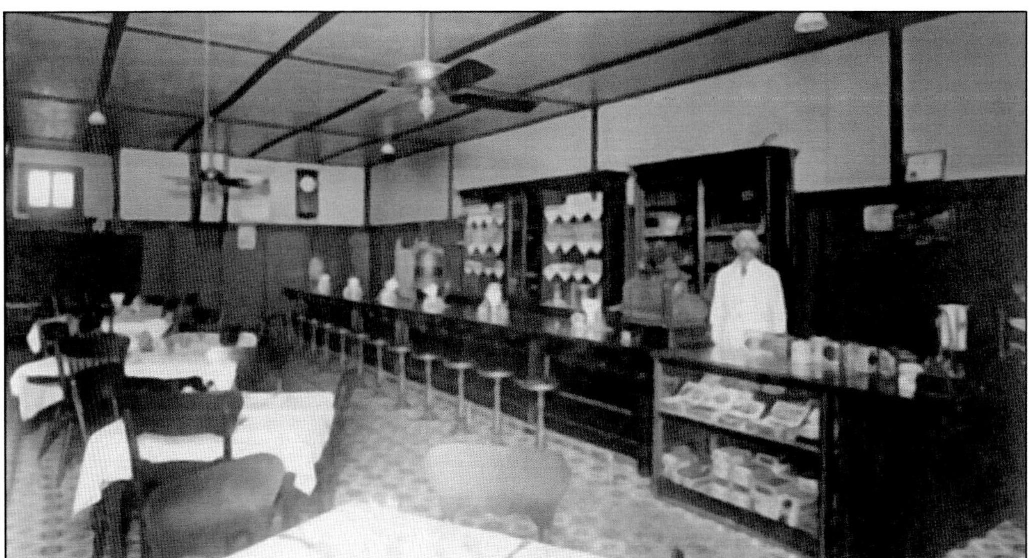

This look inside of Trent's Café on South Morgan Avenue in Downs shows us how it appeared in 1912. The 12-seat soda fountain proved to be a popular draw among old and young customers alike. The stock of tobacco goods and ornate ceiling fans are reminiscent of the times.

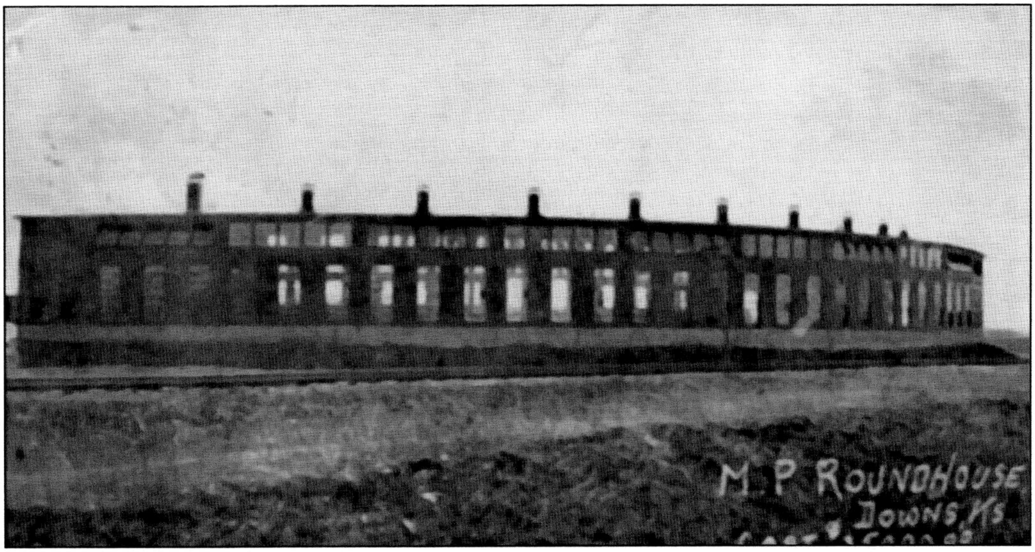

Taken shortly before fire destroyed it on July 31, 1908, this postcard view shows the second Missouri Pacific Railroad roundhouse in Downs. The ten-stall roundhouse had been completed at a cost of $35,000 in early 1907 to replace an earlier structure that had also burned.

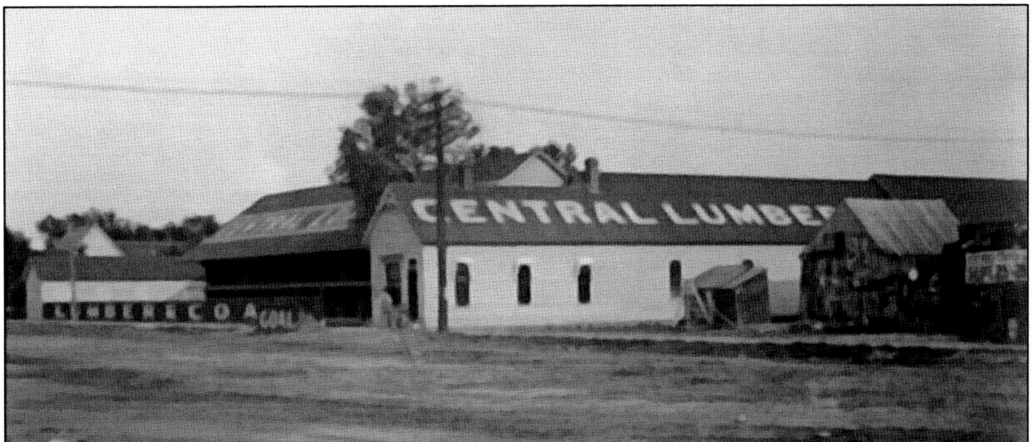

Shown here are the main offices of the Central Lumber Company on First Commercial Street in Downs around 1900. The company was formed by Henry Welty, W.H. Noll, and Marion Hardman in 1892. In 1903 this partnership dissolved and the company evolved into the Hardman Lumber Company, a large-scale lumber concern owned by Marion Hardman with yards throughout Kansas, Colorado, and Nebraska. Note the ramp in front for loading coal into wagons.

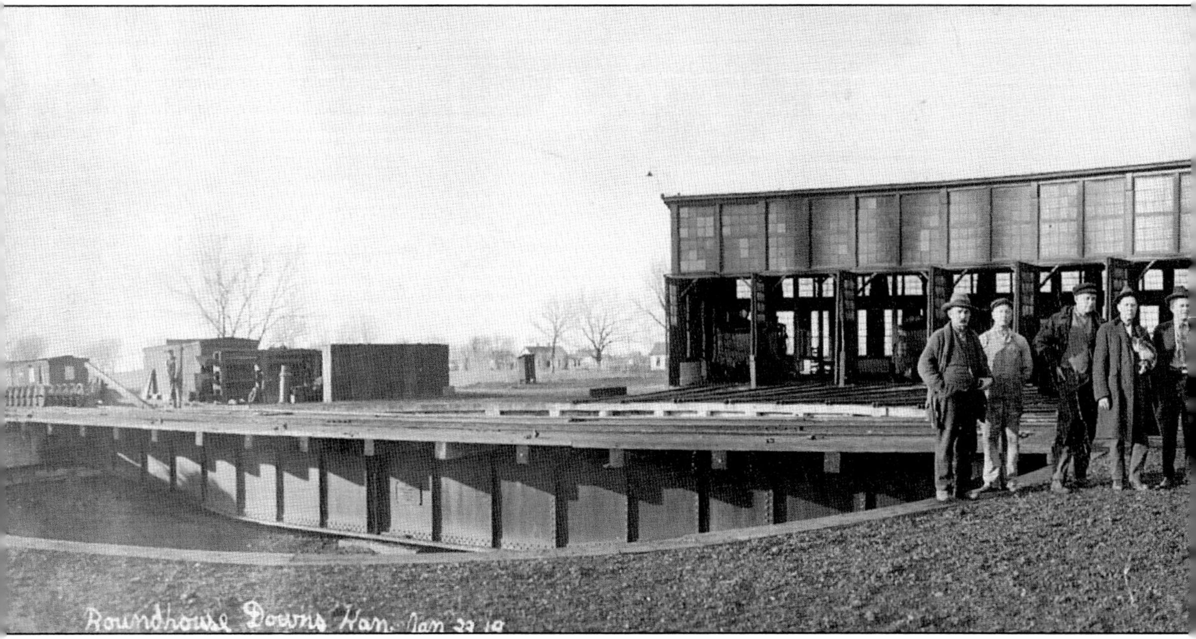

Pictured here are the Missouri Pacific Railroad roundhouse crew in front of the roundhouse in Downs. Taken on January 23, 1919, by R.H. Parrott, this was the third and last roundhouse built by the railroad after the first two burned. It was completed in the spring of 1909 and built on the foundations of the second roundhouse. To the left is the 75-foot turntable, while the water tower and other installations are to the right. Downs was founded as a division point

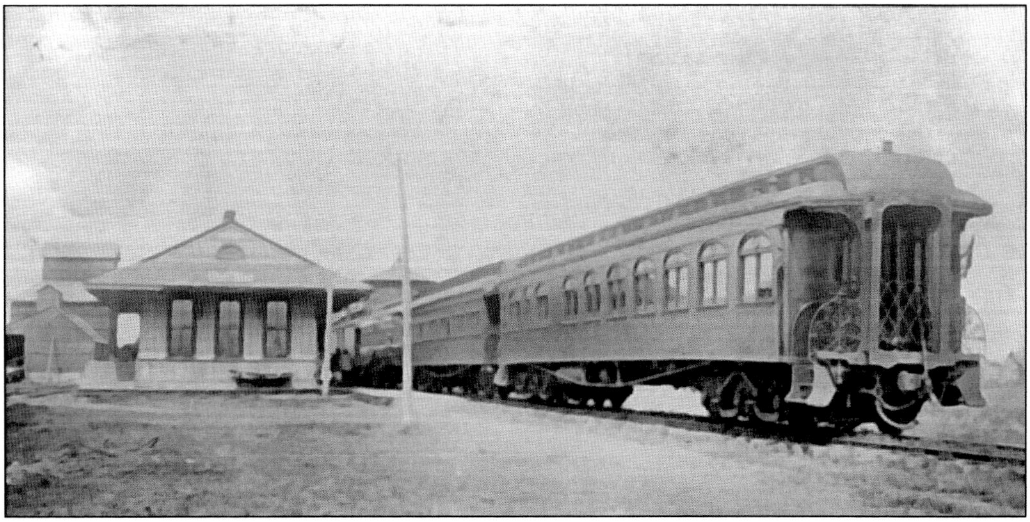

This view was taken from the east of the Missouri Pacific Railroad depot at Alton in 1910. Notice the ornamental ironwork on the rear of the railcar to the right.

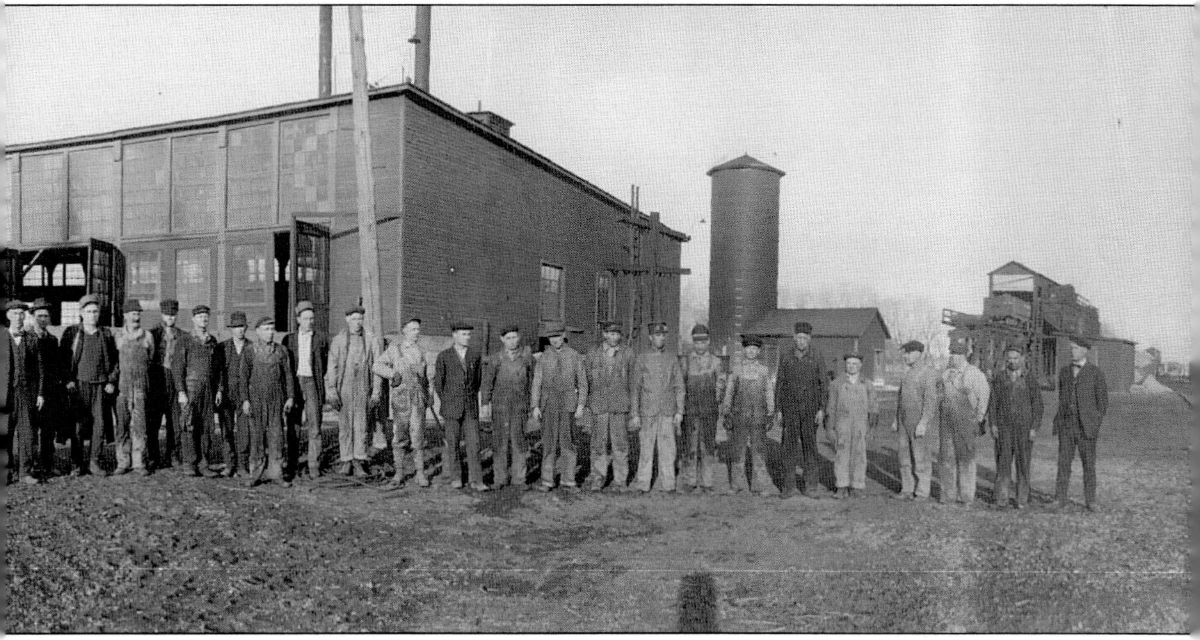

by the Missouri Pacific in July 1879. At one time 18 trains a day passed through Downs and the railroad was the largest employer in the city. Rail travel began to decline by the 1930s and periodically roundhouse stalls were torn down one or two at a time until the roundhouse and other buildings in the rail yard were gone.

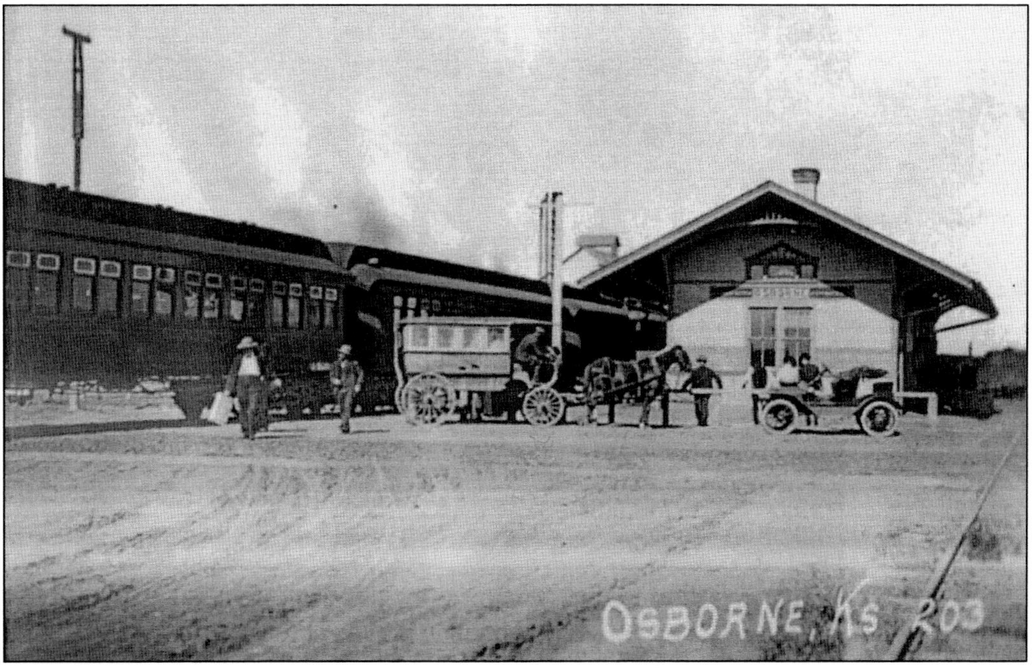

Shown here are people meeting the train at the Missouri Pacific Railroad depot in Osborne around 1910. In the center of the picture is the local taxi wagon. On the side of the depot are the signs "St. Louis, 547 miles" and "Atchison, 217 miles."

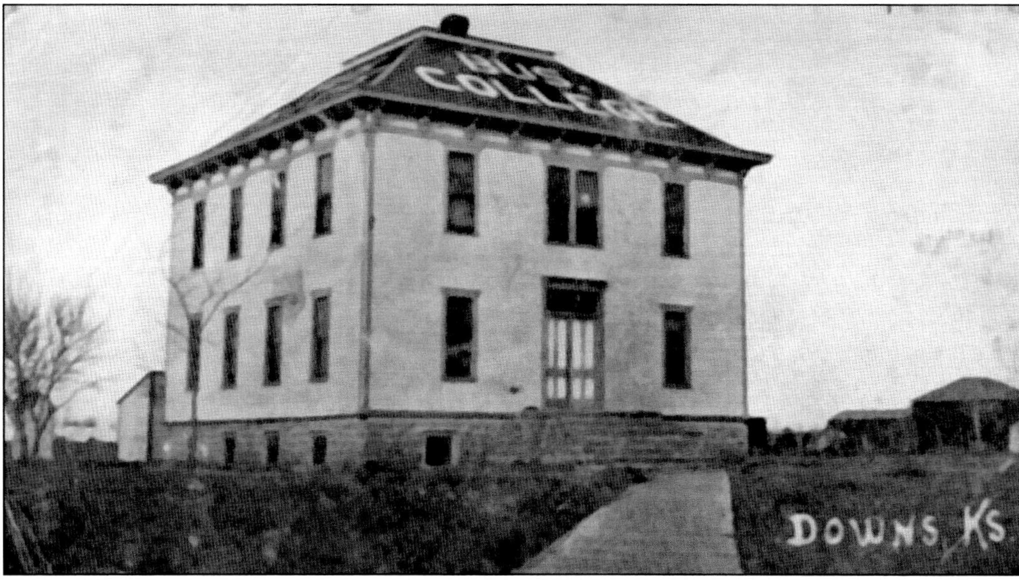

This is a postcard view of the Downs Business College, or more formally the Downs Normal and Commercial Institute. It was organized in 1901 and was operated for a stock company. Located on Kansas Street at the west edge of Downs, the college offered general and business courses. But operating costs grew too much and the Institute closed in 1909. Since then the building has housed a hospital, nursing home, and apartments.

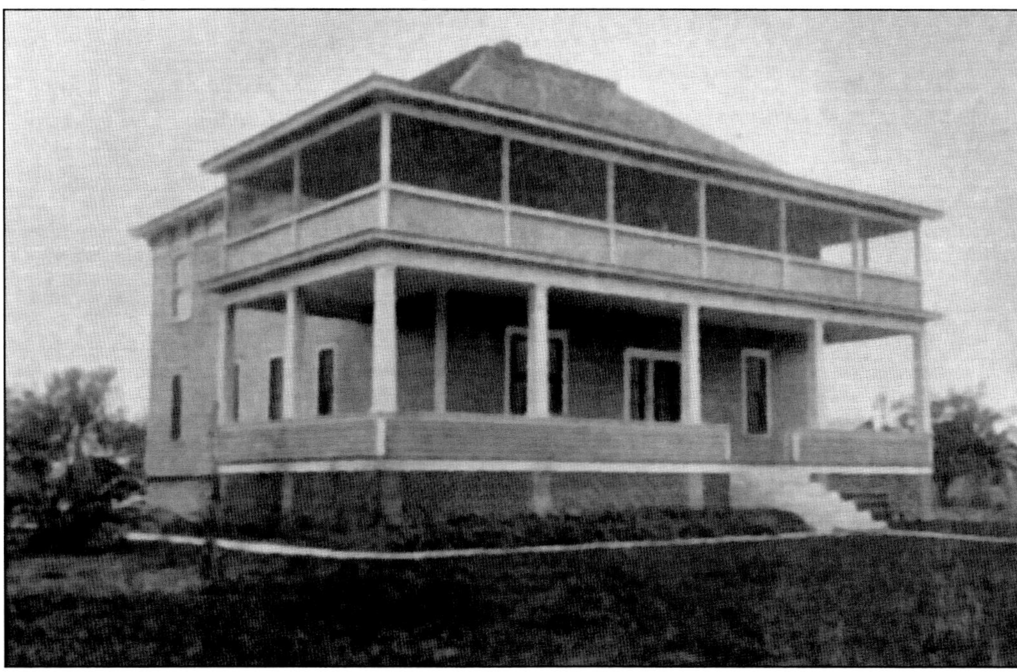

Throughout the 1920s, Dr. Jarvis Hodgson operated a hospital for Missouri Pacific Railroad employees in the former Downs Business College building. Dr. Hodgson served the medical needs of hundreds of railroad employees here. The medical care continued into the early 1930s until the dwindling presence of the railroad in the city forced the withdrawal of the railroad's support of the hospital.

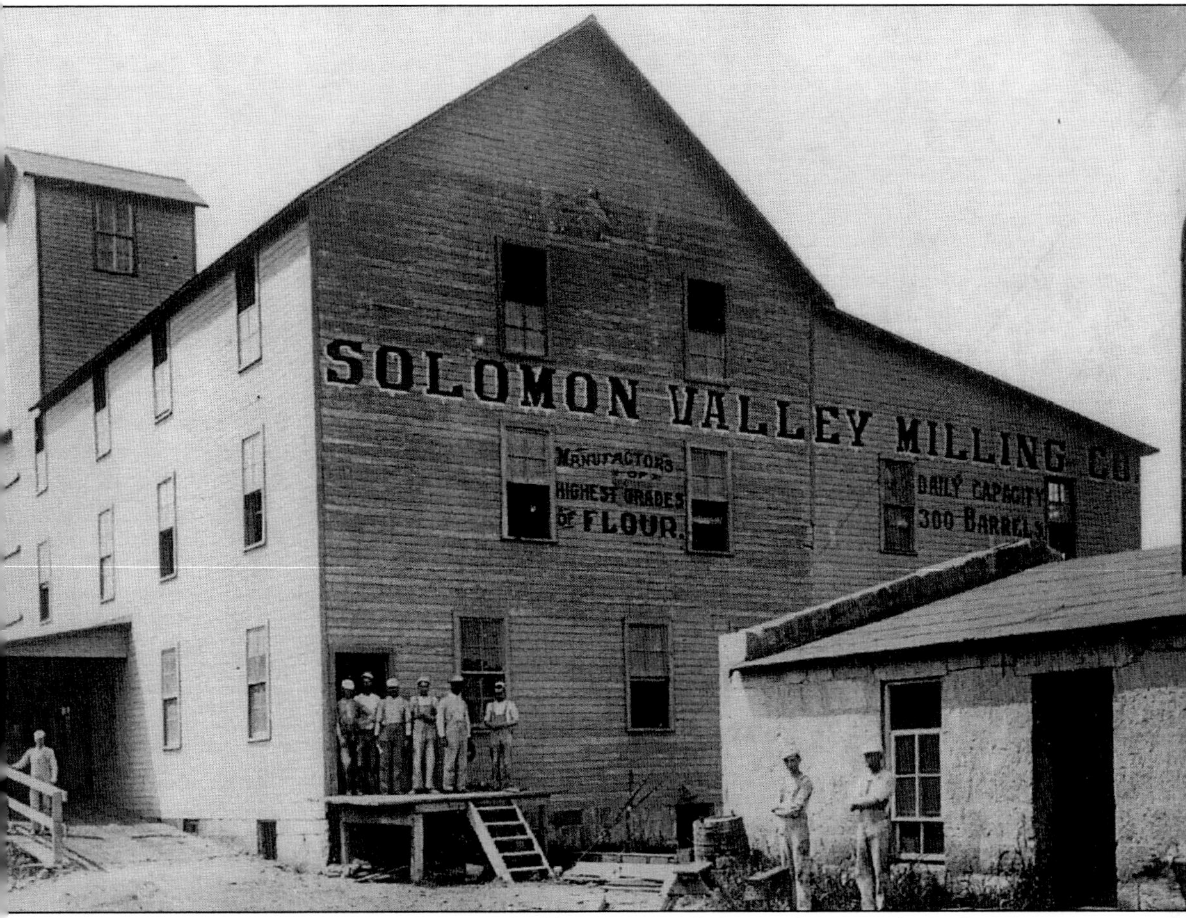

The Solomon Valley Milling Company building on North Second Street along the Missouri Pacific Railroad tracks in Osborne is pictured here. The mill was started by Ulysses Hibbs after his return from the Alaskan Gold Rush of 1898 and remained a major employer in the city for many years.

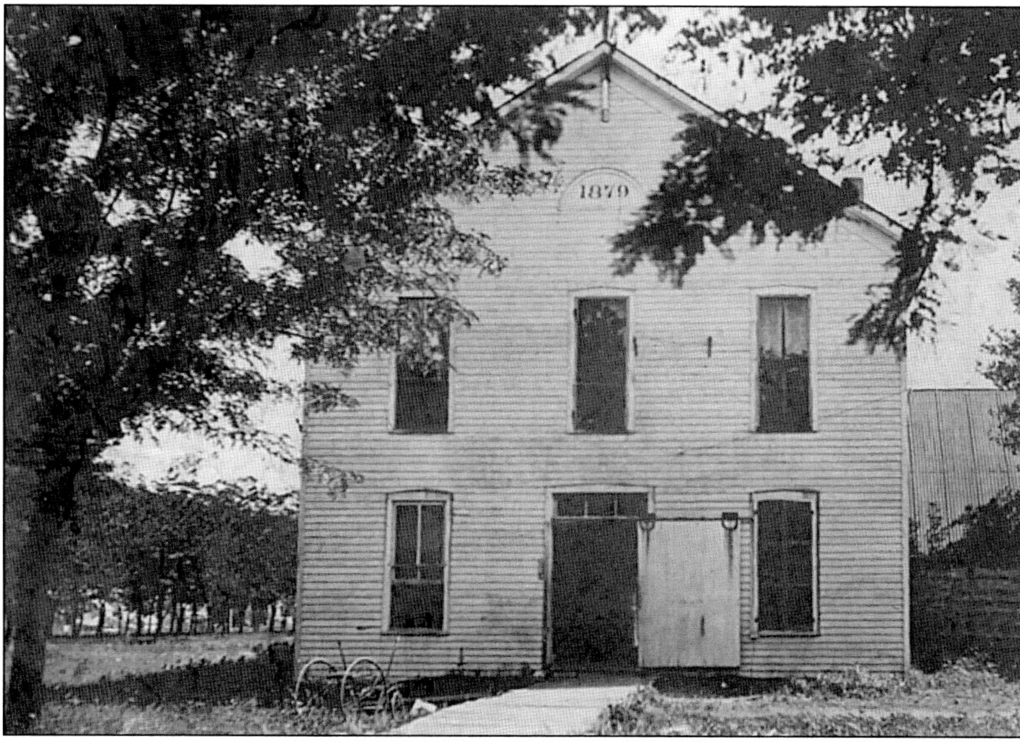

This is the north face of the second Osborne County Courthouse along West Main Street in Osborne. This photograph was taken in 1908 shortly before it was removed. The building was erected seven years after the first courthouse was destroyed in a storm in 1872. An 1879 threat to move the county seat to Bloomington convinced Osborne officials to provide funds for a new frame structure. To the right is the stone jail.

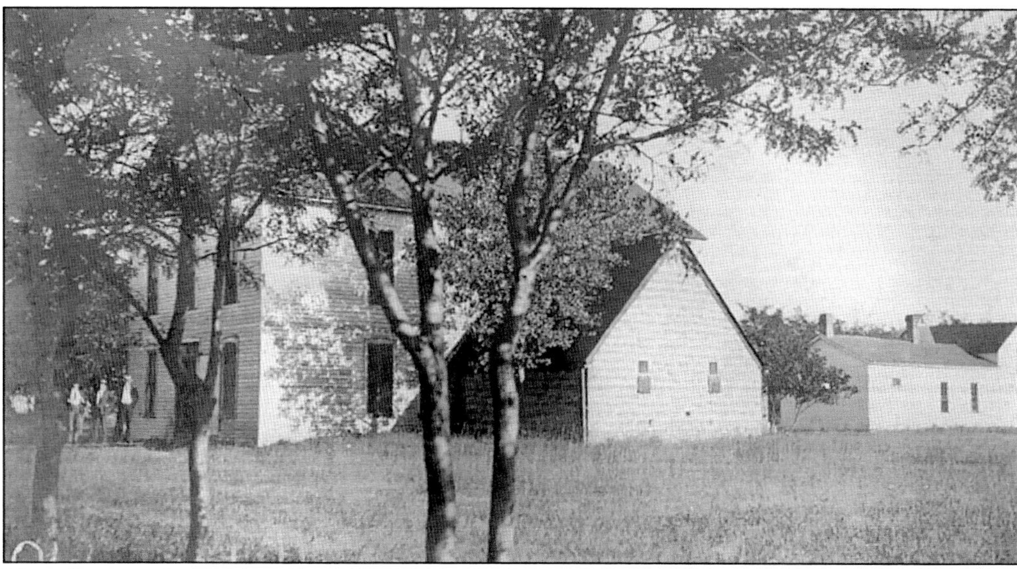

This photograph is of the west side of the second courthouse in 1908. On the right is the county sheriff's home. When the third and current courthouse was completed in 1908, the old building was sold and the timber made into two houses now located on South First Street in Osborne.

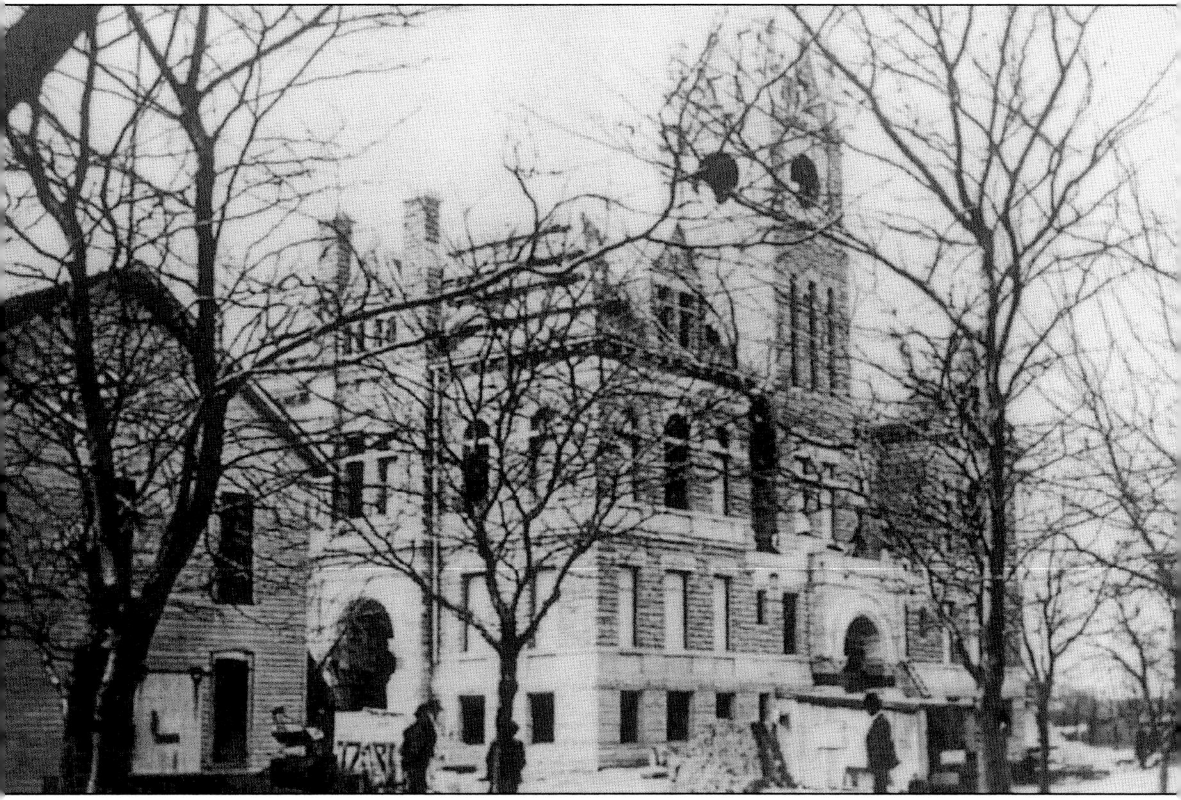

Pictured here is the current Osborne County Courthouse nearing completion in early 1908. This photo is of the north side facing West Main Street. Notice the empty windows, the lack of roofs, and especially the missing clock in the clock tower. The old 1879 courthouse, soon to be dismantled, is seen to the left. The new courthouse was designed by J.C. Holland, an architect who did several county courthouses across Kansas. Built of Cottonwood limestone from Chase County, Kansas, and Fencepost limestone from Mitchell County, Kansas, the building features several curious designs and characters carved into the rock at its entrances.

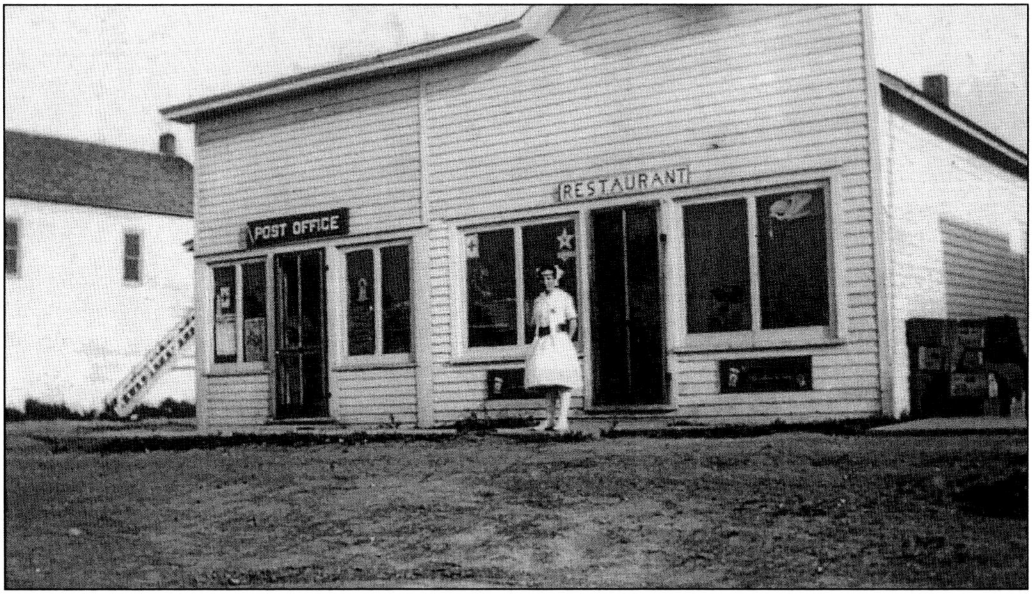

This shot of the Bloomington Post Office and Lafe Boultinghouse's restaurant shows how they appeared on Main Street in 1930. Lafe's daughter Isabella is standing in front. The post office opened in 1872 and closed its doors in 1955. To the left can be seen the Bloomington General Store, the top floor of which was a dance hall.

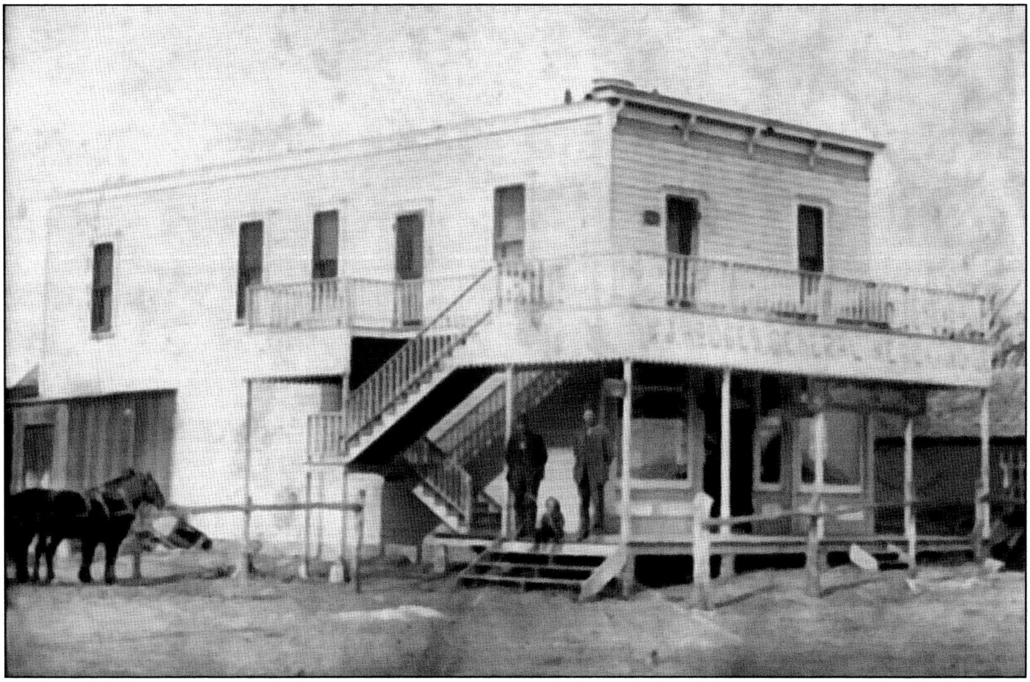

Taken *c.* 1910, this is a rare photograph of the W.J. Hodges General Merchandise Store. The store stood on the northwest corner of South and East Streets in Covert. The upstairs of the building served as family quarters for the store owners. It was built in 1903 by Leo Ruggles and was being operated by Will Hoar when the store burned down with all its contents on July 25, 1912.

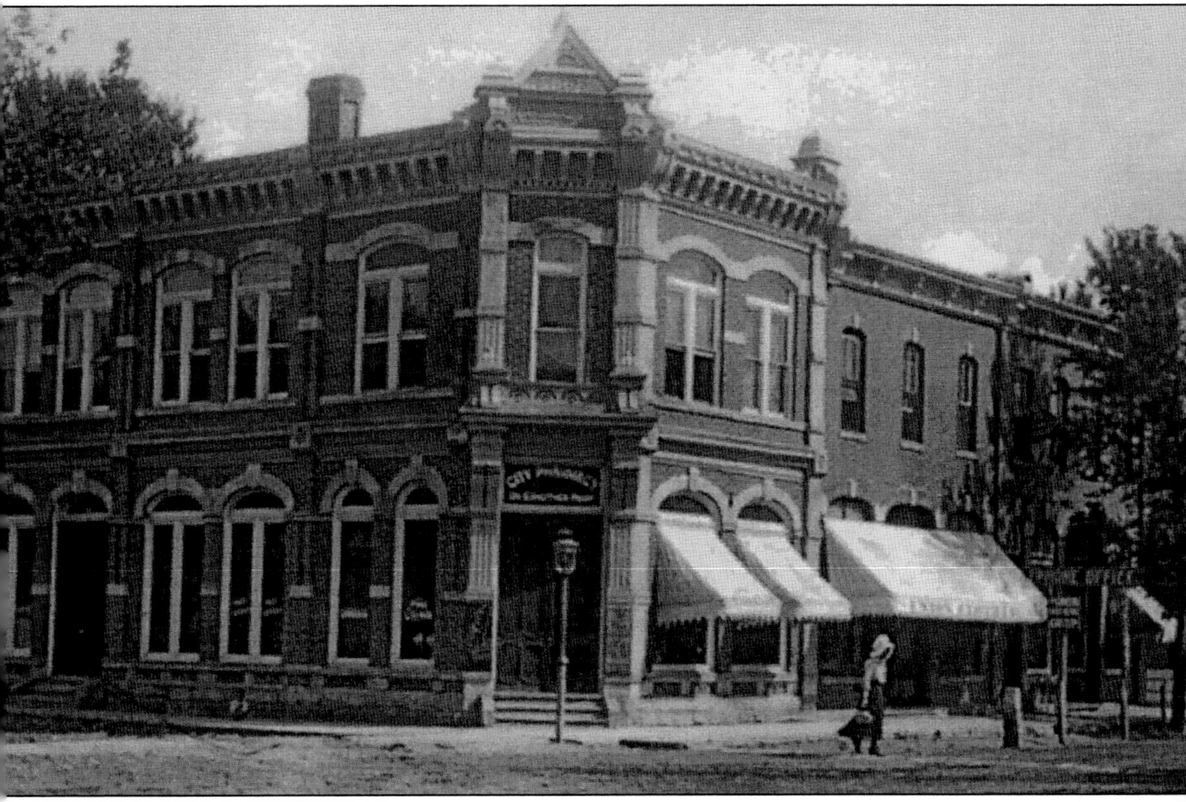

This view is of Dr. Charles Ebnother's City Pharmacy at the corner of Morgan Avenue and Beale Street in Downs shortly after 1901. The building was built for the First National Bank in the 1880s and was razed after World War II. The drugstore was famous for its soda fountain, "said to be the finest in Kansas west of Beloit," according to a 1914 newspaper account. Dr. Ebnother, a native of Switzerland, suffered tragedy when his son died of influenza in Scotland at the end of World War I. The news hastened his own death within a few months. The building site was later torn down and is now a parking lot.

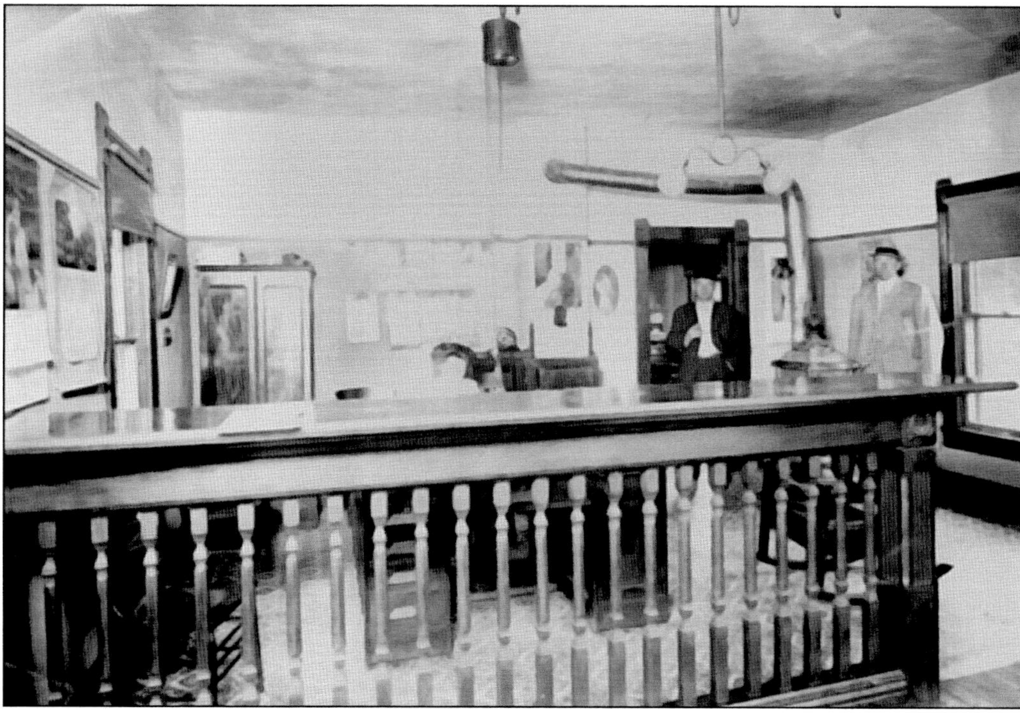

This is the inside of the office of the Rice-Johnz Lumber Company in about 1910 on East Railroad Street in Downs. A glimpse of the safe can be seen behind the secretary's desk. An interesting feature is the telephone hanging down in front of her that is attached to the ceiling.

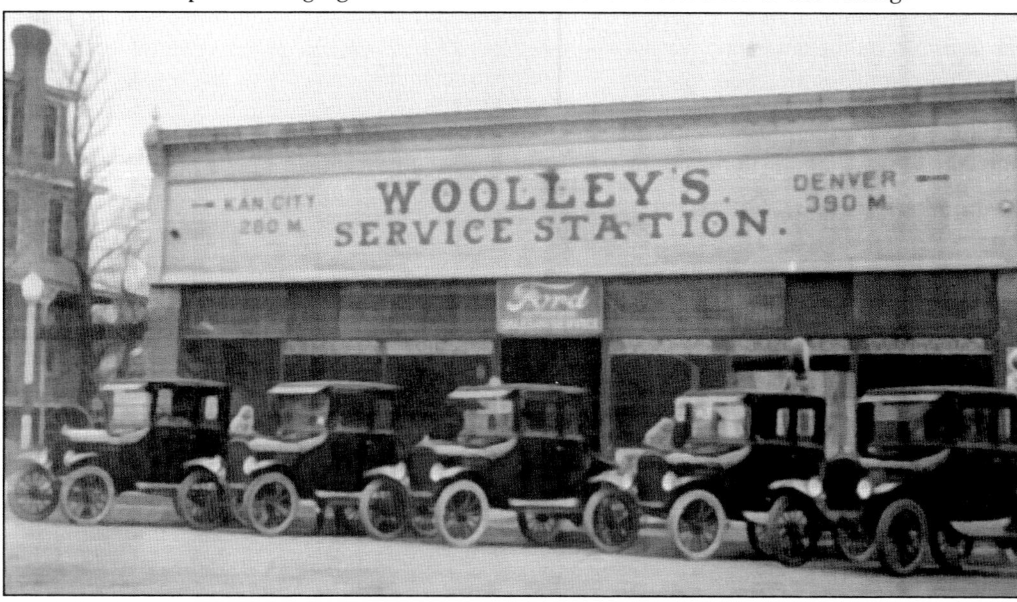

Sam Woolley's Implement Company and Service Station is seen here as it looked in the 1920s on West Main Street in Osborne next to the Alamo Hotel. Harry and Sam Woolley organized the Woolley Implement Company in 1907 and it soon became one of the largest implement firms in western Kansas. Notice the street lamp and the bulldog figureheads. The bulldog is the mascot of Osborne High School's athletic teams.

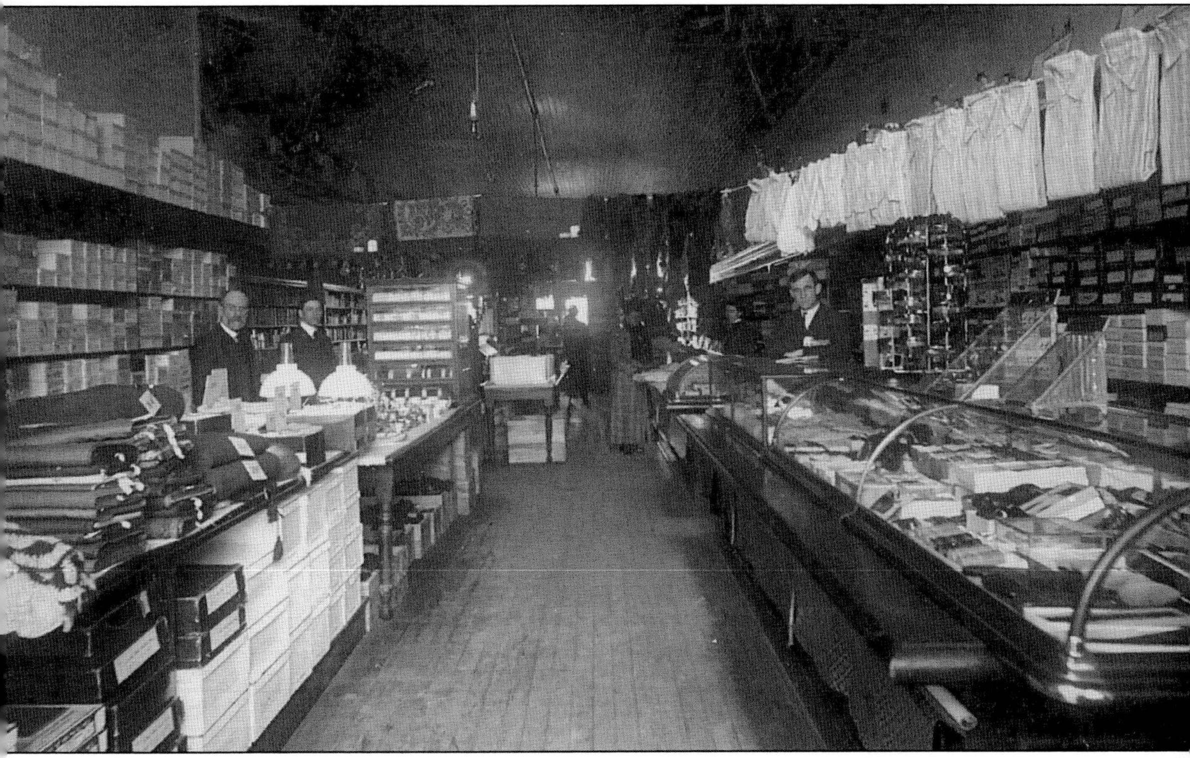

This photograph is of The VanWormer-Craig Clothing Company on West Main Street in Osborne in about 1915. Several items of interest include the shoe shelves on the left, the underwear in the boxes at bottom left, the sunglasses on the revolving stand on top of the right counter, and the rugs and fur stoles draped across the ceiling of the store.

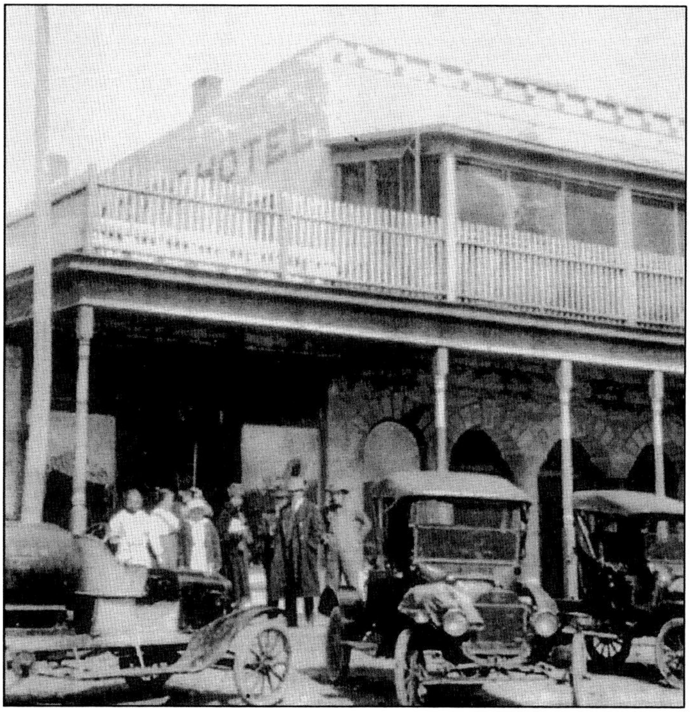

A family gathering at the Pacific Hotel and restaurant on North First Street in Natoma is shown here, taken around 1910. Built by A.A. Saum in 1906 and named for the nearby Union Pacific Railroad, Saum's father Raymond hand-carved the native limestone arches and pillars—seen in the right of the picture behind the vintage automobiles. The building also housed a restaurant and other businesses. After the demise of local passenger trains, business at the hotel dried up and it was closed in the 1960s. The vacant building was finally razed in 1976.

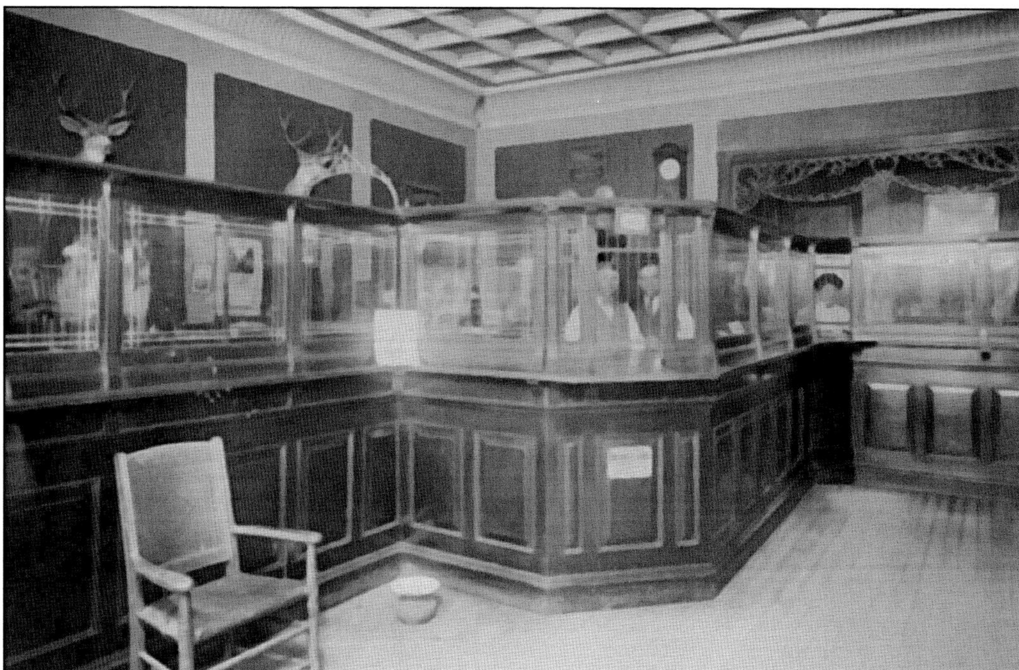

This photograph shows the lobby of the State Bank of Downs in the early 1900s. The bank was the Bank of Downs when it built a two-story stone structure on the southwest corner of Commercial and Morgan Avenues in 1884. Eight years later the bank failed and the State Bank of Downs was formed by the Harrison family. In 1976 the bank moved to a new location two blocks to the north.

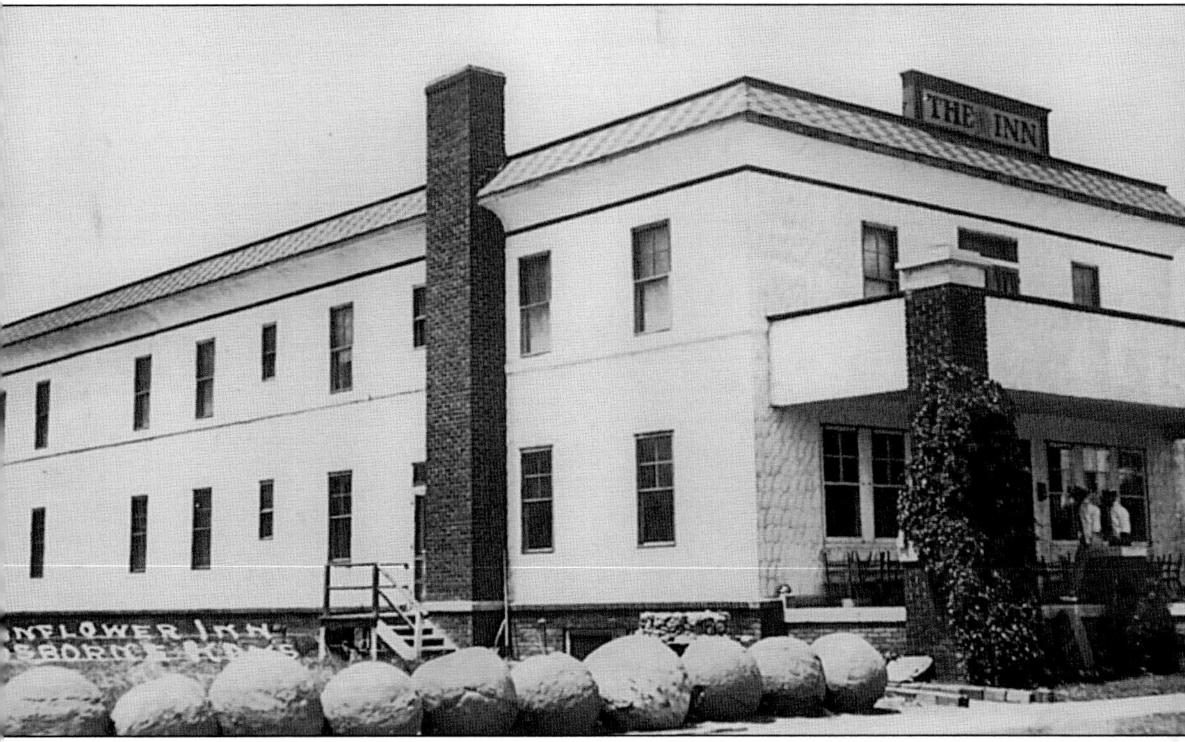

Pictured here is Sherman Benson's art deco-style Sunflower Inn as it looked upon its opening in July 1924 at the southwest corner of First and Washington Streets in Osborne. At the time, the Sunflower was considered the finest building ever constructed in the city and boasted 24 sleeping rooms, seven of which had a bath and toilet, with each room being equipped with a Simmons steel bed topped by a Sealey mattress. The Sunflower operated under various owners into the 1970s but now stands vacant. The row of boulders, called septarian concretions, are iron-based nodules native to the area. They range in size from a few inches to over 9 feet in diameter. These concretions were found south of Osborne during the construction of a new road and were brought into town to decorate the grounds of the inn.

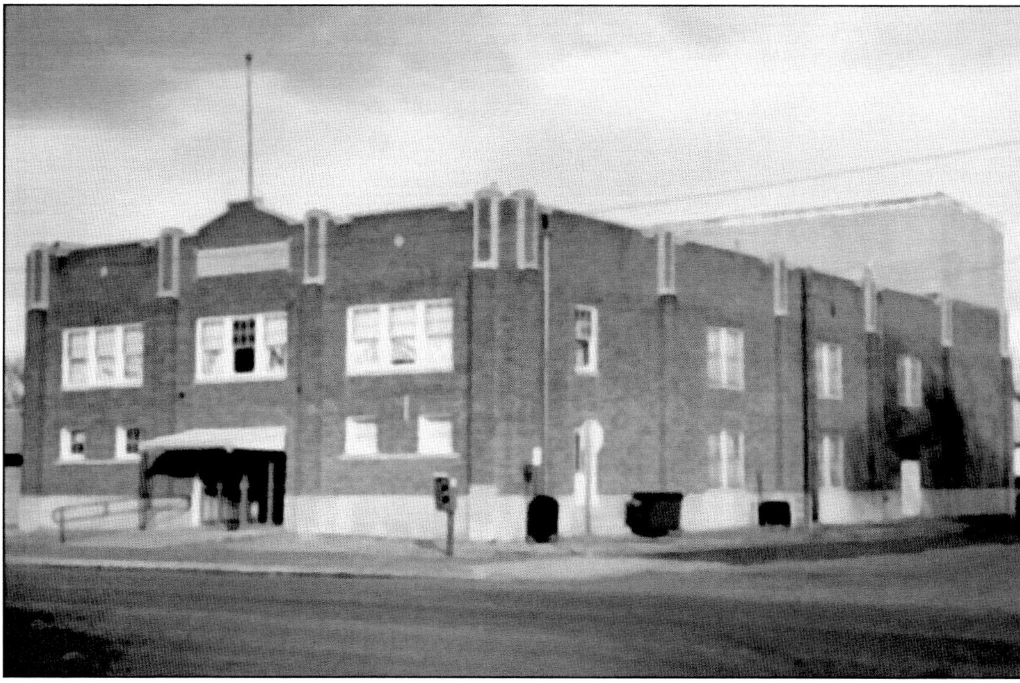

This is a current view of the Downs Memorial Hall. The hall was built with donated funds as a memorial to those who served in World War I and remains the county's only World War I memorial. Located on South Morgan Avenue, the hall hosts numerous activities year round and features the original tin ceiling and painted stage curtain.

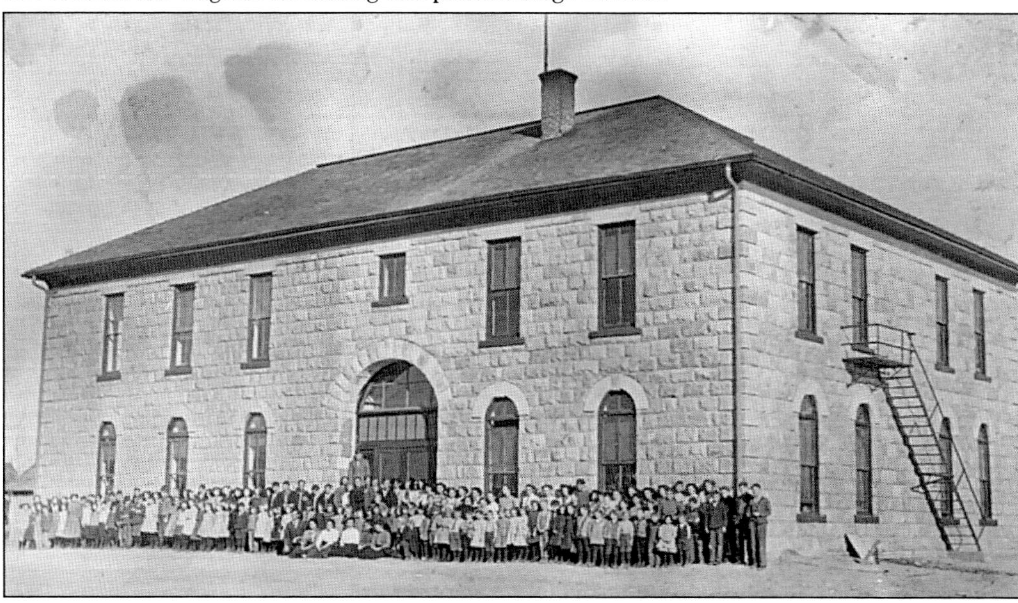

Photographed here is the Osborne Carnegie Library upon its completion in 1913. Located in the City Park on West Main Street, the structure was placed on the National Register of Historic Places in 1987, the only such registered site in Osborne. The library was built with a $6,000 grant from steel magnate Andrew Carnegie and served the city for over 80 years until a new adjacent building was erected in 1994.

Three

People and Homes

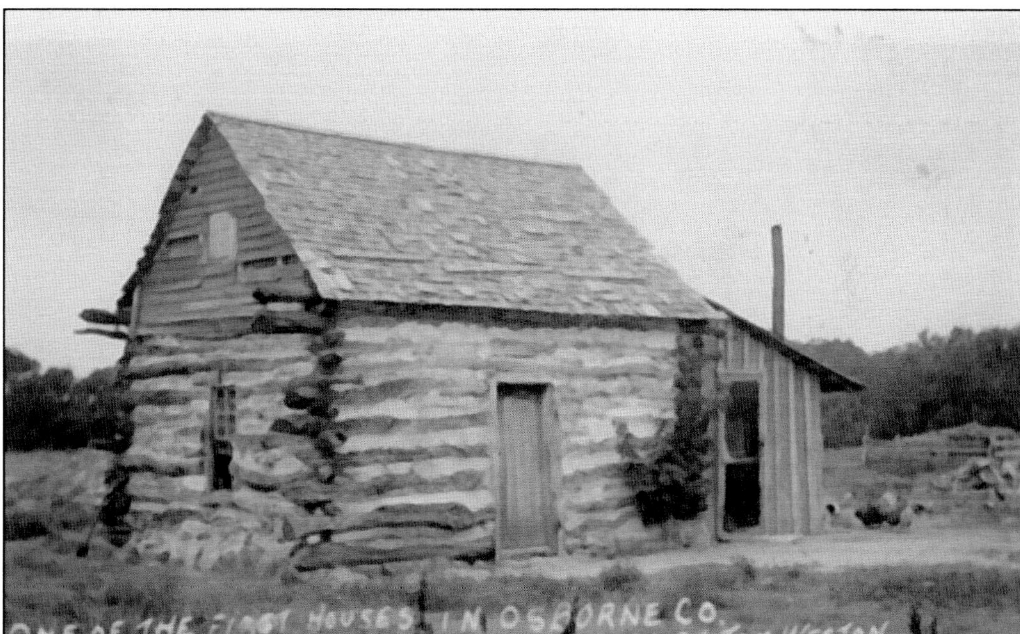

This is the Thomas Weston log cabin, built in June 1870 along Covert Creek, 13 miles from the present site of Osborne. Weston's daughter America was the first child born in Osborne County. In July 1870, a colony of settlers including Jeff Durfey arrived here and erected the Weston Stockade around the cabin. The cabin was used for nearly 20 years before it was torn down in the late 1880s.

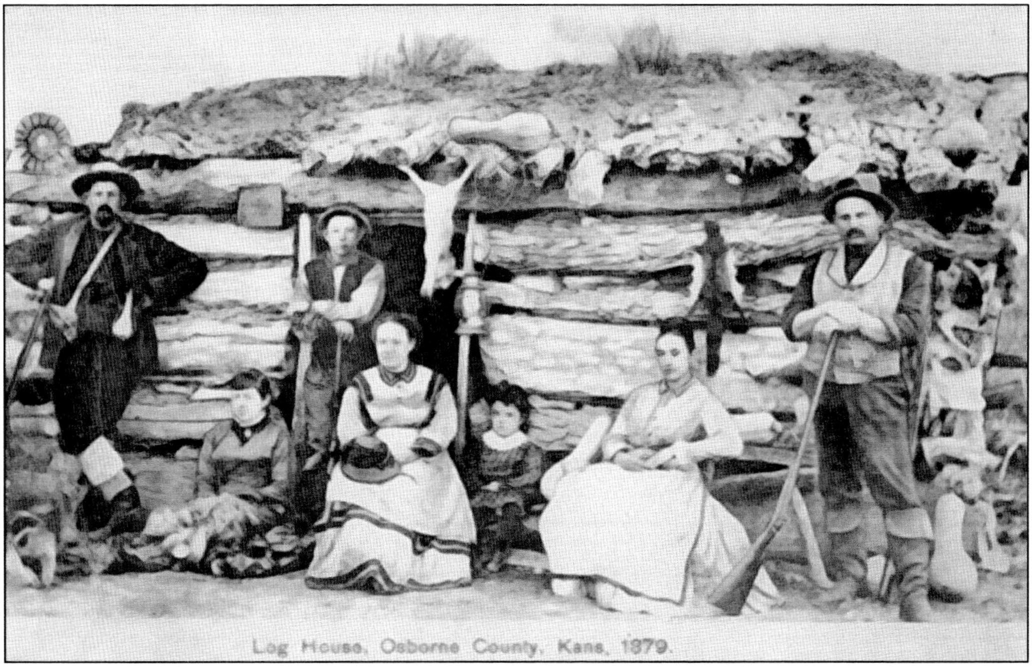

This 1879 postcard picture is of the John Stadiger farm residence located 3 miles east of Osborne. Notice the grass and gourds growing out of the sod roof along with the various animals and skins hung up to dry.

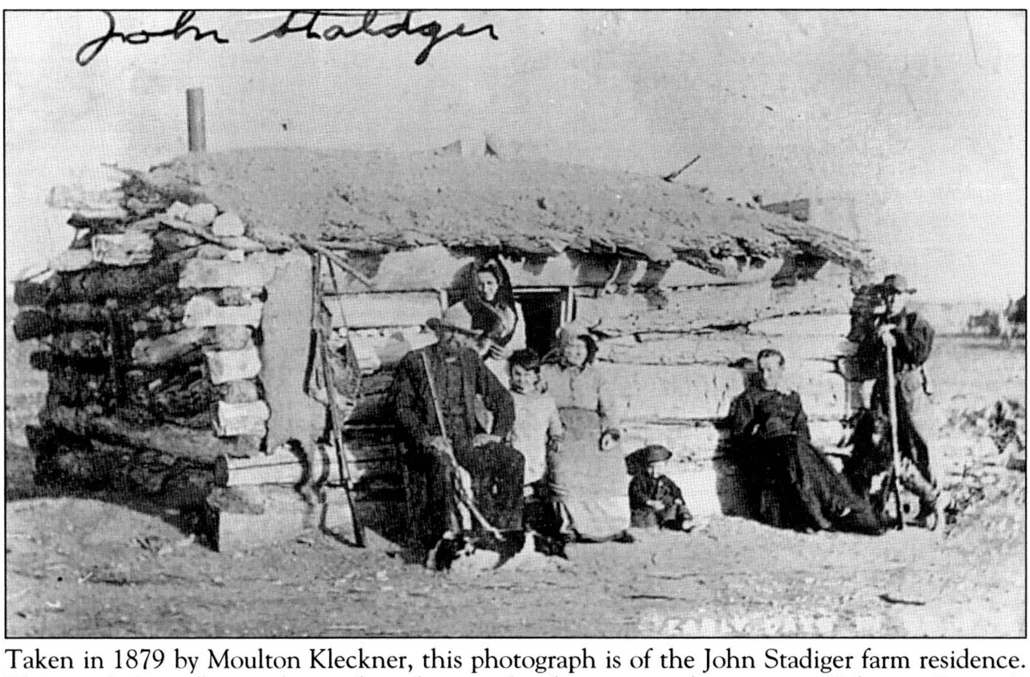

Taken in 1879 by Moulton Kleckner, this photograph is of the John Stadiger farm residence. The rough log cabin with a sod roof was a familiar site at this time in Osborne County's history. Stadiger, a native of Bethlehem, Pennsylvania, stayed on this farm for only a few years before moving on.

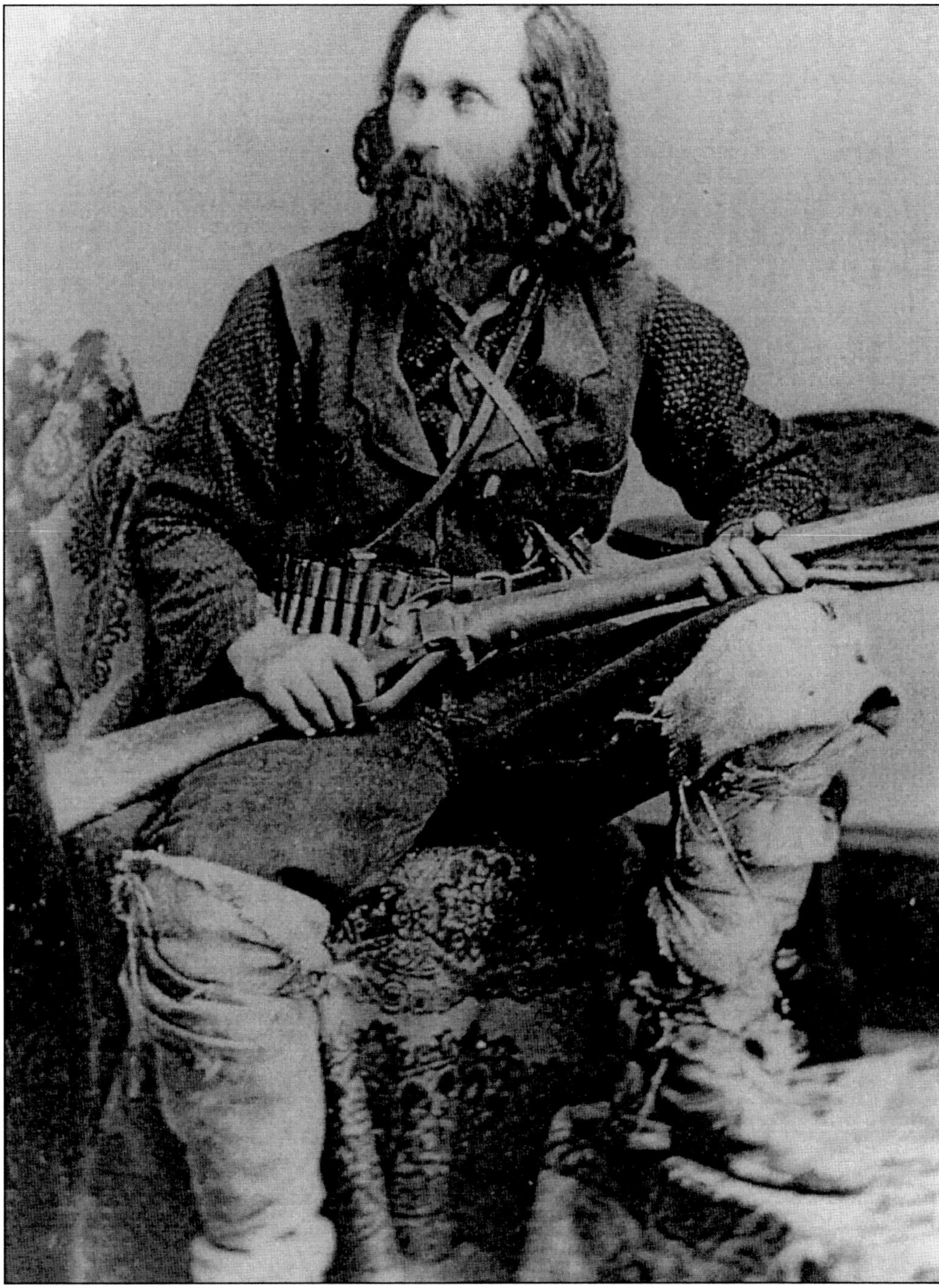

This 1870s portrait shows Jessie Hendricks, a buffalo hunter and U.S. Army scout who was a contemporary of "Buffalo" Bill Cody and Jeff Durfey. Around his waist are the bullets for his buffalo gun while his lower legs are wrapped as protection against burrs, snakes, and other potential problems on the prairie. The frontier era of Osborne County lasted for nearly ten years, until 1880, by which time men such as Hendricks had either settled down on a farm or had moved farther west.

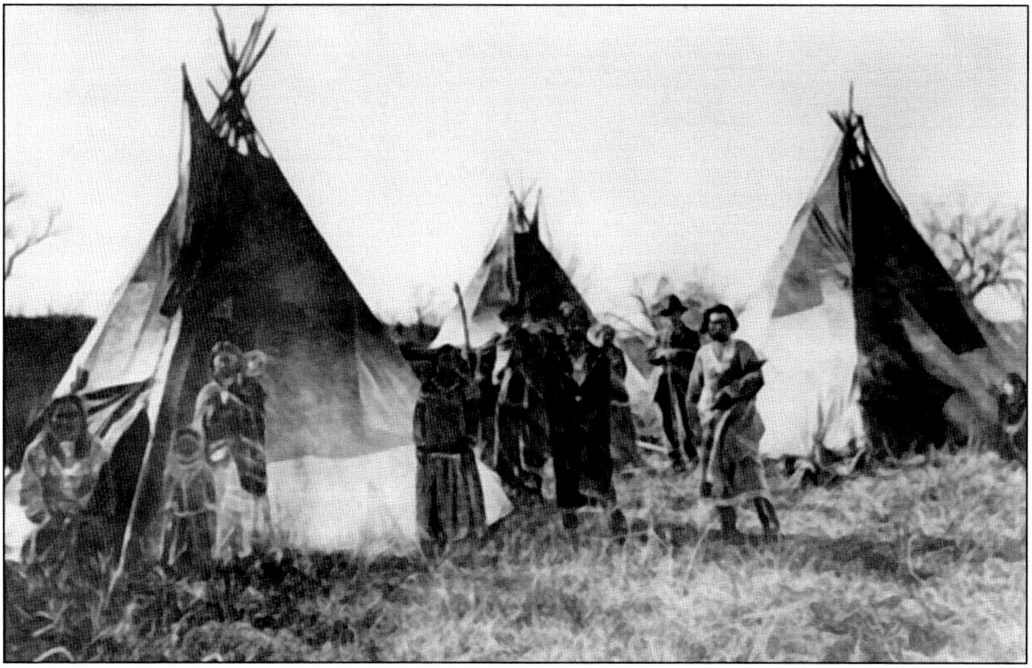

Here is another photograph by Moulton Kleckner this time showing Omaha Indians camped on the South Fork Solomon River west of Osborne in 1879. Two Indians, Zacharias Bones and Running White Bear, insisted that a white man be in the photograph so that it would not take their souls—otherwise they would not let the photograph be taken. So white settler John Meyer can be seen in the center background dressed as an Indian.

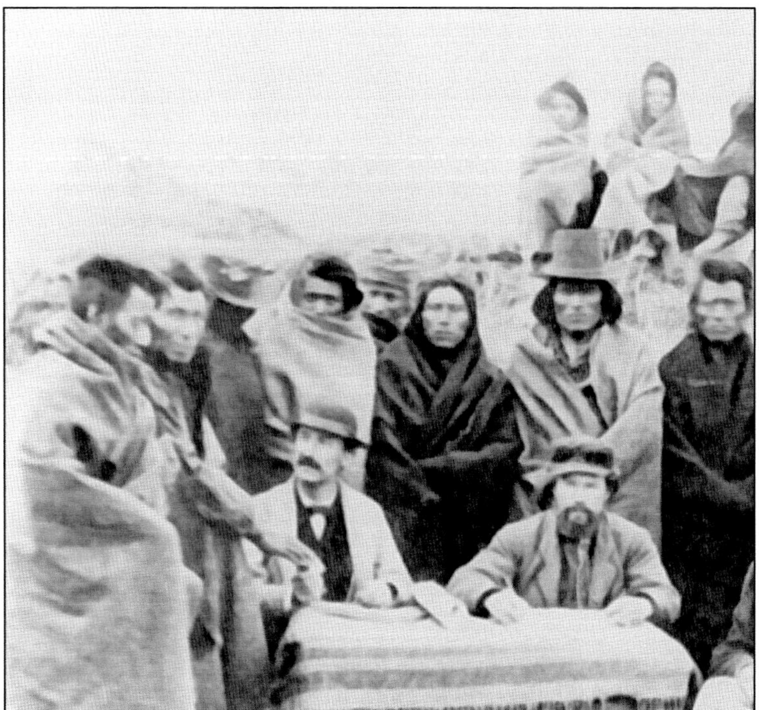

Moulton Kleckner captured this scene in 1879 of Omaha Indians receiving county rations from a three-member committee at their camp on the South Fork Solomon River west of Osborne. Seated on the left is William P. Gillette. The Omahas came west to hunt buffalo and were distressed to discover that the white man had now settled so far out over the plains, and that they had to travel far in order to hunt.

Pictured here is Thomas Jefferson Durfey, better known as Jeff Durfey. Jeff arrived in Osborne County in July 1870 from Wisconsin and joined the large numbers of early white settlers who made their living hunting buffalo on the Great Plains. He was a friend of the famous "Buffalo" Bill Cody, who in 1911 stated that Durfey was the only man he would ever admit could outshoot him.

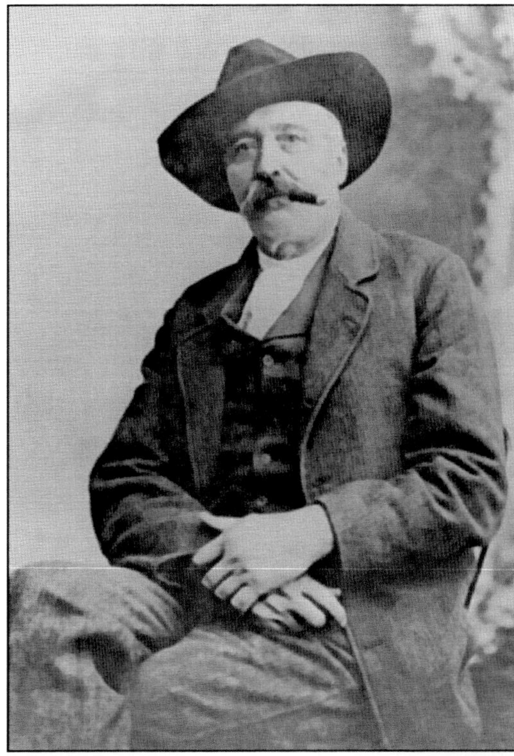

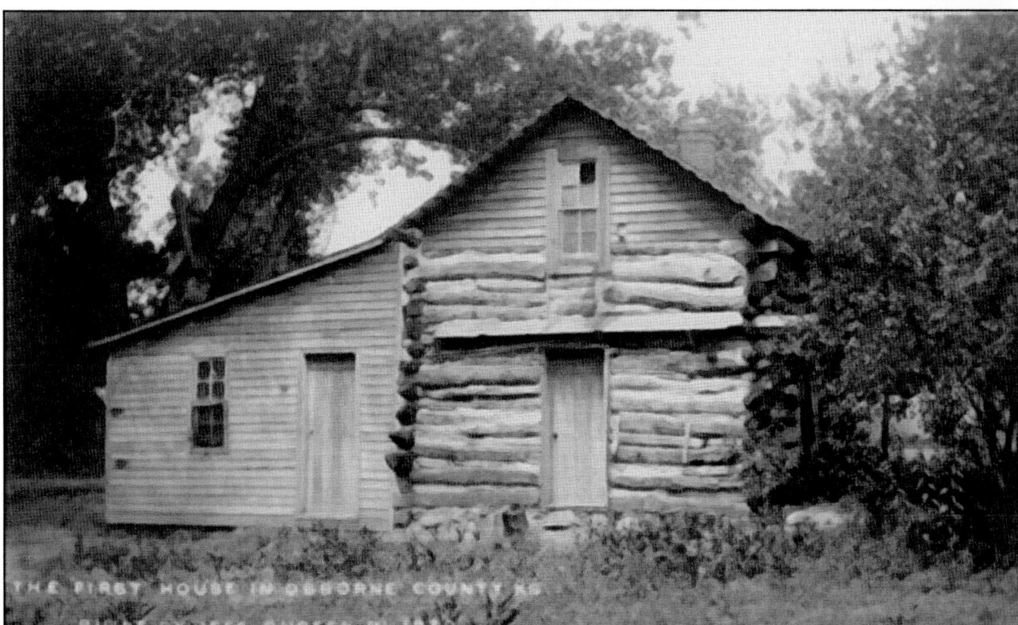

In August 1870 Jeff Durfey located his homestead near the center of Osborne County. While he did not build the first home in the county as this 1910 postcard attests, his cabin is still on its original site and is now the oldest building standing in the county. The lean-to was added sometime after 1900. Durfey became the first large-scale wheat farmer in the county and remains a local legend.

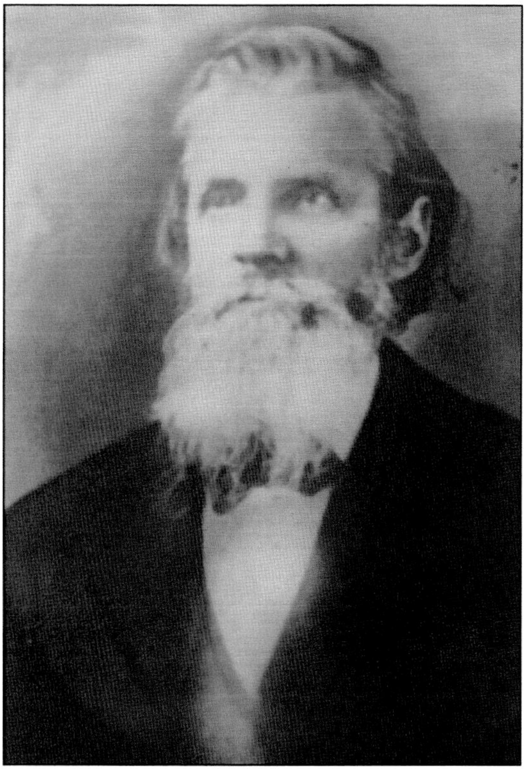

This portrait is of Hiram C. Bull taken early in 1879. Bull was Osborne County's leading citizen during its formative years. A New York native, he had been Wisconsin's Quartermaster General and attained the rank of major in the Civil War. He was Osborne County's first probate judge and was serving as a Kansas state representative when he was gored to death by his pet elk on October 12, 1879.

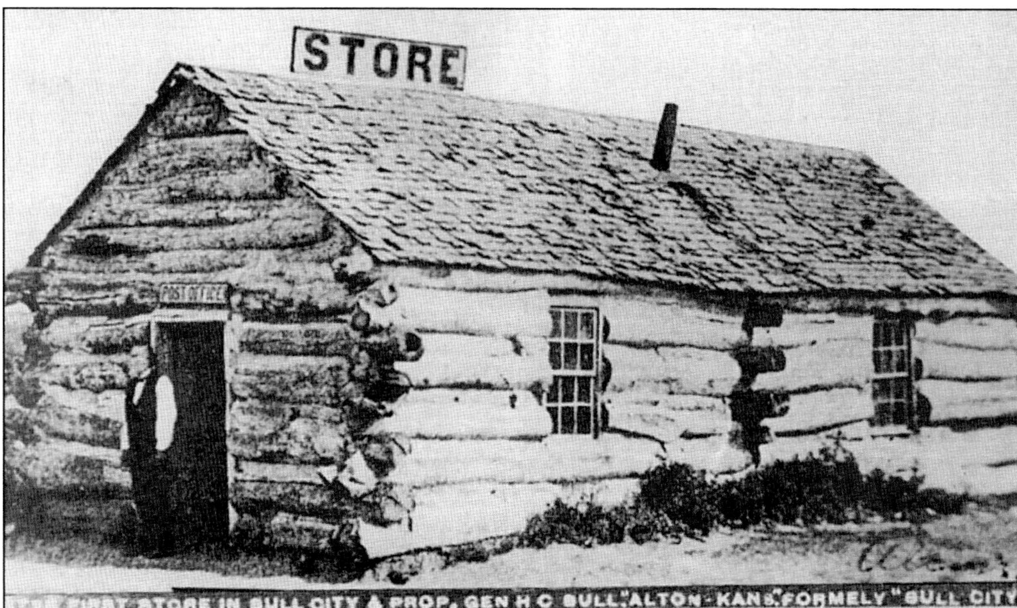

This late 1870s postcard photograph shows Hiram C. Bull and his log general store in Bull City. It was built in January 1871 and was the town's first building. The front room housed the store while the back room was the family quarters. Goods stocked were from as far away as New Orleans, St. Louis, and San Francisco. Bull died in 1879 and the city was renamed Alton in 1885.

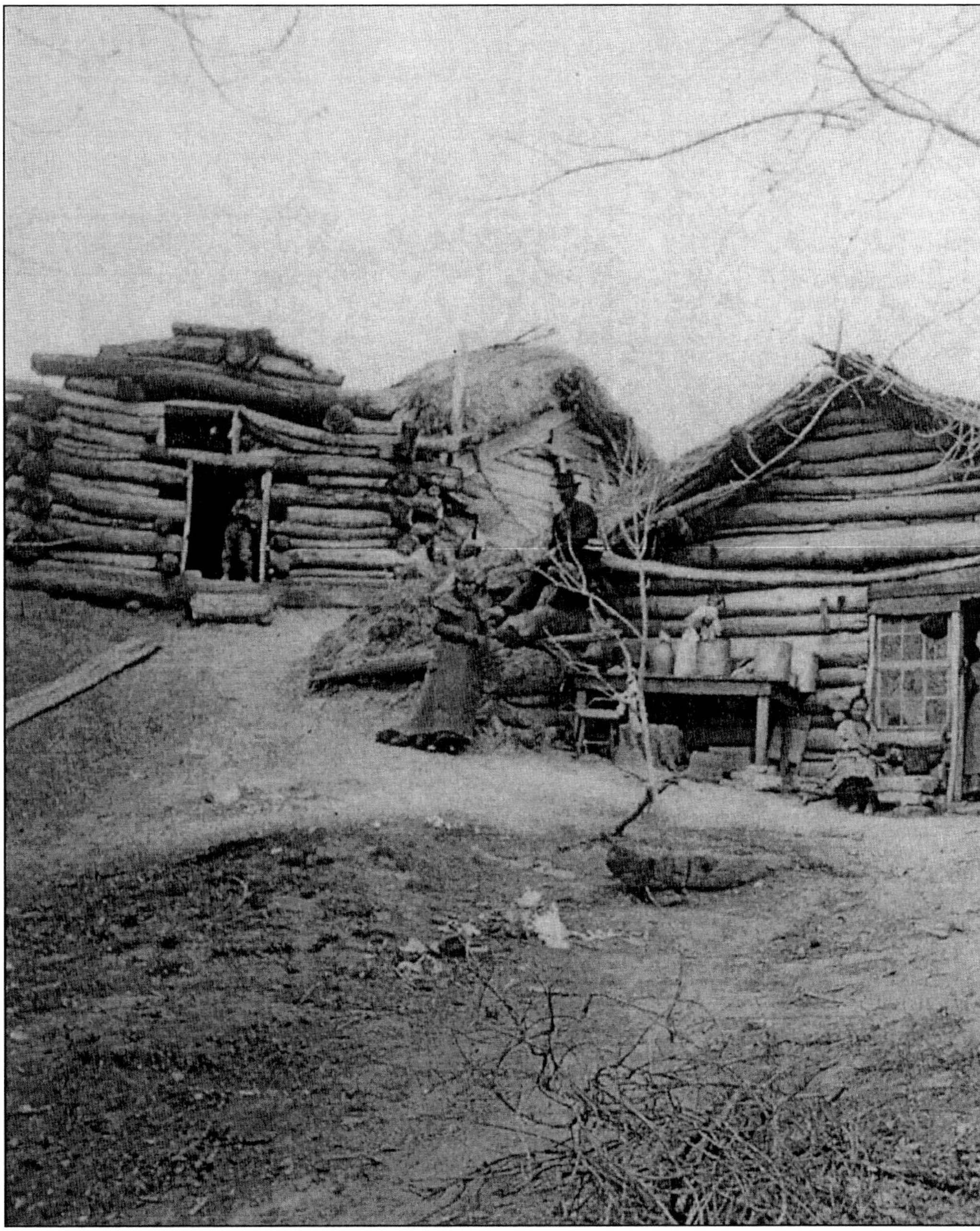

Located on the north bank of the South Fork Solomon River a mile west of Osborne, this view is of the William Goodlad family homestead. Taken in 1878 by Moulton Kleckner, the photograph clearly shows how these dugout cabins were constructed, with a single main beam down the center and covered by sod. The man seated in the center is Adam Smith.

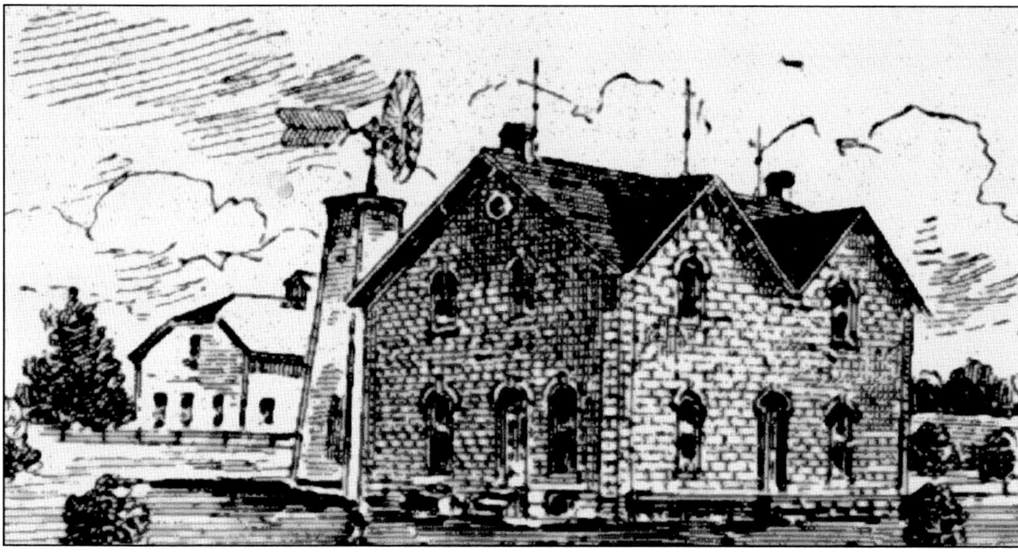

This 1884 sketch is of the Reverend Russell Osborn farm residence located 3 miles west of Alton. It was built by him in 1883 from native limestone near the site. In 1892 Osborn was elected to his only political office of any kind, the first and only Populist Party Kansas Secretary of State. Shortly after his taking office, the Legislative War of 1893 between the Republican and Populist Parties broke out.

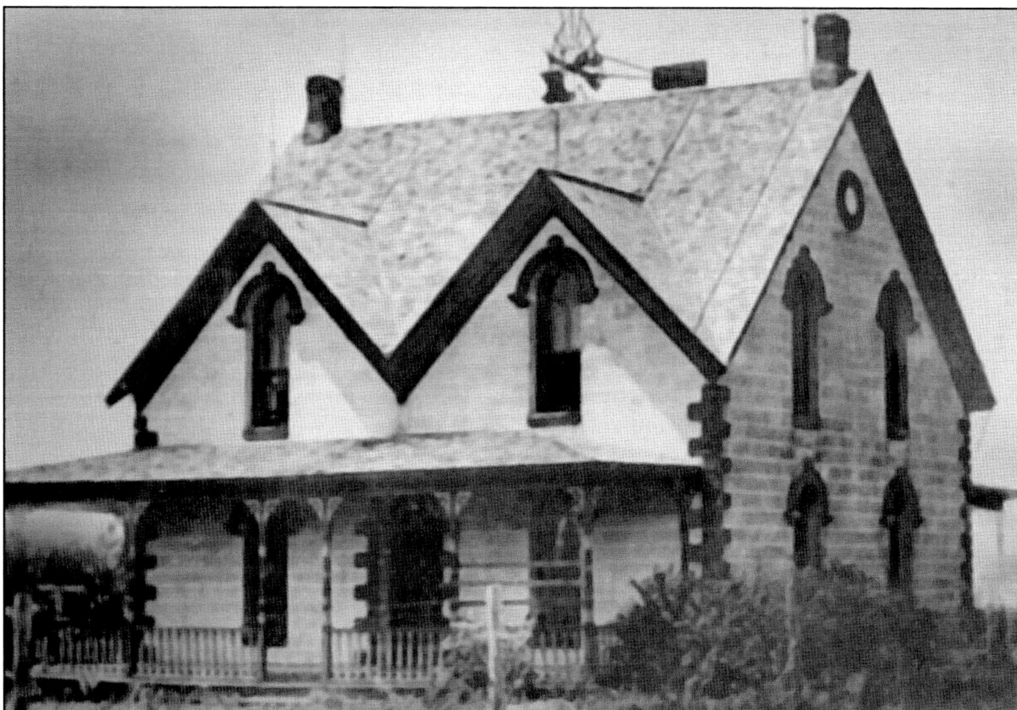

Pictured here is the Reverend Russell Osborn farm residence in the early 1900s. In this photograph porches can be seen, having been added to the stone home which still stands and is owned by Reverend Osborn's descendants. The home was built with walnut-framed windows and doors. The windmill seen at the rear of the house is also still standing.

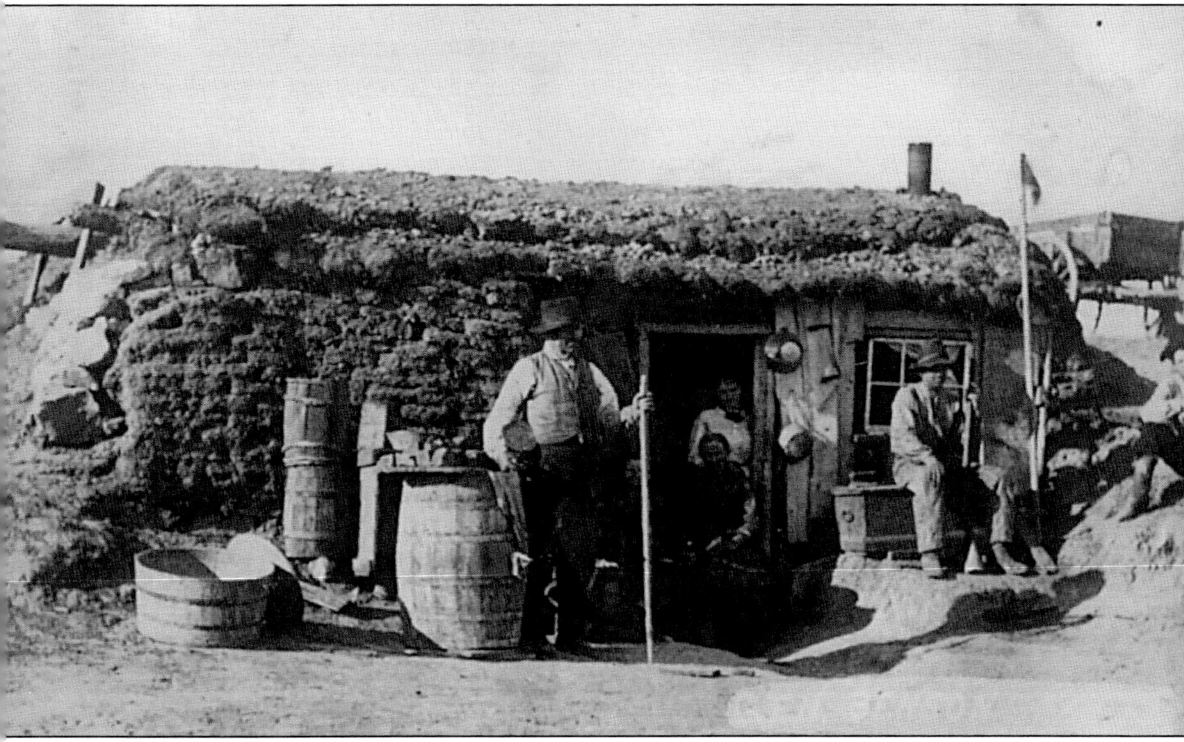

This photograph shows the Martin M. Mohler sod dugout, located 3 miles southwest of Downs, as it appeared in 1879. Mohler was one of the first three graduates of Northwestern University. He staked out a claim in eastern Osborne County in 1871 and was well respected for his views on farming the new land. In 1888 Mohler became the first Kansas Secretary of the Board of Agriculture from Western Kansas. His son Jacob, born in this sod home, followed in his father's footsteps and became the state's Agricultural Secretary from 1914 to 1949. It was Jacob who created the image of Kansas wheat being the finest in the world.

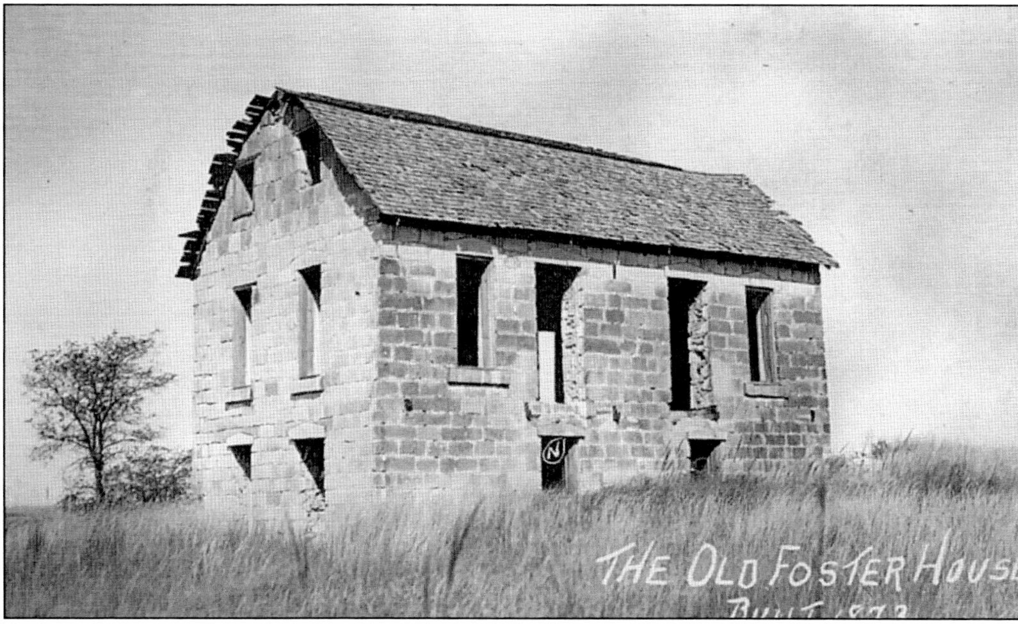

This 1929 postcard picture shows the Reverend Richard B. Foster home, built in 1873 on the divide between Osborne and Portis. The two-story native limestone structure was a county landmark for decades. The abandoned house often served as shelter in rain or at night for many a traveler before it was torn down in 1930 and the stones used for the tees at the nearby Osborne Country Club Golf Course.

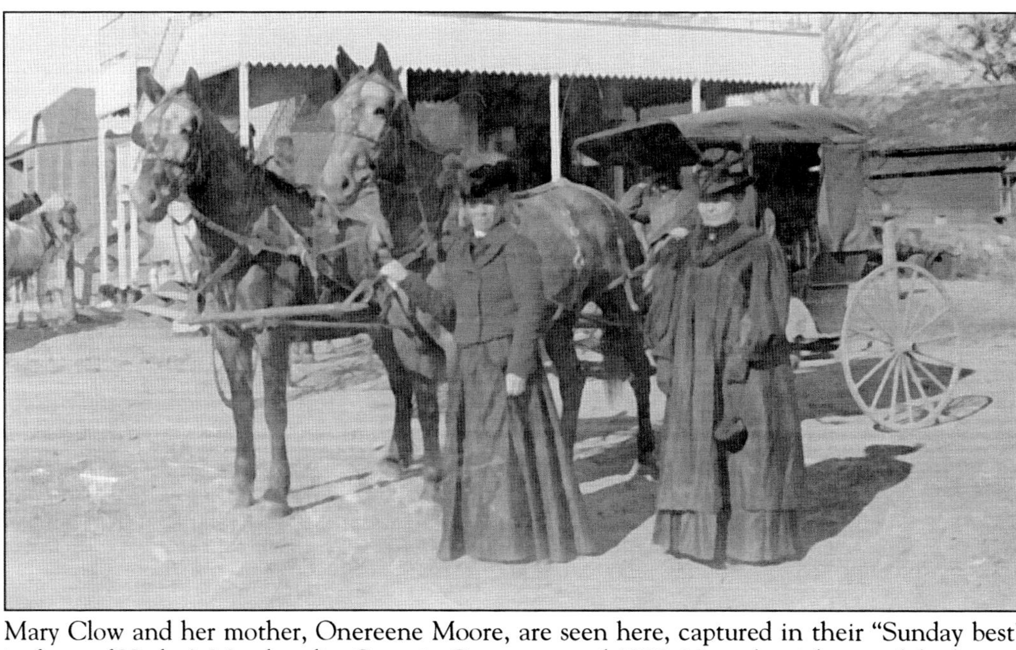

Mary Clow and her mother, Onereene Moore, are seen here, captured in their "Sunday best" in front of Hodge's Merchandise Store in Covert around 1910. Note the richness of the horses' harnesses and of the buggy.

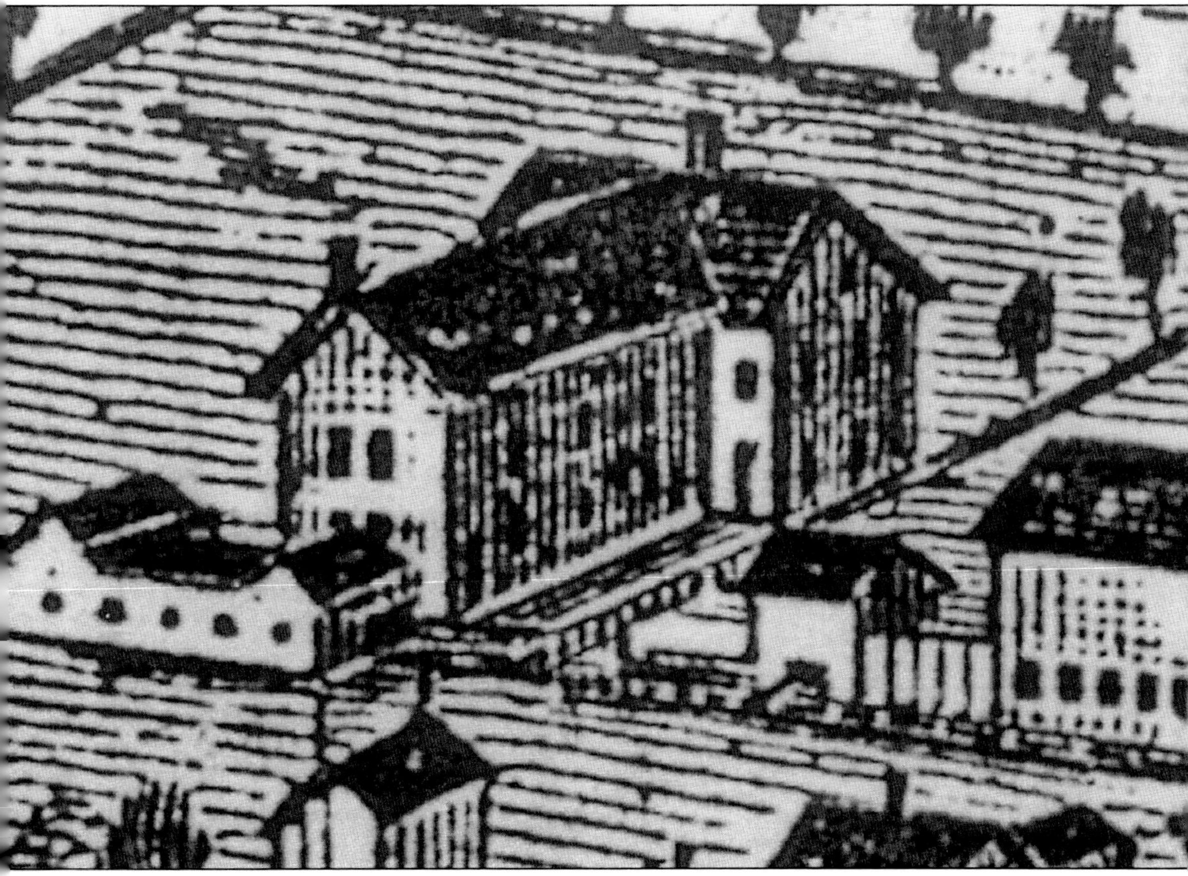

Taken from an 1879 newspaper sketch, this is the only known picture of the two-story frame Solomon Valley House in Osborne. The building was built in 1872 by Calvin Reasoner on West Main Street to serve as both his home and as a boardinghouse. After a windstorm destroyed the first stone county courthouse in late 1872 it also became the unofficial county courthouse and home to most of the county offices. This arrangement continued until 1879, when rumors arguing the need to move the county seat from Osborne because the city would not build a proper courthouse induced city officials to finally do so and erect a new frame structure. The boardinghouse continued for many years under the ownership of Mrs. Reasoner. When it was torn down in 1919, it proved to be a difficult job, as the frame walls had been filled with concrete some years before. The building's site is now a parking lot.

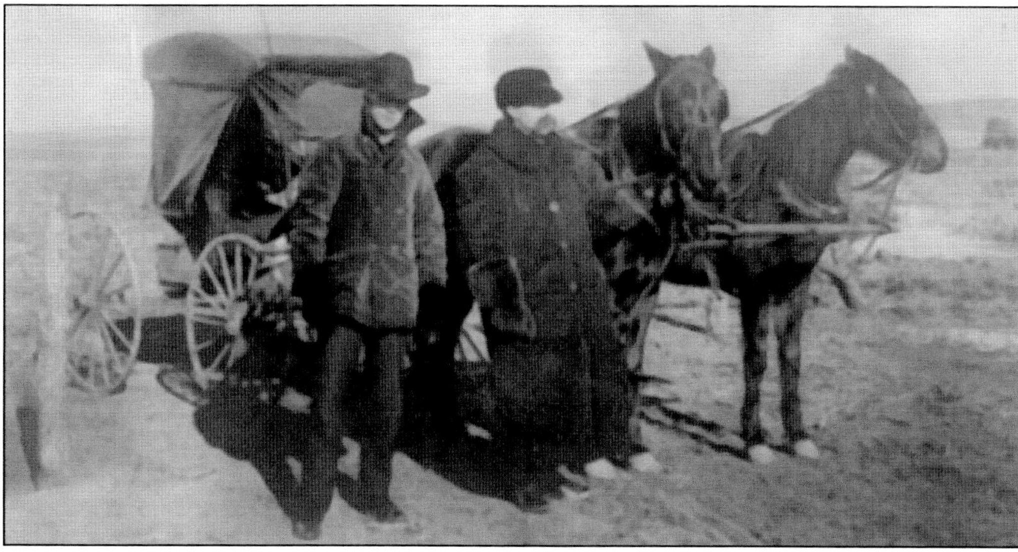

Dr. Tasso O. Felix, on the right, was one of the true horse-and-buggy doctors. His dedication to making house calls at all hours of the day and night in all kinds of weather in the Downs area was much appreciated among his fellow citizens.

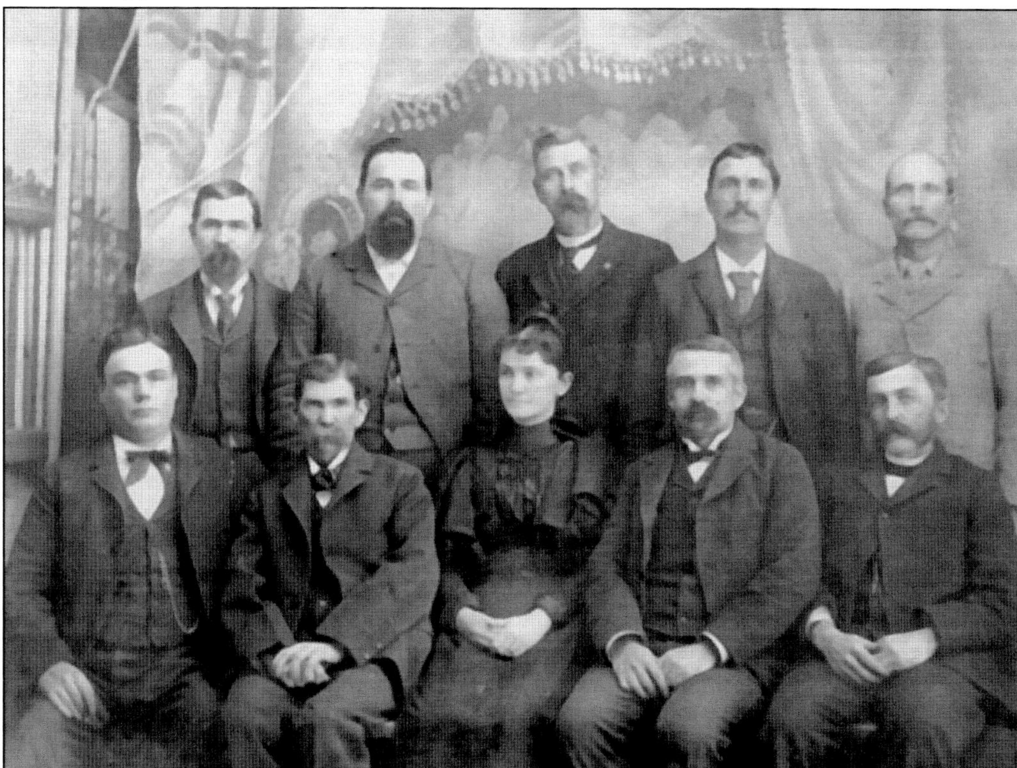

Pictured here are the 1894 Osborne County officials at the beginning of their terms of office. The woman in front center is Etta Cross, the newly elected county superintendent of schools. The school superintendent's office was the only county office ever held by a woman for nearly 40 years before the election of Laura Ward as county register of deeds in 1908.

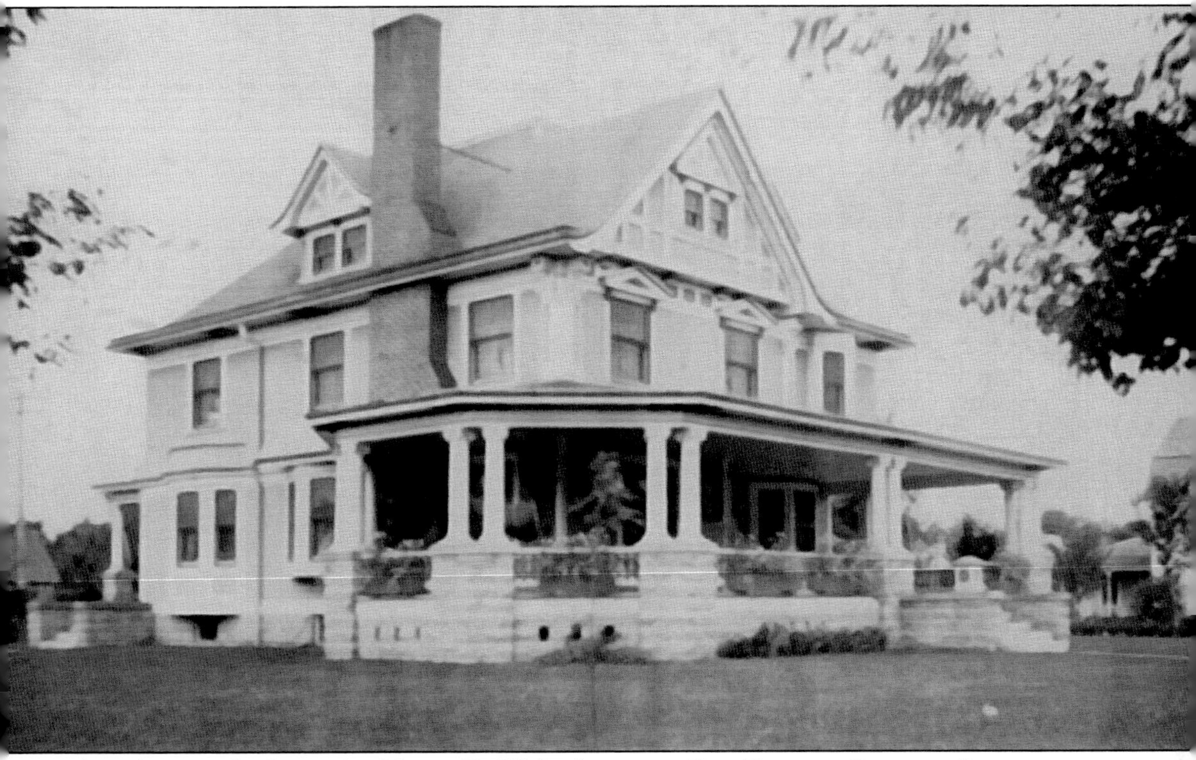

This photograph shows the Henry H. Welty home on East Division Street in Downs as it appeared on July 28, 1908. It was built by Welty in 1904 at a cost of $20,000 with a carriage house in the rear costing a further $1,000. The house was used later as a private hospital by Dr. Jarvis Hodgson and was the longtime home of the Marion Hardman family. It is currently the largest private residence in Osborne County.

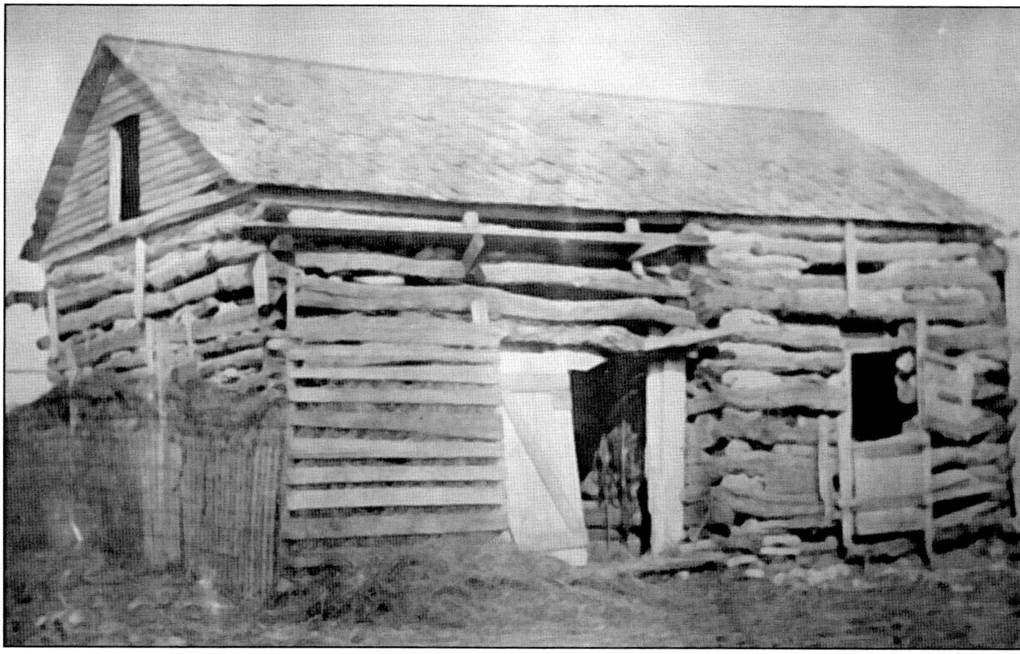

Shown here are the remains of the Jeremiah Quigley log cabin, built in 1872 13 miles south of Alton, as it appeared around 1930 when it was being used as a barn. In the photograph the log construction can be clearly seen, chinked between with mud mixed with sand and lime. Though this one is no longer standing, three others can still be found in Osborne County that continue to remind current generations of the county's frontier heritage.

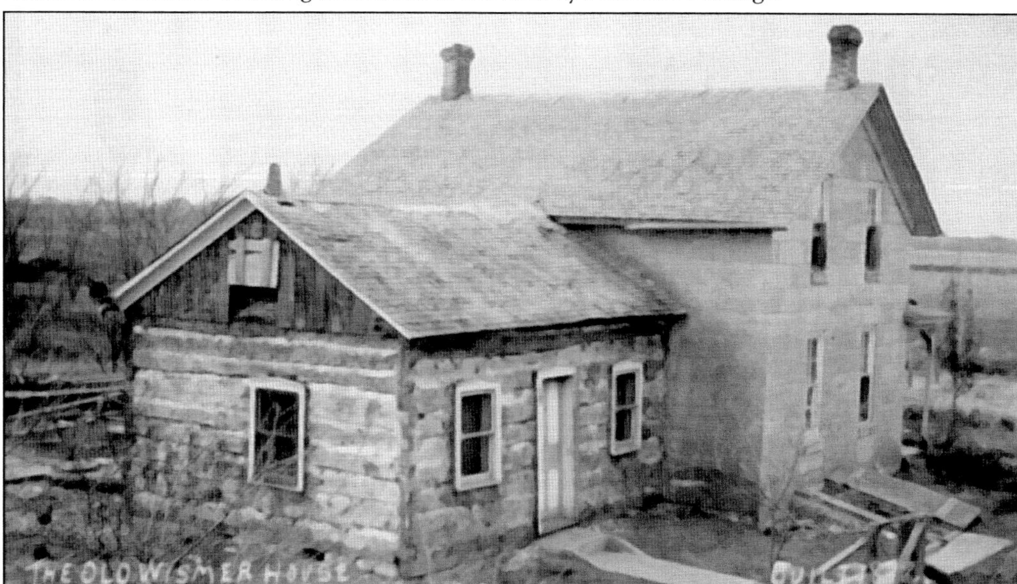

This photograph of the Jacob Wismer farm residence on Kill Creek in west-central Osborne County was taken *c.* 1910. The 1872 log portion is symbolic of the first homes a majority of the white settlers erected while turning their homesteads into productive farms. The later two-story native stone addition attests to the more prosperous and stable farm life the industrious family has earned after several years of struggle.

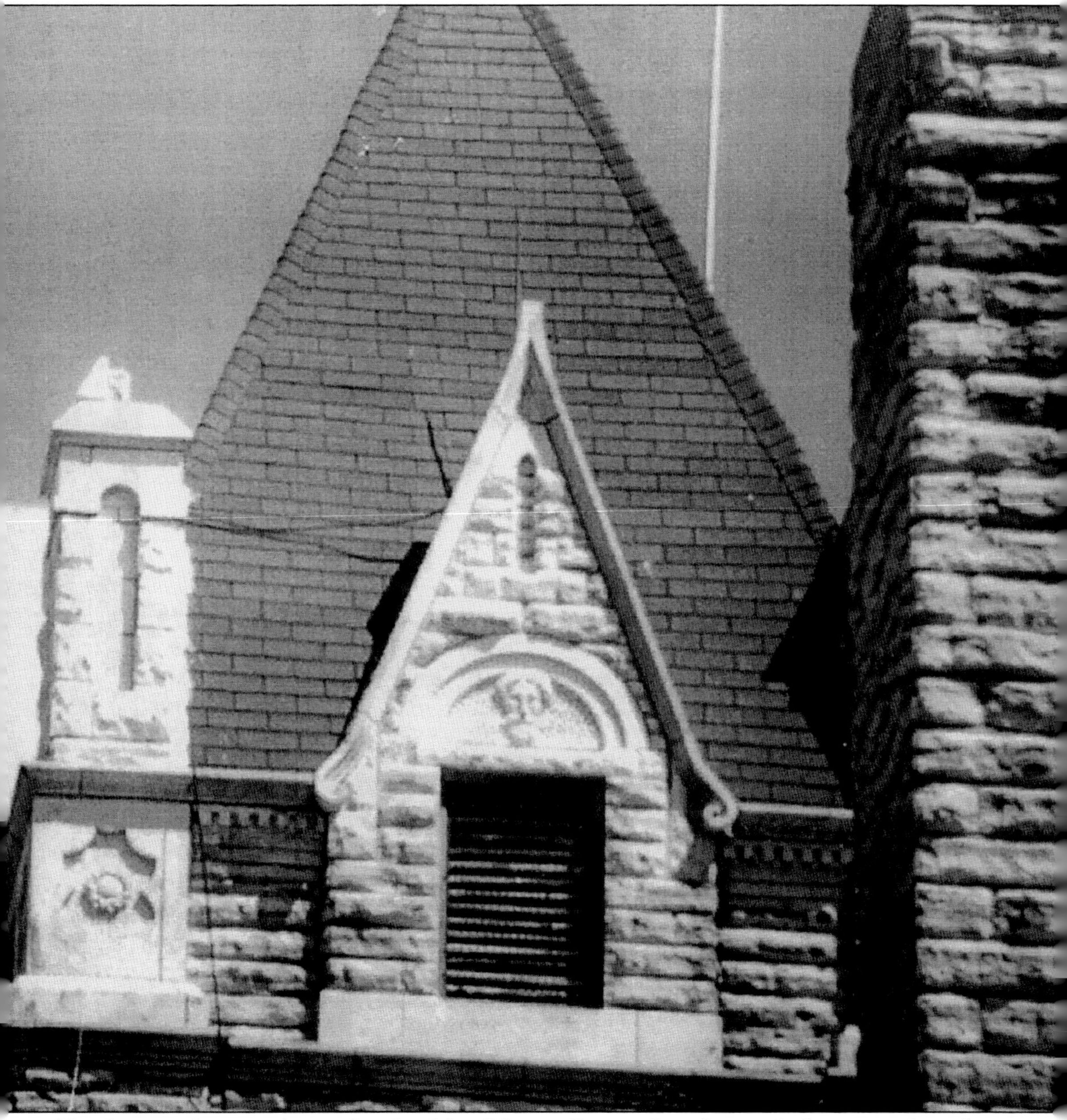

The face seen here on the south side of the Osborne County Courthouse clock tower is that of John Wineland, an early county settler. John then lived across the street from where the new courthouse was being erected in Osborne. The story told of the face is that in 1907 and 1908 he would daily visit the construction site and "suggest" to the stonemasons how they might go about their job. Finally the masons' foreman told John that if he did not stop visiting them they would carve his face in the rock. He did not stop and the stonemasons kept their word.

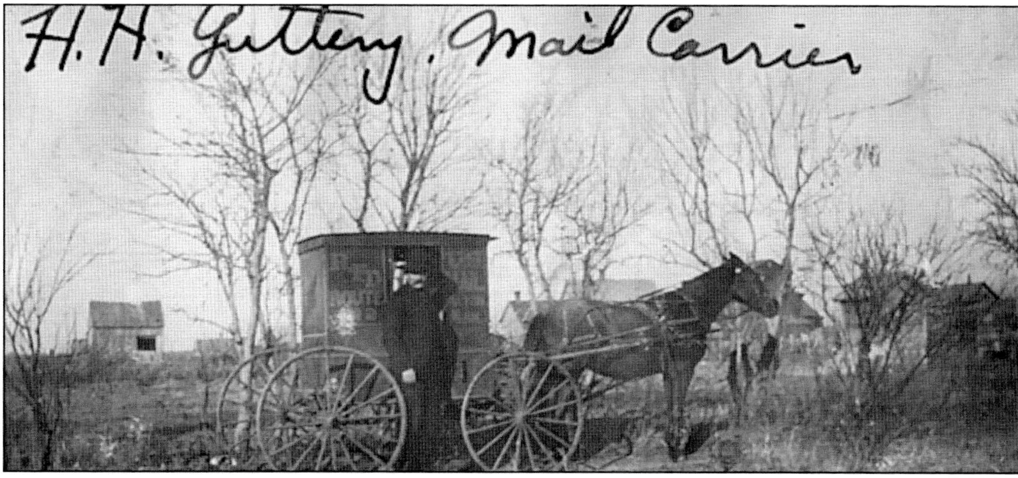

This view of Harry Guttery and his mail wagon in Alton was taken in the early 1900s. As the postal service and other federal branches continued to modernize, Harry would soon trade in the wagon for a mail car.

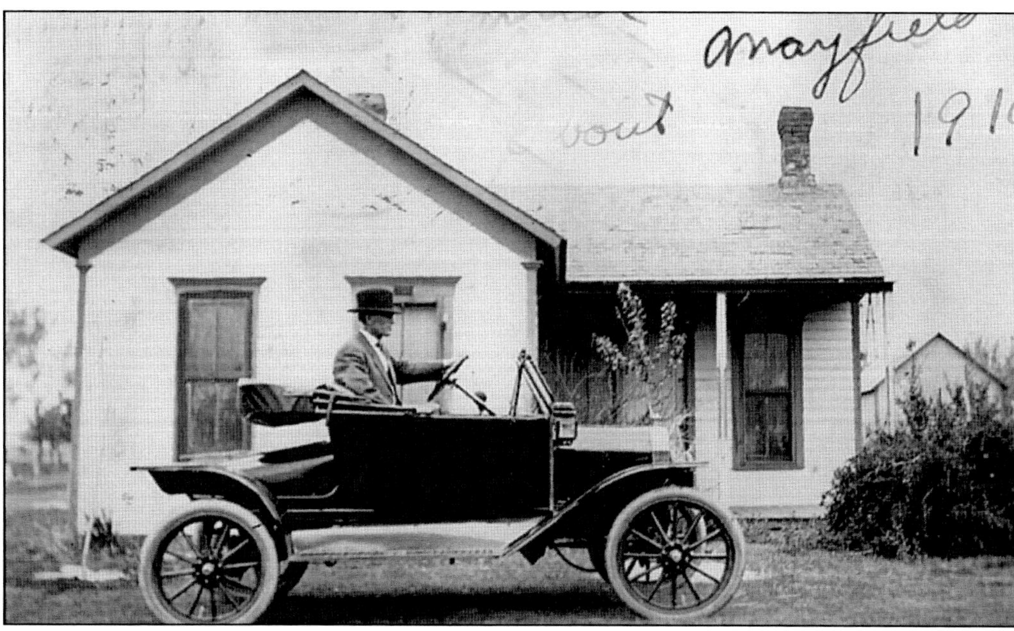

Sheridan Mayfield, the mail carrier in Portis around 1910, is pictured here. The photograph denotes that the change from wagon to car has taken place in the Portis post office.

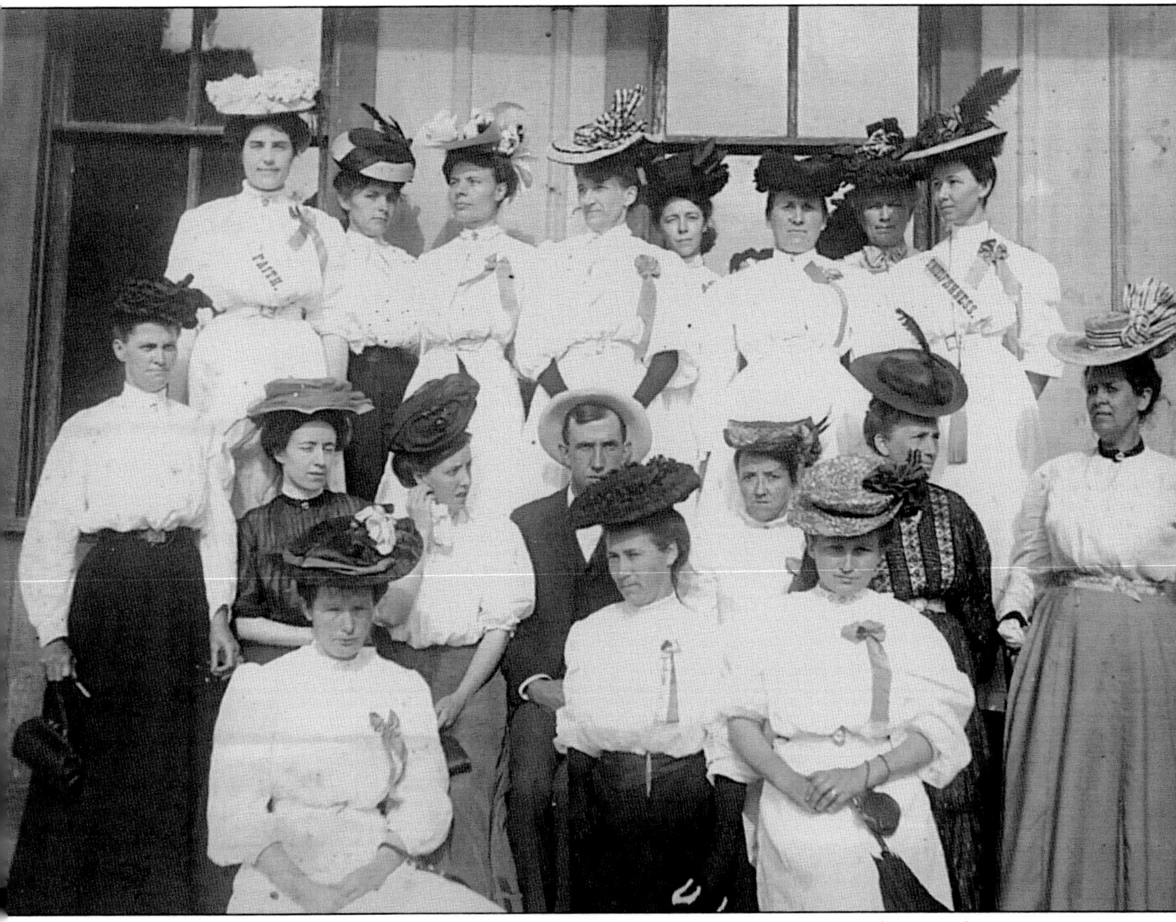

Dressed in their finest for this group photograph taken around 1910 are the worthy matrons of The Noble Grands' Association of the Osborne Rebekkah Lodge. Standing on the extreme right is my great-grandmother Viola Rothenberger, a longtime officer. The Rebekkahs were a sister lodge to the International Order of Odd Fellows and wielded a large influence over social and political issues in any community where a chapter was organized. Amid the hats and ribbons can also be seen a coin purse, opera spectacles, an umbrella, and one seemingly unhappy patron from the Odd Fellows Lodge.

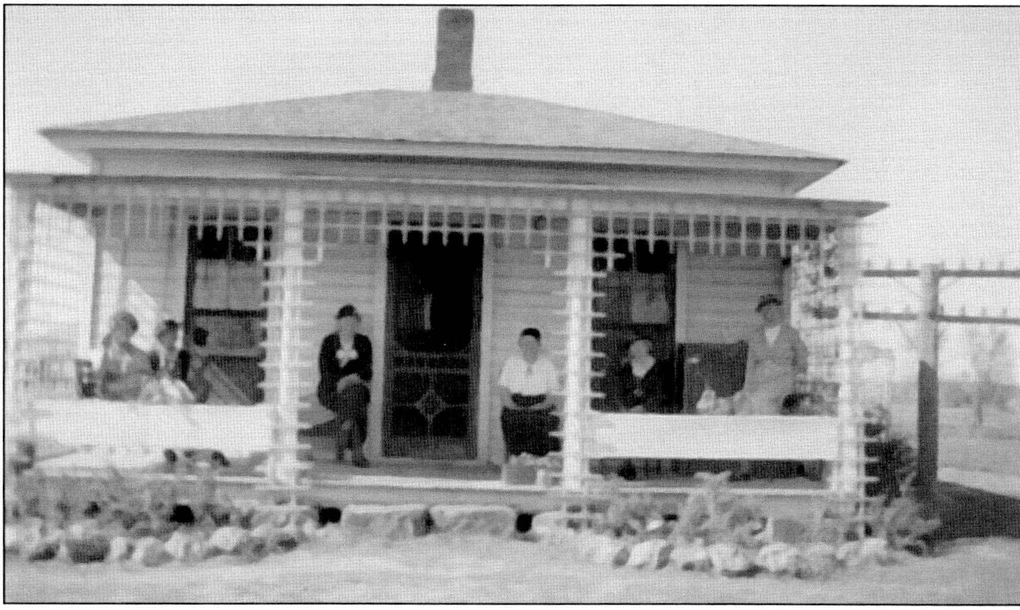

A gathering of friends are pictured here on the porch of the Julia Shaw residence on Main Street in Bloomington in the 1930s. The Shaw home at this time housed the Bloomington Telephone Company, as can be seen from the pole on the right of the home.

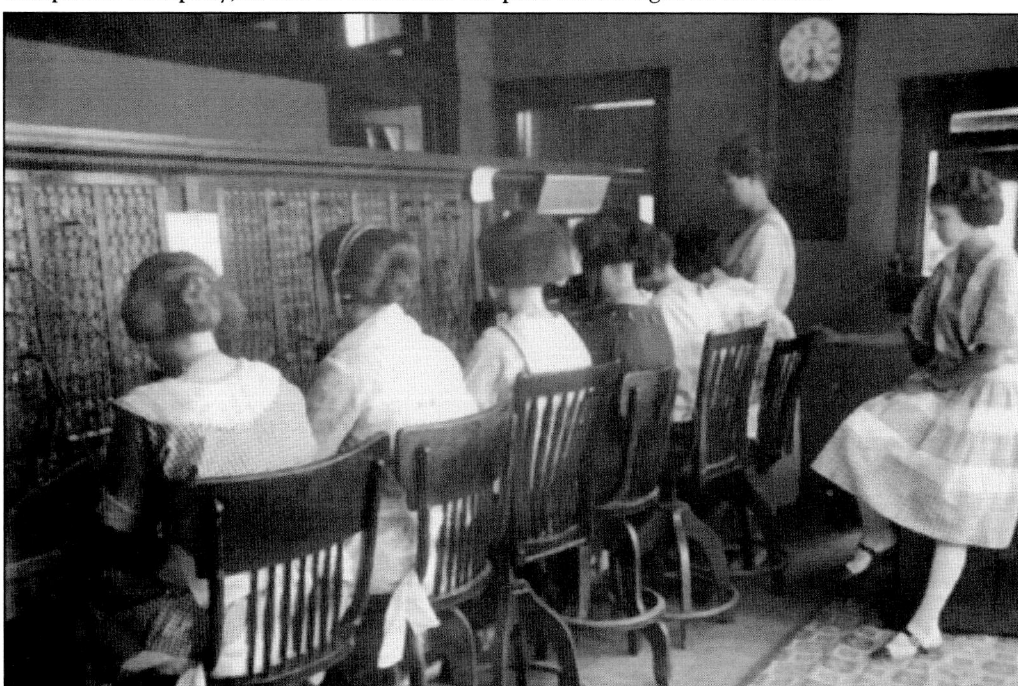

This photograph shows six operators of the Downs Western Telephone Company, as seen in the early 1920s. The company was owned by Charles Dittman and housed in the Ebnother Pharmacy. On one particular weekend the operators concluded that they should be paid more, and when their demands were not met they staged a walkout from 6 p.m. Saturday until the following Monday morning. The ensuing panic assured the ladies their raise.

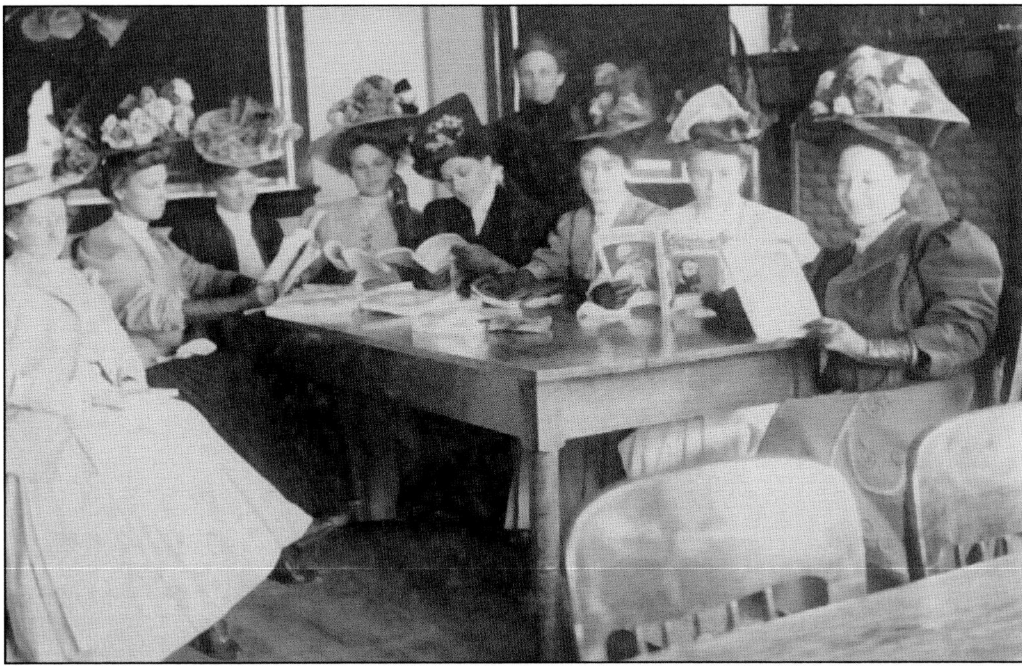

This literary society meeting in Downs took place on May 3, 1908. The group of finely dressed ladies are shown absorbed in the reading of such periodicals as *Everbody's Magazine* and *Cosmopolitan*. Notice the fireplace mantel and other interesting items in the room.

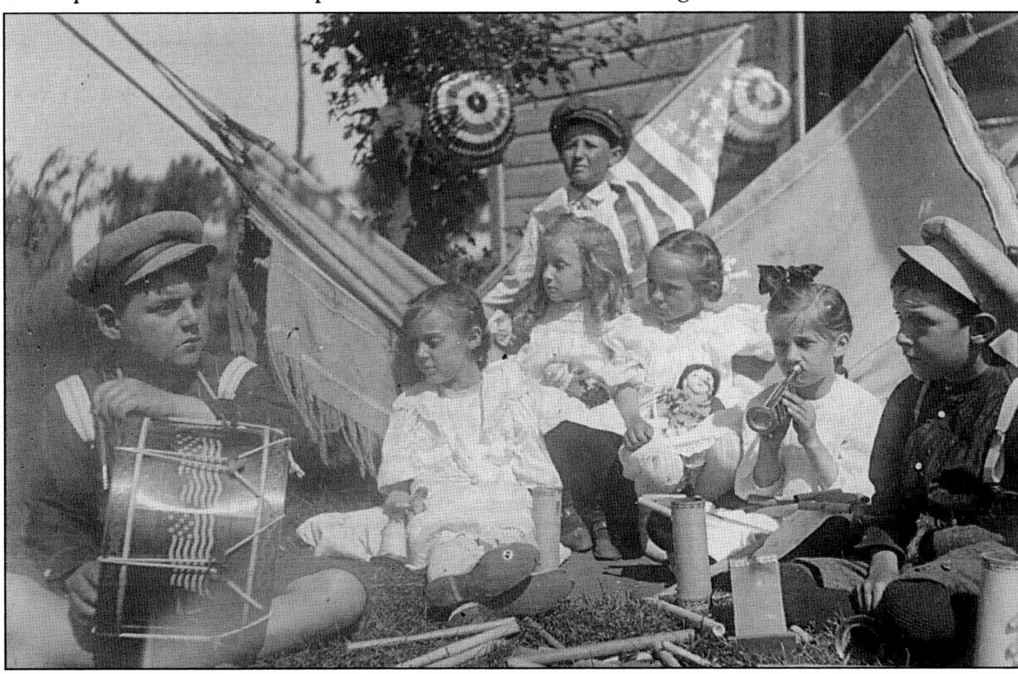

A group of young revelers are pictured here at a Fourth of July picnic sometime after 1900. The girl at center left is holding a horn made from a cow's horn, while the girl at center right is holding a china doll. The finery of the children's clothes, the kaleidoscopes, and the fireworks in the foreground complete the scene.

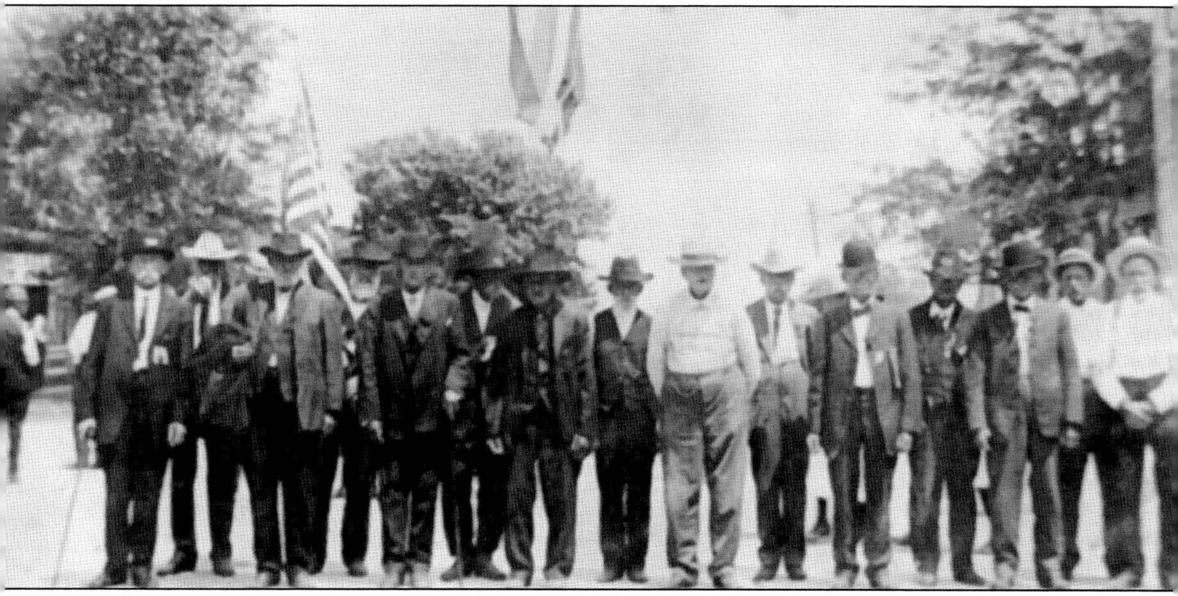

This photograph shows the members of General Bull Post 106, Grand Army of the Republic, participating in Alton's Decoration Day parade in 1913. Over 60 percent of Osborne County's early settlers were Civil War veterans and they remain the largest group of veterans buried in the county. The Alton post was named after General Hiram C. Bull, co-founder of the town and a Civil War veteran. The last Alton post member passed away in 1933, while the last Civil War veteran in the county died five years later.

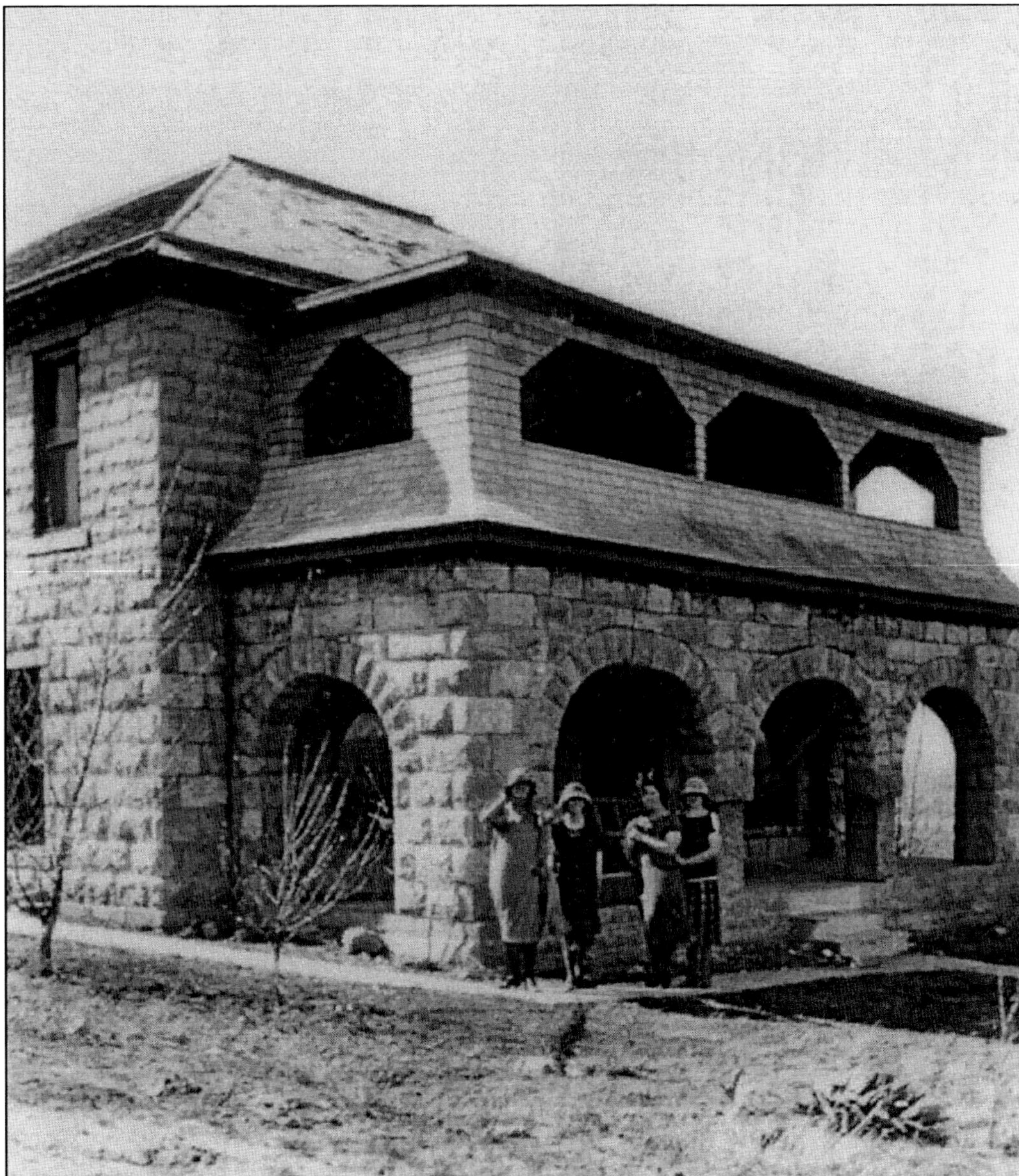

This picture from the 1920s shows the William Craig home that was located at the foot of Craig Hill a half mile south of Natoma. Craig tore down the nearby Sunny Kansas Sanitarium in 1914 and used the native limestone blocks to build his own ranch home. The sanitarium had been built in 1911 to promote better health for tuberculosis sufferers, but had never attracted the numbers of patients for which it had hoped. The arches that form the front porch of the house once formed the sanitarium's main entryway. The house was lived in for many years until it was razed sometime after 1981.

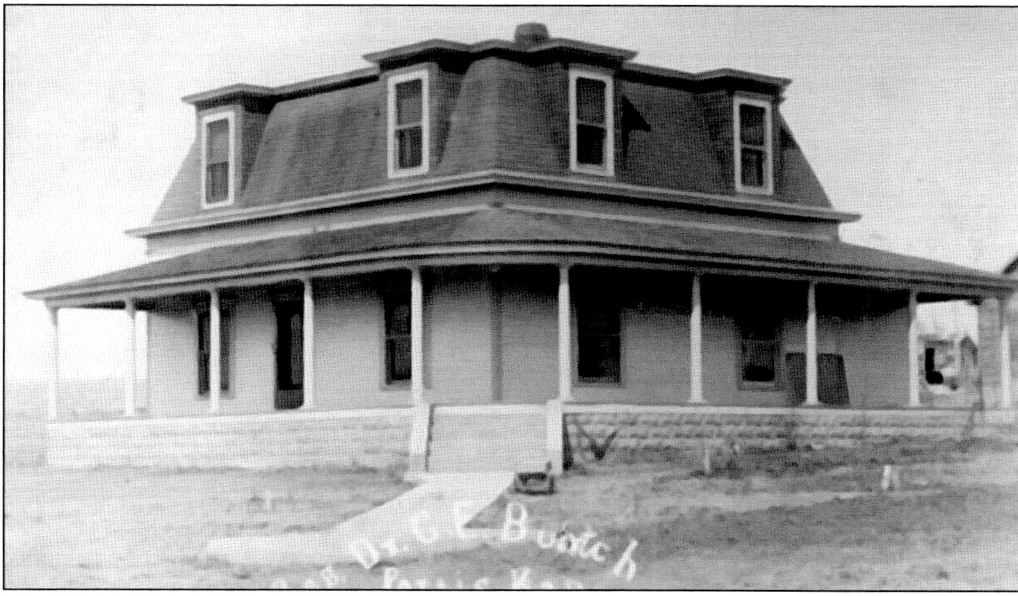

Taken in 1925, this photograph is of the Burtch home and hospital in Portis. Dr. Claude Burtch moved into this home when he moved into the city and opened his private hospital here. It was enlarged many times over the years until the good doctor passed away in 1952. Today the house stands vacant.

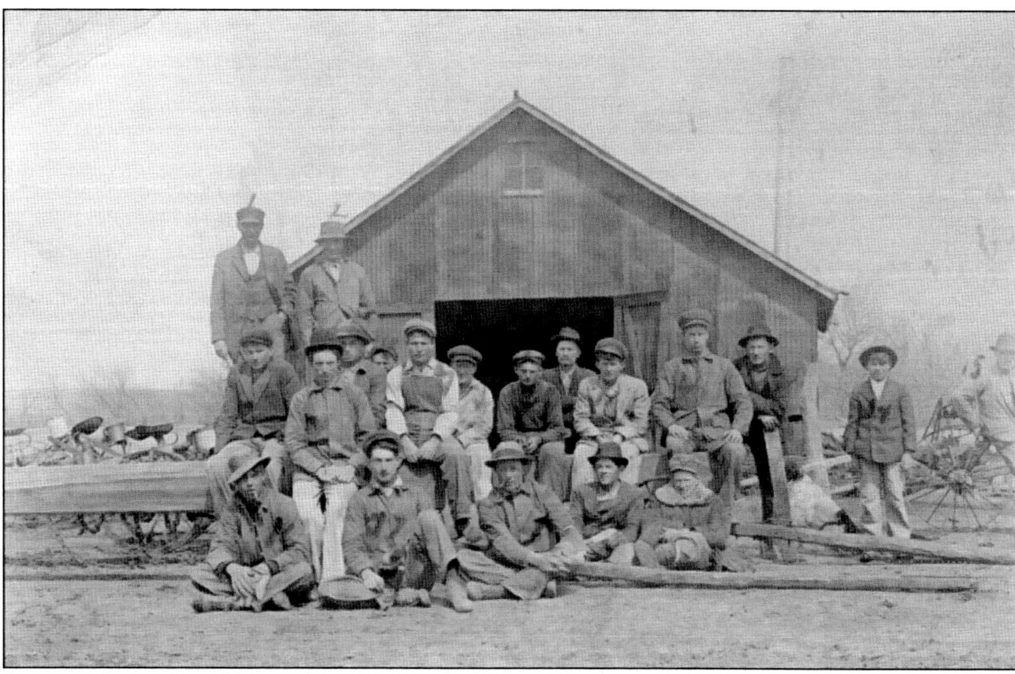

Some of the men and boys of Covert are shown gathered together in April 1913 at a blacksmith shop. Notice the various farm implements in the background in both the left and right sides of the photograph.

Four

SCHOOLS AND CHURCHES

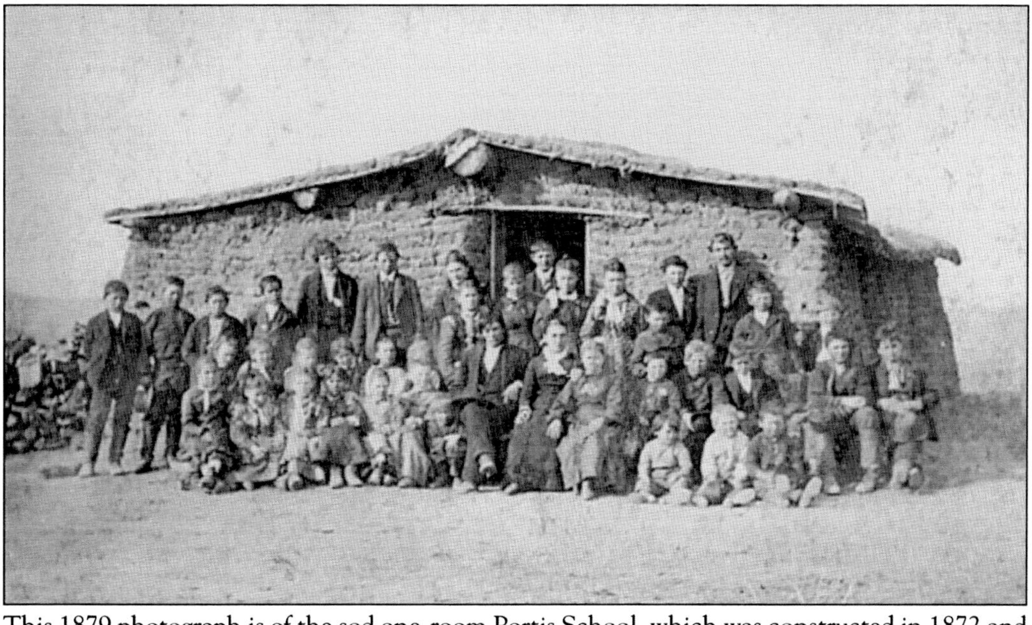

This 1879 photograph is of the sod one-room Portis School, which was constructed in 1872 and stood a short distance north of Portis in Smith County, Kansas. In 1879 the school district's boundaries were changed and a new one-room frame building was built inside the Portis city limits in 1880.

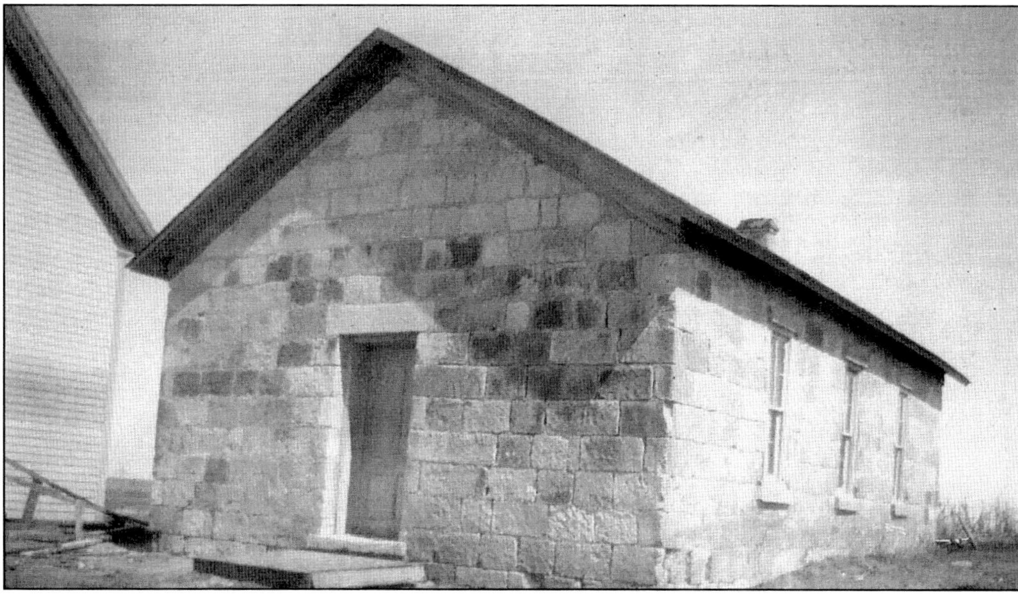

This view shows the first Lawrence Creek United Brethren Church shortly before it was torn down in 1894. The native limestone structure was built in 1874 and was the first church building erected in Osborne County. Located 7 miles west of Portis in extreme northern Osborne County, the old stone church was replaced by the new frame building glimpsed on the left.

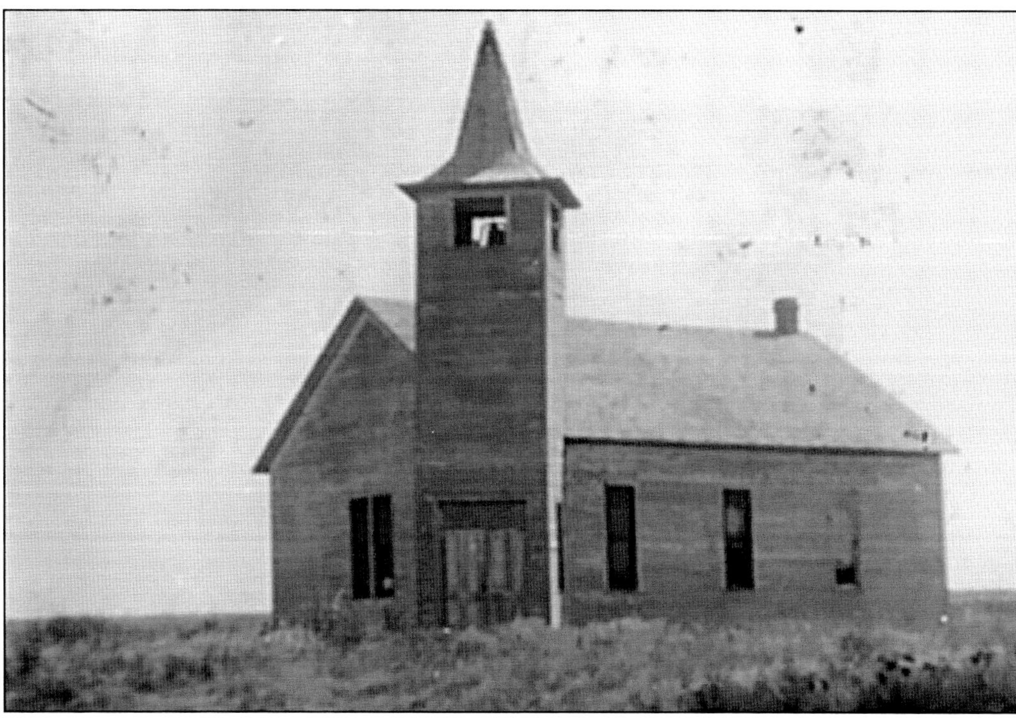

Shown here is the Mayflower United Brethren Church as it appeared in the 1930s. It was built in 1905 on a site located 7 miles southwest of Portis in northern Osborne County. Services were held here for nearly 75 years until the building was sold in 1977.

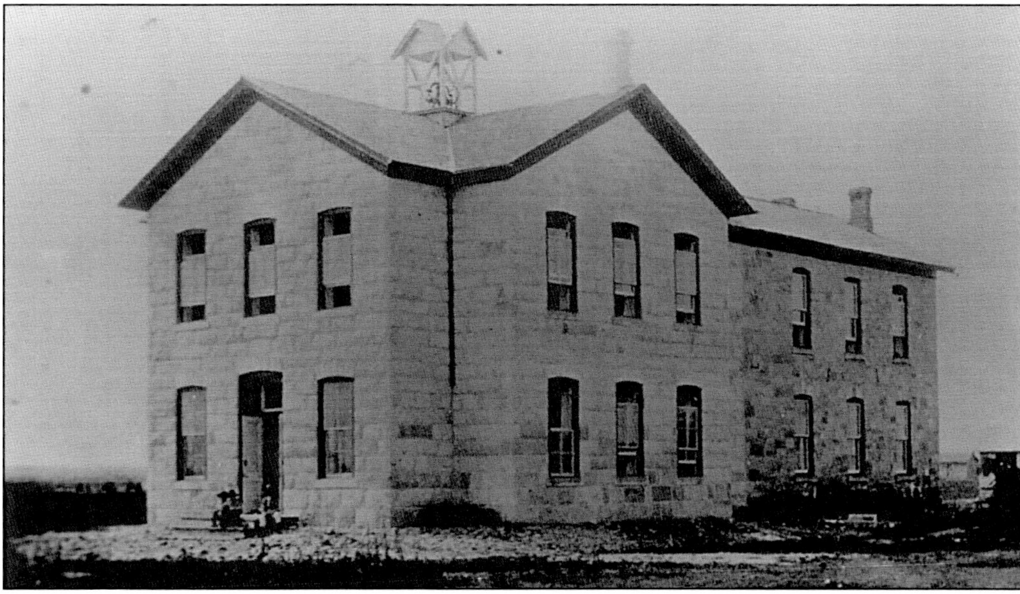

Taken in the late 1870s this view is of Osborne's first school building, built in 1872 of native limestone near the northwest corner of Second and Washington Streets. The two-story school was topped with a bell tower that also served as a warning device against approaching Native American raiders, an event that never happened. The building housed the first high school in 1883–87 and served as the city's grade school until it was torn down in 1910.

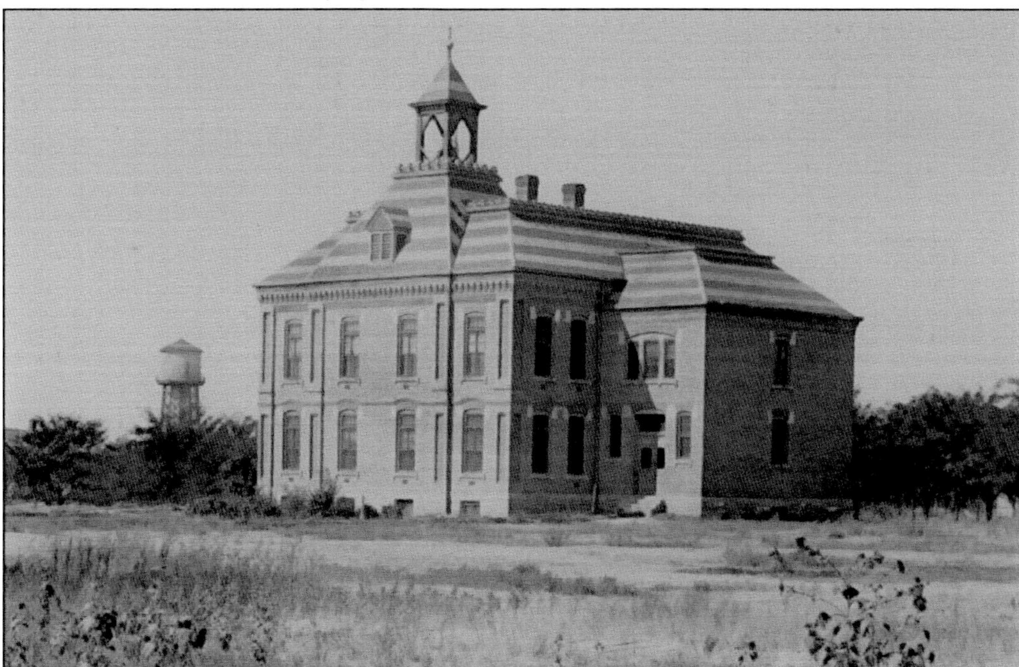

This photograph is of the second Osborne High School as it appeared in 1895. Constructed in 1888, the schoolhouse was fashioned of bricks handmade in Osborne. After 1910 it served as the grade school until 1929 when it was dismantled. In the left background the city water tower can be seen. It then stood in the northeast corner of the Osborne City Park.

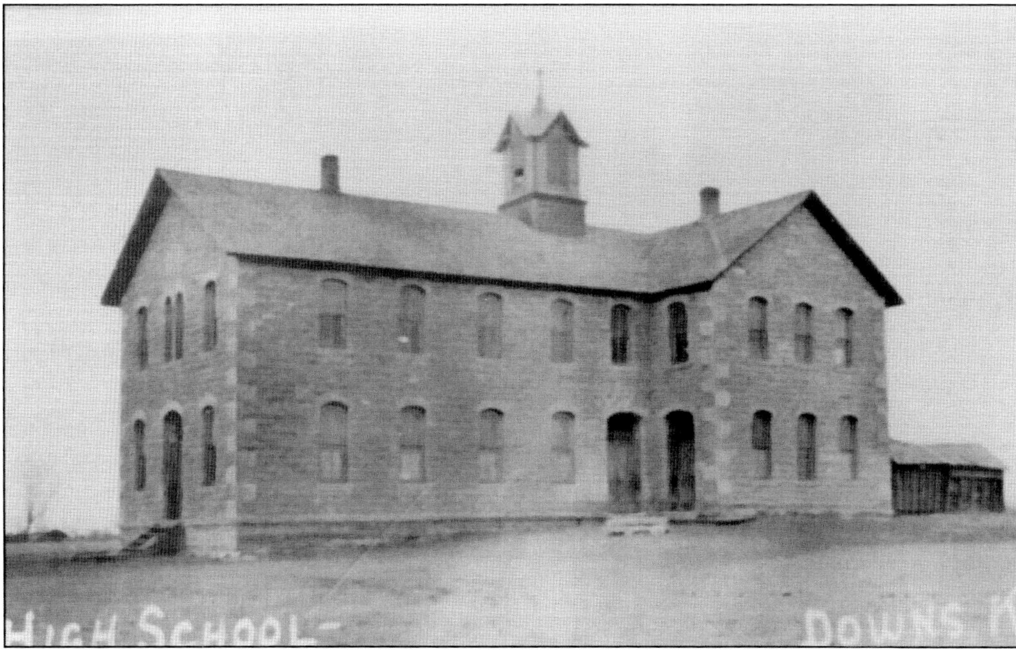

The first school building constructed in Downs was the North School. Built of native limestone in 1880 with an addition in 1884, the structure became home to Downs High School in 1900. It was razed in 1908 to make way for a new school building. Some of the old school's stones were used in the new structure to symbolize the school district's bridge with its past.

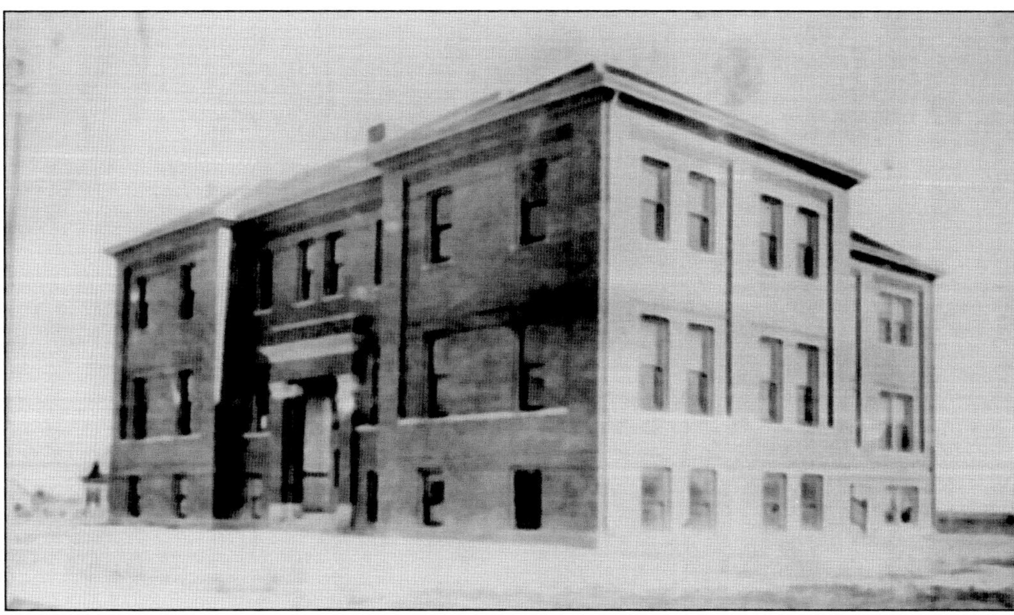

Pictured here is Downs' new brick high school building as it looked upon its completion in 1908. A fire on January 18, 1929, seriously damaged the structure, and a new high school was built the next year. The top floor of the burned building was removed and the lower half then housed the grade school and later the junior high grades. The building was torn down in 1998.

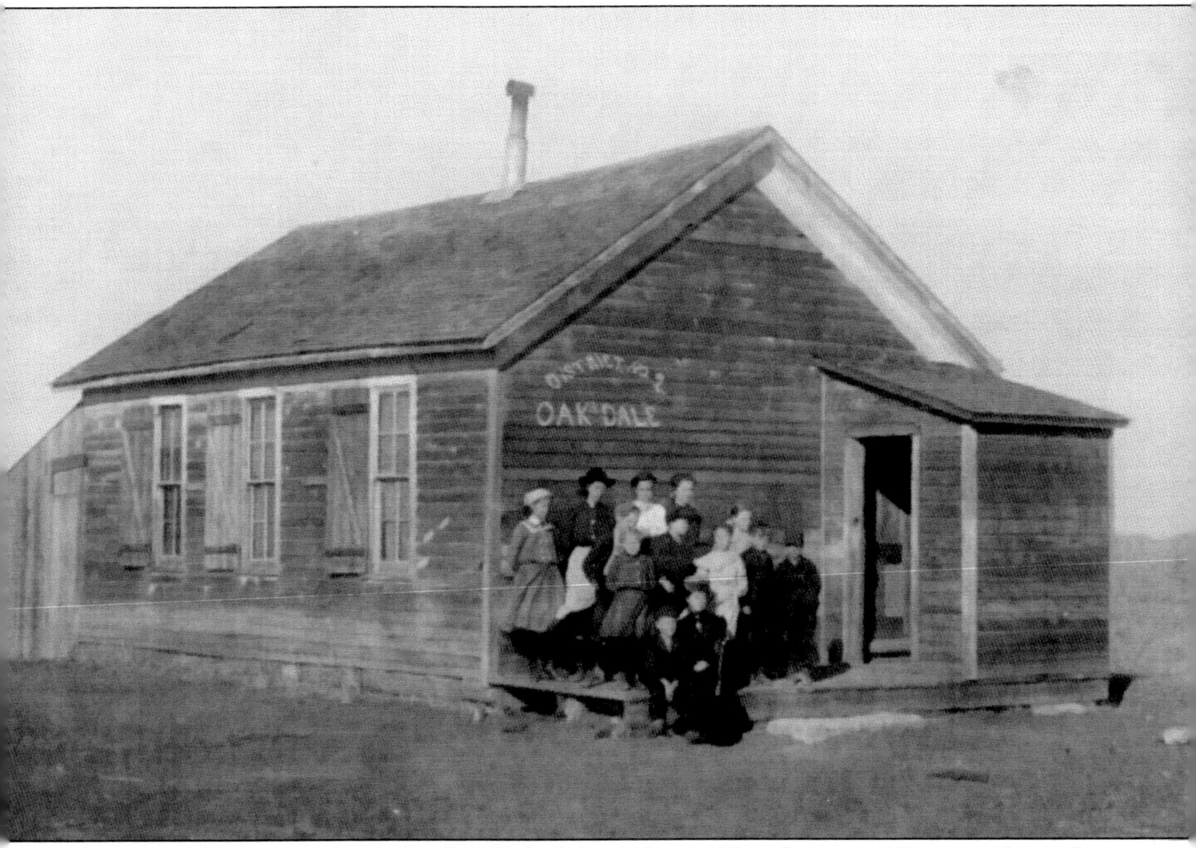

This 1890s photograph shows the Oak Dale School, located 2 miles east of Downs. Although a school term was held the previous December, in April 1872, Oak Dale became the second school district to formally organize in Osborne County. In 1970 Oak Dale became the last rural one-room school in the county to close. Notice the seated teacher wearing her finest clothes and sporting a fur hat.

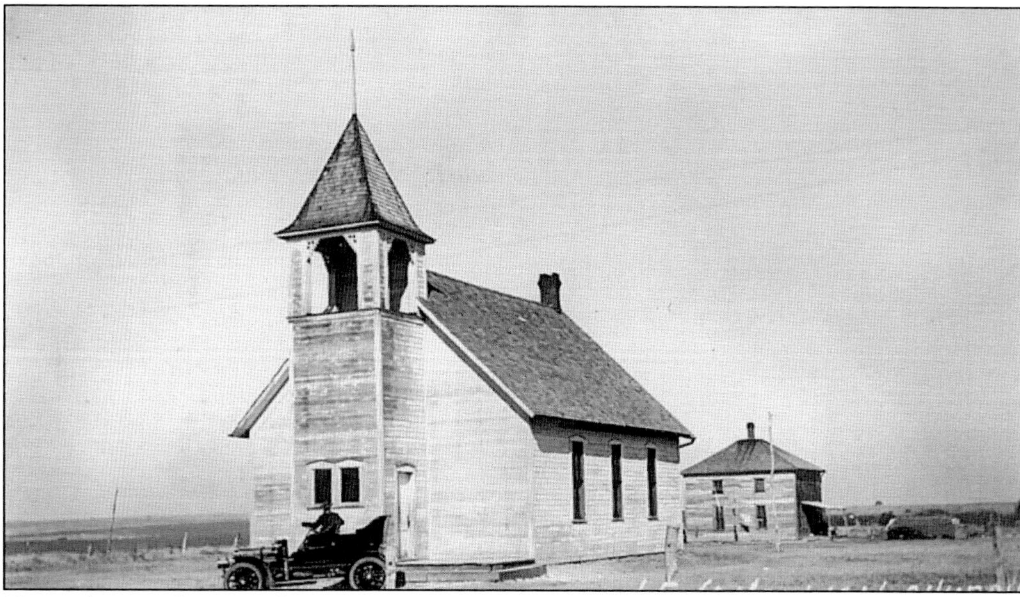

Shown here is the second Zion Evangelical Church and parsonage from about 1908. Located 5 miles southwest of Bloomington, the first "Little White Church" was built in 1877 and was the church located the farthest west on the plains in Kansas. It began as a Mennonite church, then it became Evangelical United Brethren, and finally was known as the Kill Creek United Methodist Church. It was torn down in the mid-1990s.

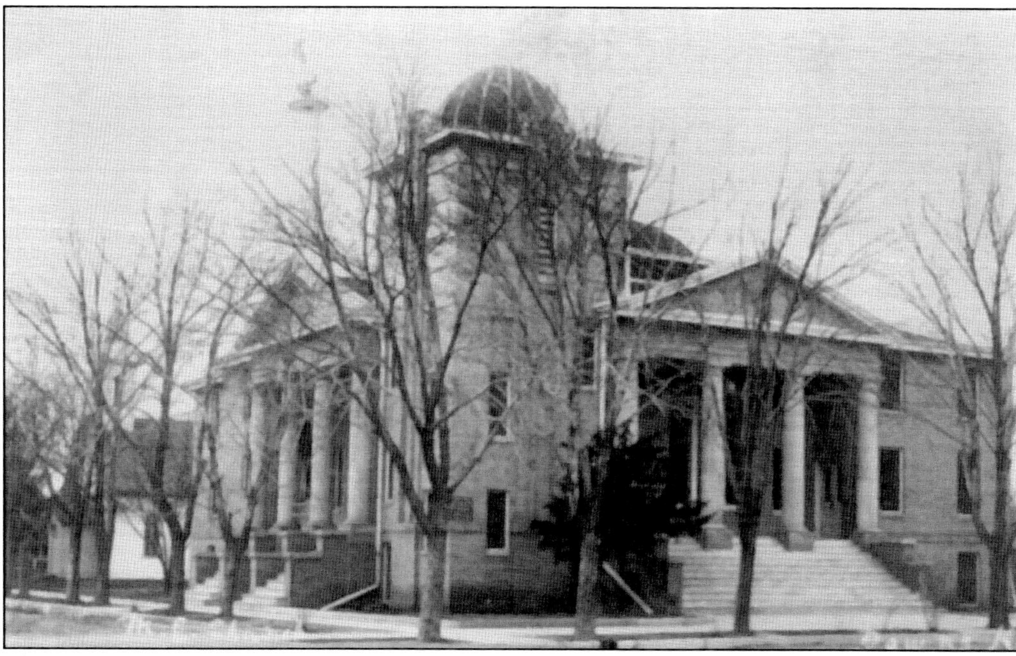

This is a postcard view of the United Methodist Church located at the northwest corner of Blunt Street and Morgan Avenue in Downs. This was the second church edifice, built at a cost of $25,000 in 1916 with a seating capacity of 650 people. The church was organized in the city in 1880 but can trace its roots in the area back to 1872. It remains as one of the more striking architectural structures in Osborne County.

Pictured here is the Union Congregational and Baptist Church in Bloomington as it appeared in the 1920s. The church structure was built in 1879 and served the village for many years until the church body disbanded. It was then used as a community hall. In 1986 the church was sold and shortly thereafter it was torn down.

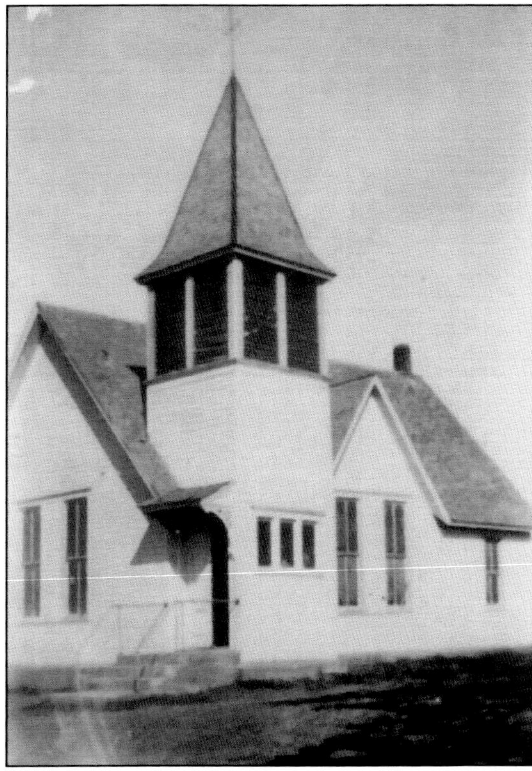

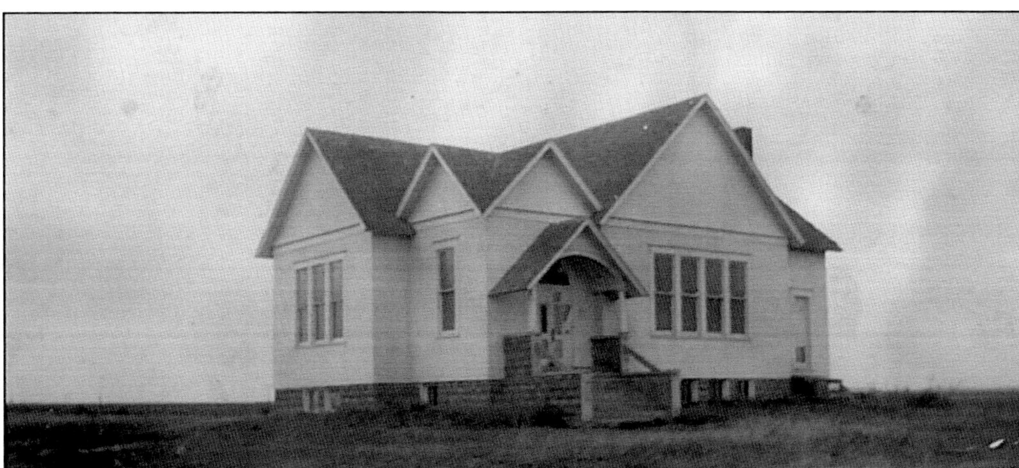

This photograph is of the Beulah Methodist Episcopal Church in the early 1930s. It was located 7 miles southwest of Osborne. A Methodist class had been organized in the area in 1879 but a church structure was not built until over 25 years later. This is a photograph of the second church that was completed in 1917. It was sold in 1951 and dismantled.

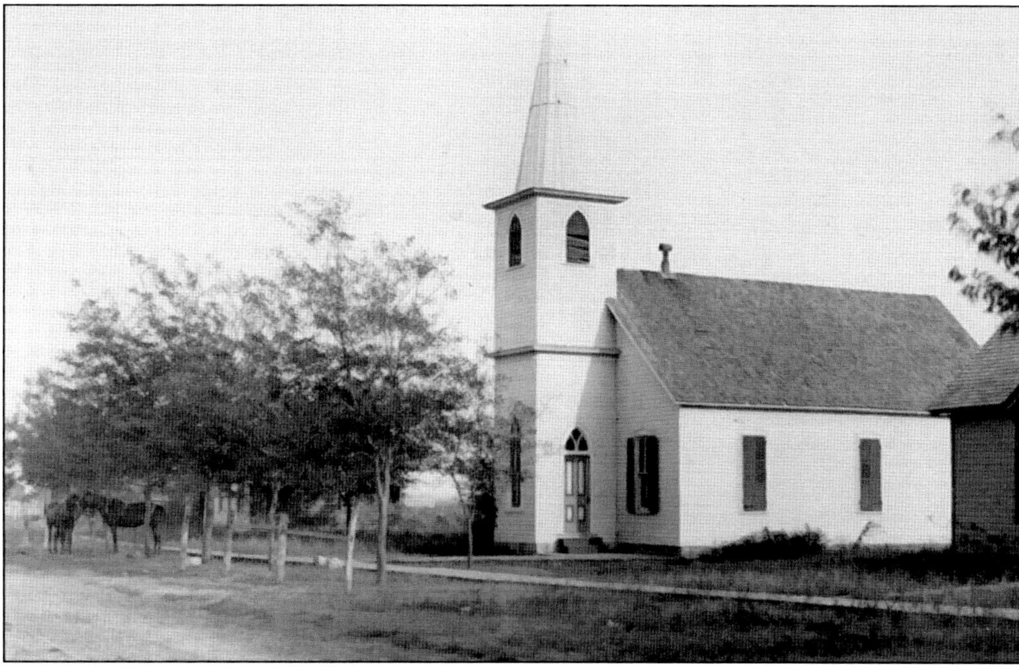

This 1895 picture of the Congregational Church, located at 121 West New Hampshire Street in Osborne, was by C.W. Buell. It was dedicated in 1878 and was the first church structure built in Osborne. The Congregationalists were first organized in 1872 by the Reverend Richard B. Foster. By 1902 a new church was built half a block away and this building was then sold. It is now a private home.

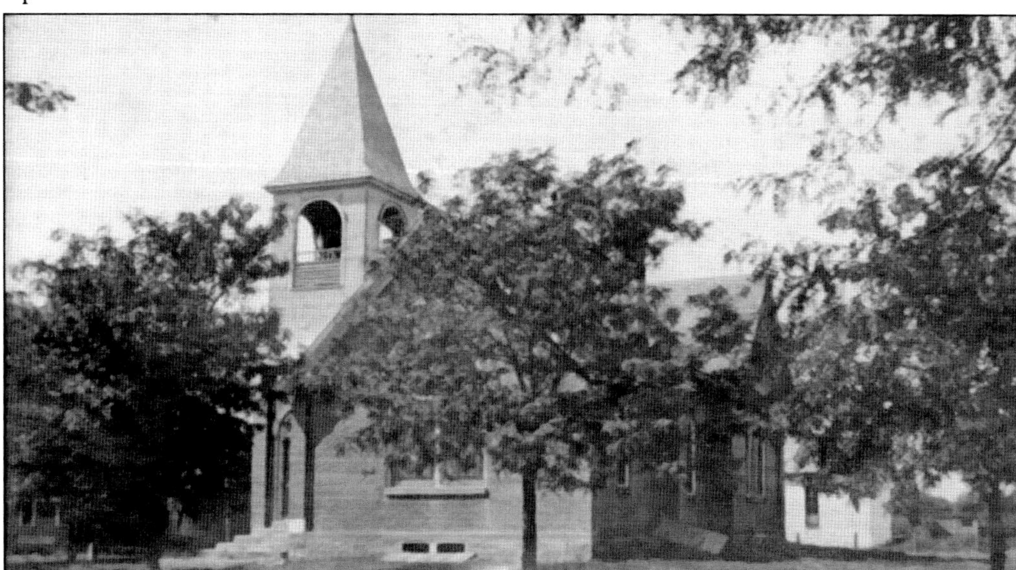

The second Congregational church building in Osborne is shown here as it appeared in 1916. The church was dedicated in 1902 at the corner of Second and New Hampshire Streets and the basement was named Foster Hall after Reverend Richard Foster. The Congregationalists merged with the Presbyterian church in 1948 and the Veterans of Foreign Wars bought the vacant building. It is the current home of the Bible Baptist Church.

This is a good view of the rural Corinth Center Schoolhouse, School District Number 122, located 4 miles southeast of Downs, as it appeared in the late 1920s in eastern Osborne County. Between 1872 and 1889, 128 rural one-room school districts were formed in Osborne County. The majority of these met in frame school buildings such as the one depicted here. District 122 was organized in 1886 and closed in 1948.

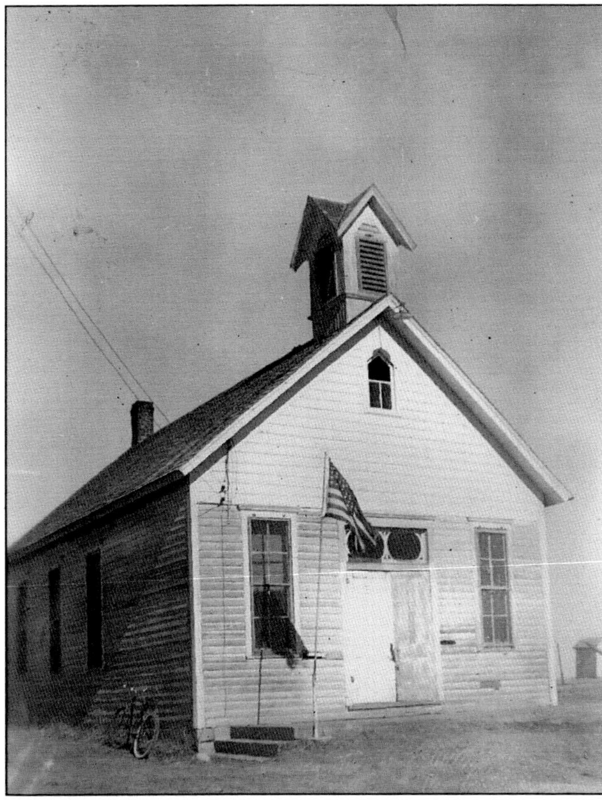

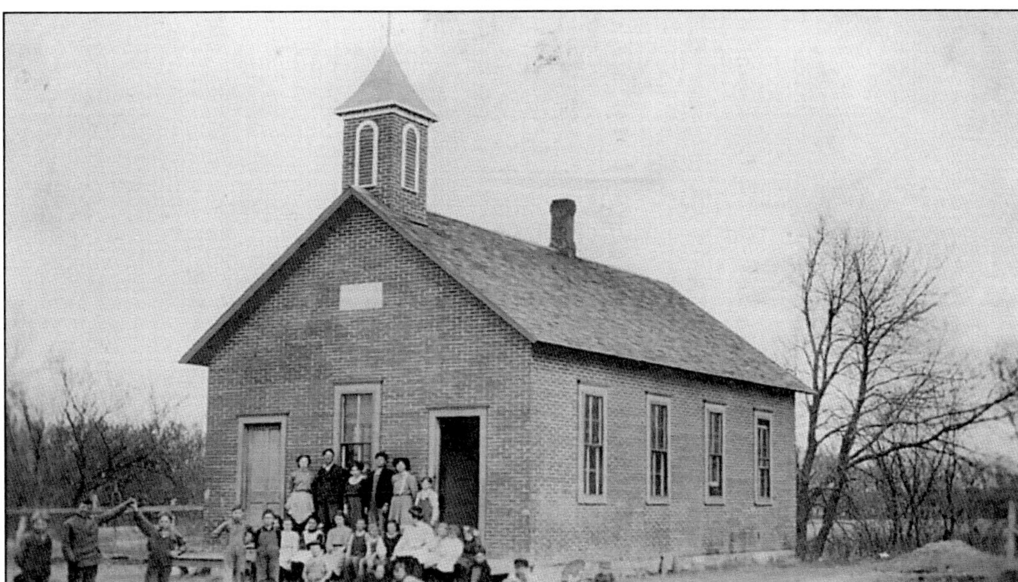

Pictured here is the student body standing in front of the Greenwood School, which stood 6 miles southeast of Osborne along Twin Creek. It is not known when the picture was taken. Rural brick schoolhouses were a rarity in Osborne County where the conventional frame structure was preferred. The Greenwood School District was formed in 1876 and closed in 1947. The building was later torn down.

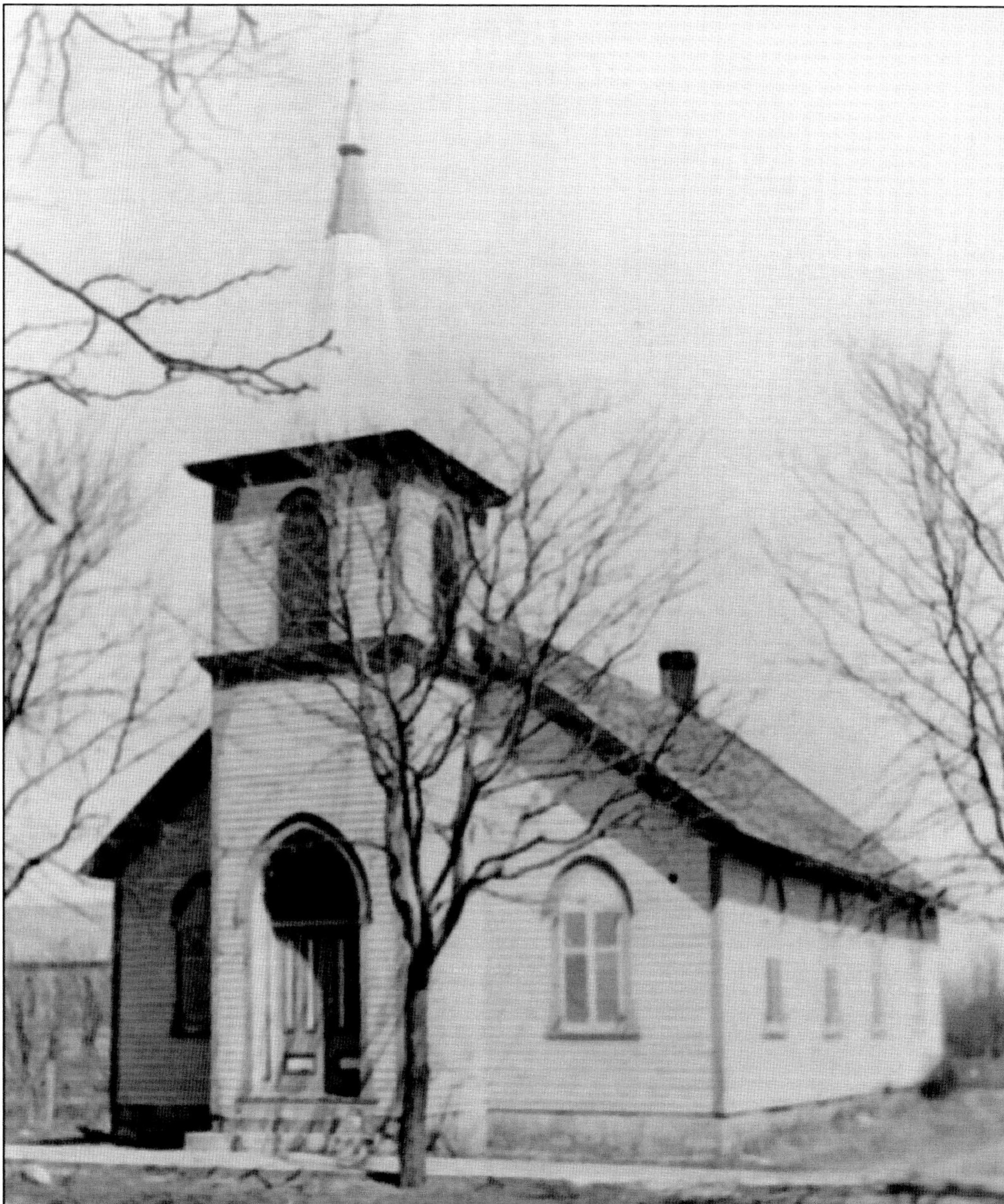

In 1875 the city of Osborne built its first public building, known popularly as the town hall. Used for an occasional home talent play or for county court sessions, from 1879 to 1910 it was the home of the Presbyterian Church—the occupants when this picture was taken. Later it was used as a shop, first by Sherman Benson and then by Harold Dunkleberg, until it was torn down in 1964.

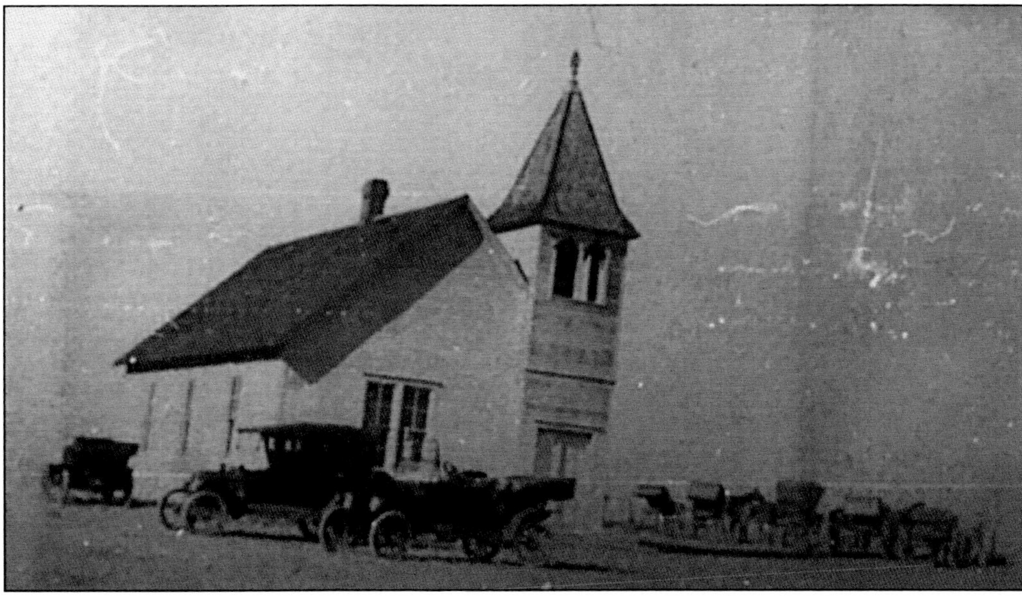

Taken in the 1910s, this is a photograph of the Bristow Baptist Church. The Bristow Baptists started in 1881 and when they were large enough erected this church structure, located 10 miles southwest of Osborne. But by the mid-1920s, attendance declined and the church building was sold and torn down. In this picture it is interesting that all cars are parked on the left and the buggies are parked on the right.

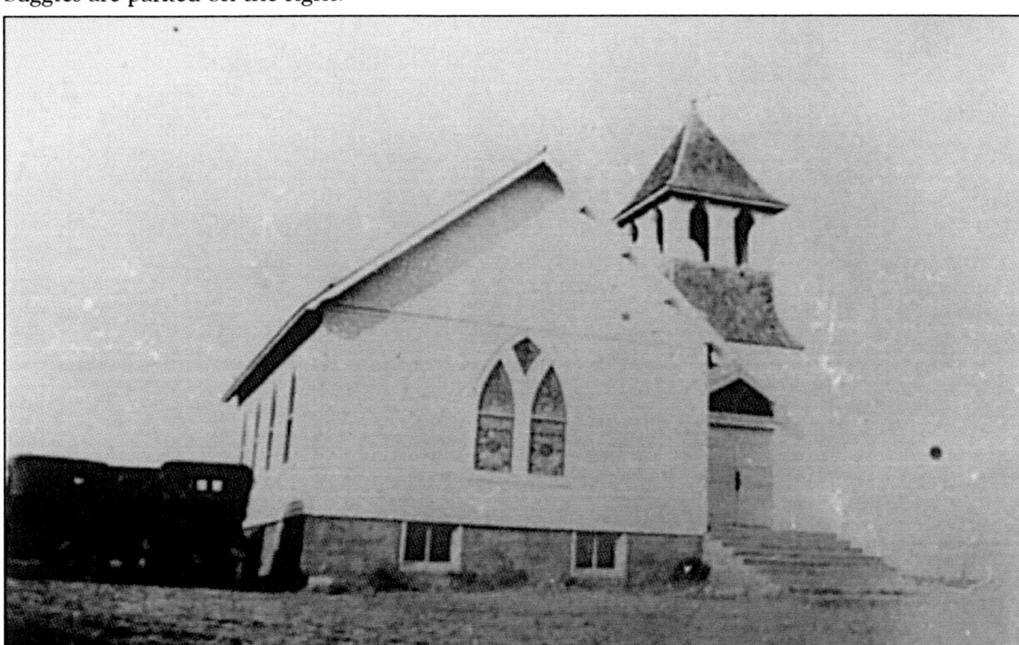

Shown here is the second Bristow Methodist Church building as it appeared in the early 1920s. The church was organized in 1872 and after the first church structure burned, this building was built and dedicated in 1918. It was located 9 miles southwest of Osborne in the Bristow community. This second church structure was struck by lightning and destroyed by the consequent fire in 1957. The Bristow Methodists then chose to disband.

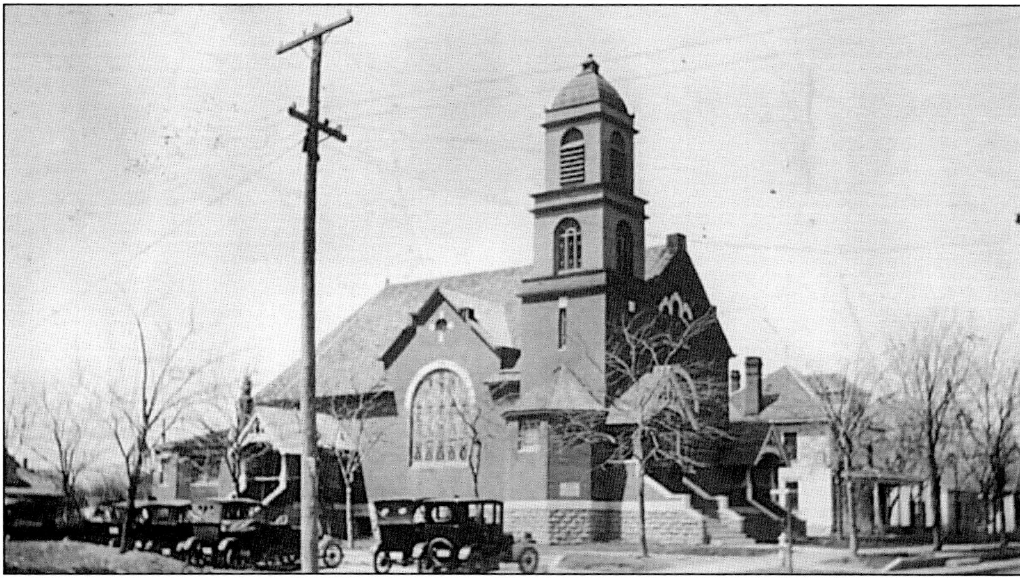

This photograph shows the United Church of Christ in Osborne taken sometime before 1920. It is located at the corner of First and Washington Streets and was dedicated as the new Presbyterian Church in early 1911. Thirty-seven years later the Osborne Congregational Church merged with the Presbyterians and the church was renamed. The building's distinct copper dome is an Osborne landmark.

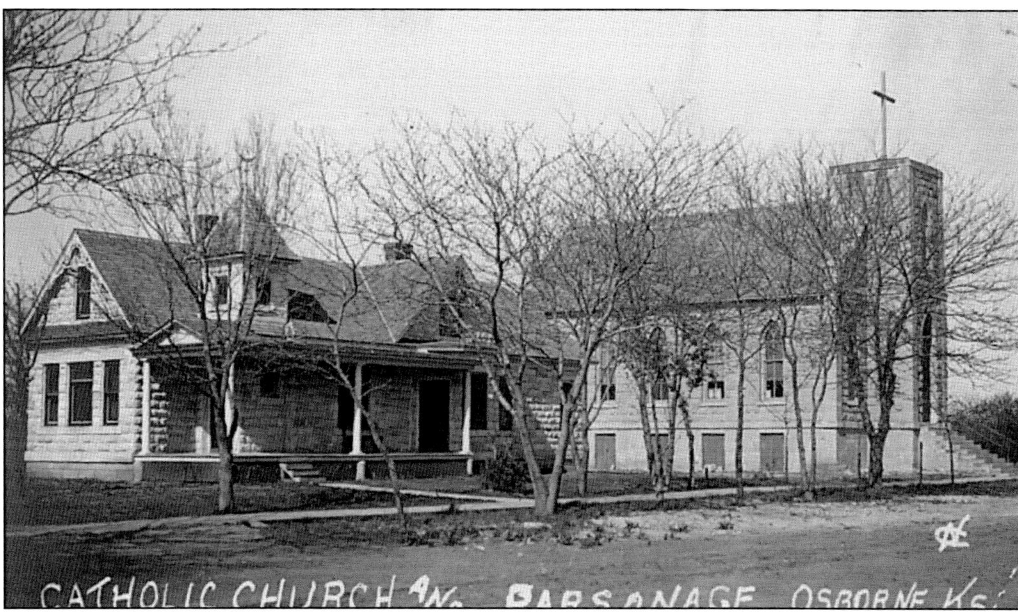

This is the native stone Osborne Catholic Church and rectory, shown here from around 1910. Located at the corner of Elm and Washington Streets, the church structure was built in 1880 to house the Osborne Moravian Church. The Catholics bought the building in 1900 and used it until 1957, when a new church was built at the site. The rectory was replaced with a more modern home in 1962.

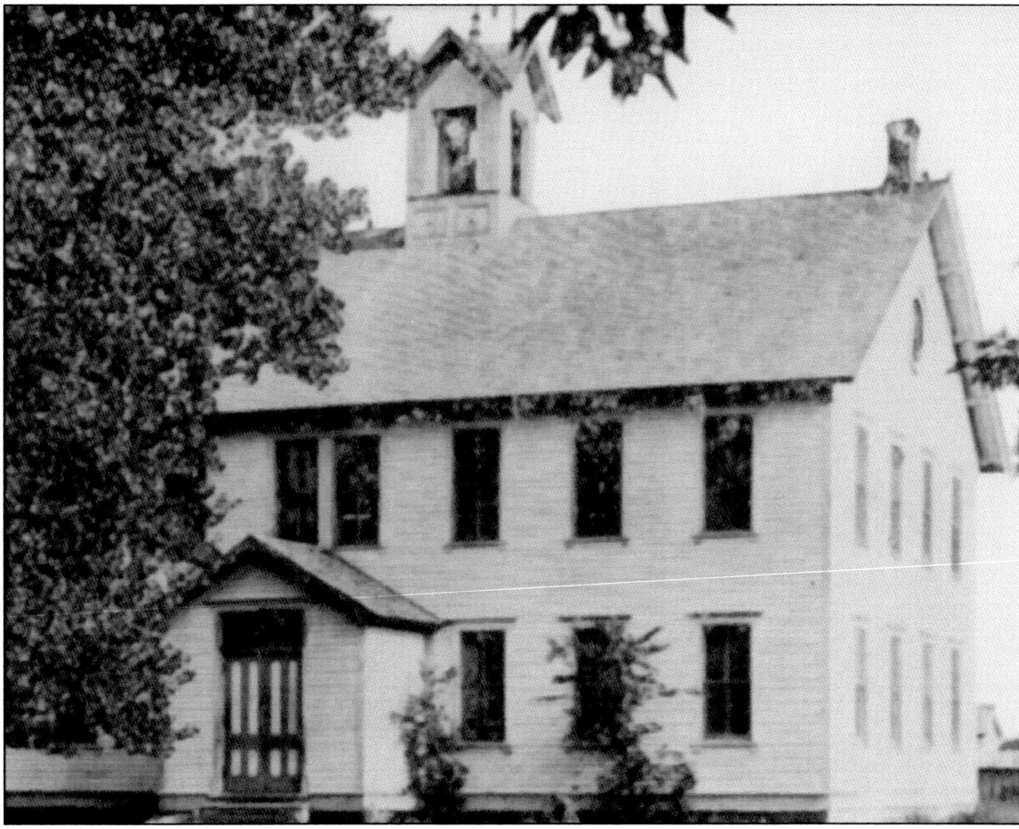

Built in 1890 to accommodate a growing student population, the two-story frame South School was located in Downs on the southwest corner of Second and Ray Streets. Ten years later the high school took over the building and remained there until 1908, when a new school structure was built in the north of town and the South School was then sold.

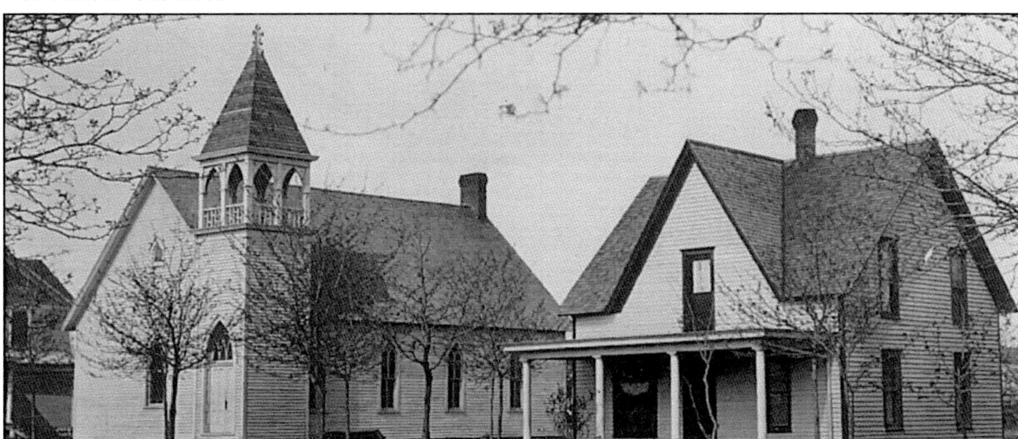

This postcard view shows the Christian Church and parsonage on North Second Street in Osborne. The church was organized five years before the first house of worship, shown here, was completed in 1897. In 1954 this building was moved to Stockton, Kansas, and the parsonage was moved to South Elm Street and is now a private home. A new church was dedicated on the same site as the first on July 17, 1955.

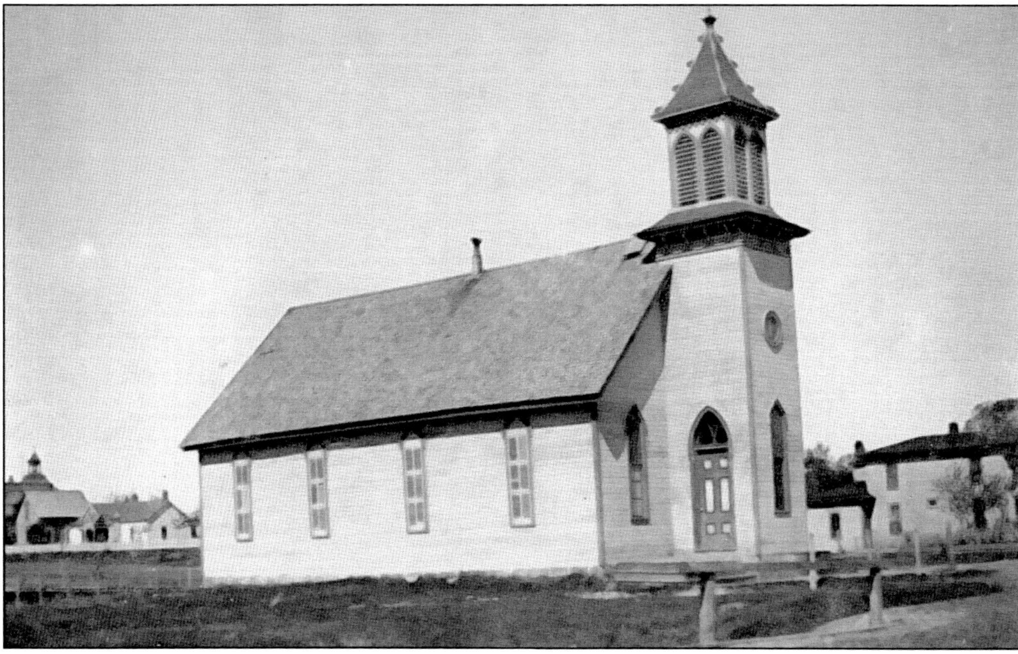

Pictured here is the first Methodist Episcopal Church as it looked on the northwest corner of Third and Main Streets in Osborne in 1905. The first Methodist church class in Osborne was organized in 1872. This church building was built in 1885 for $2,000. In 1891 the bell tower was added. Years later a larger church was needed, and in 1905 the old church was replaced by a new church.

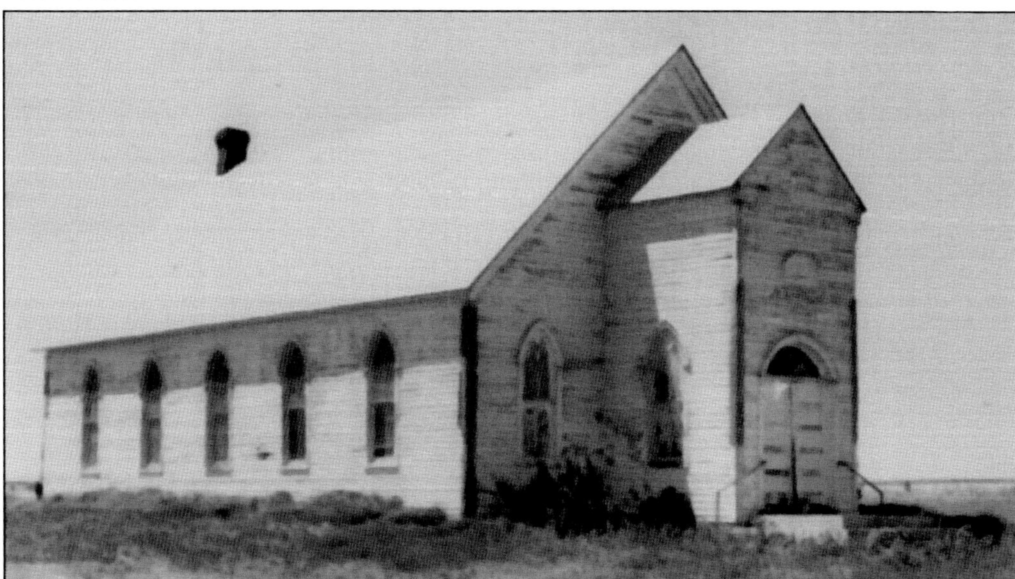

The Delhi Methodist Church was organized in 1882 and a large religious structure was built on the north end of the Delhi Cemetery in the early 1900s in southeastern Osborne County. It closed in 1920 and was used sporadically through the next few decades for services and as a community hall. The church building was sold in the 1980s and moved to a neighboring farm to be used as a barn.

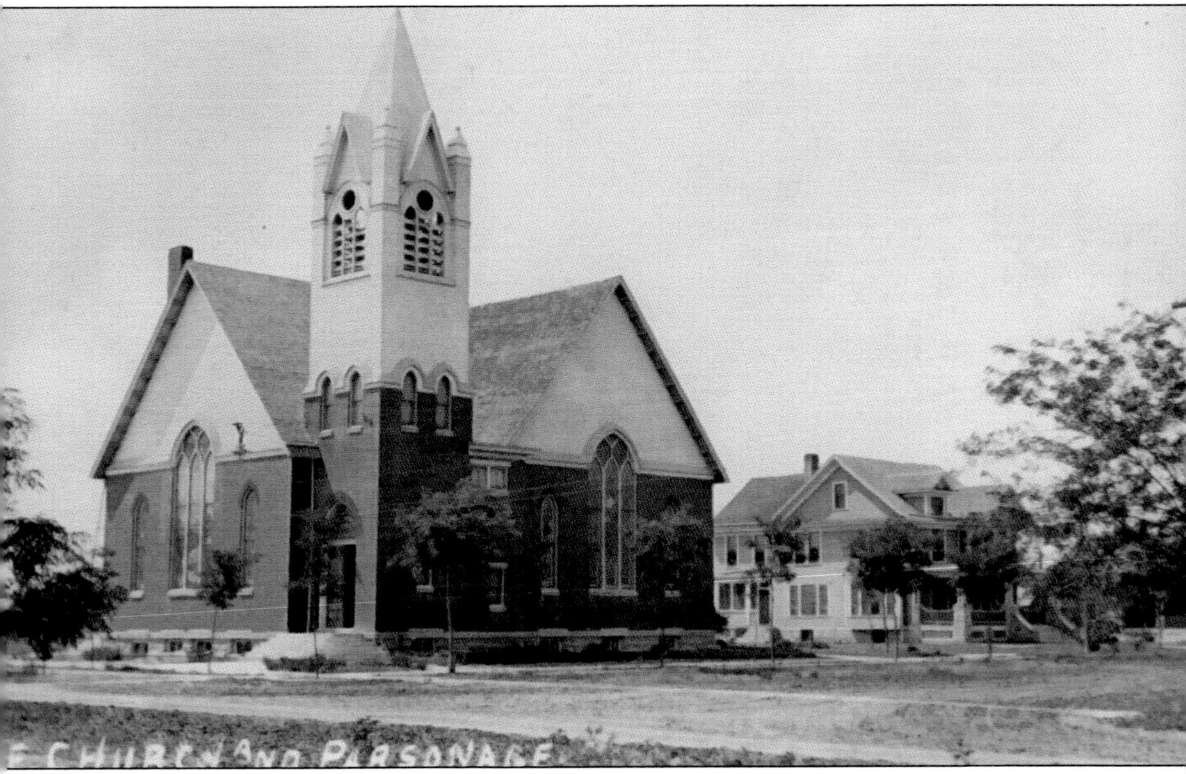

Shown here is the second Methodist Episcopal Church and parsonage at the corner of Third and Main Streets in Osborne around 1920. This church was built in 1906 at a cost of $14,000. The basement was completely remodeled in 1919 and named the Ford Parlors after longtime church benefactor Joseph P. Ford. Since then the church has been enlarged several times. In 1965 the parsonage was sold at auction and moved to make way for a new one-story brick home.

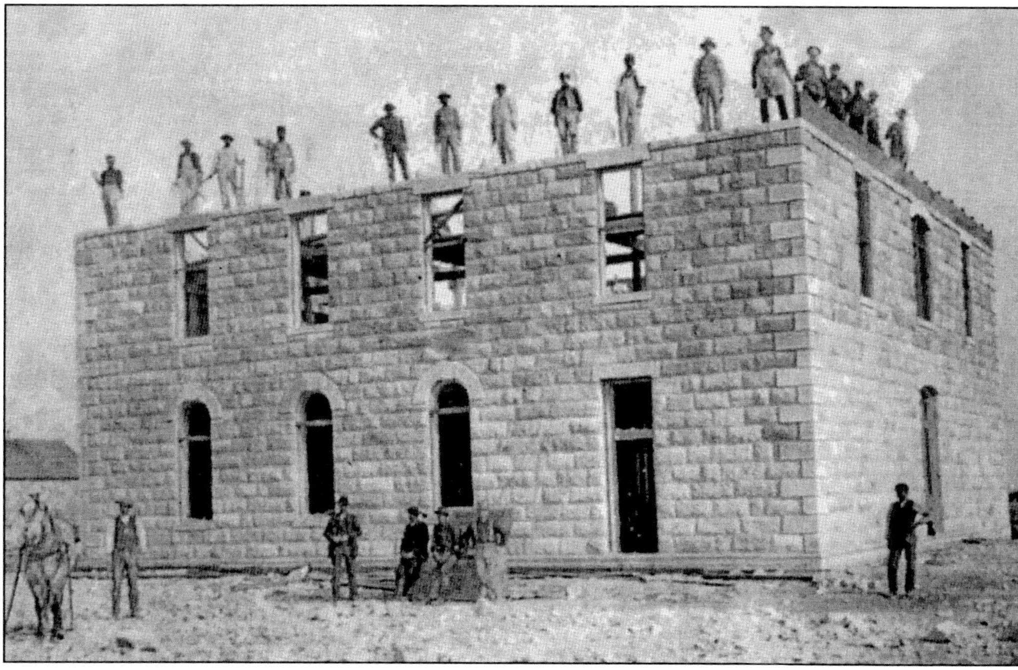

Organized on August 2, 1872, School District No. 15 in Bull City had outgrown two previous schoolhouses by 1883. The two-story structure, shown here half completed on East Second Avenue, was constructed of native limestone quarried from the bluffs a mile south of town for the purpose. The building served the city's educational needs for the next 27 years.

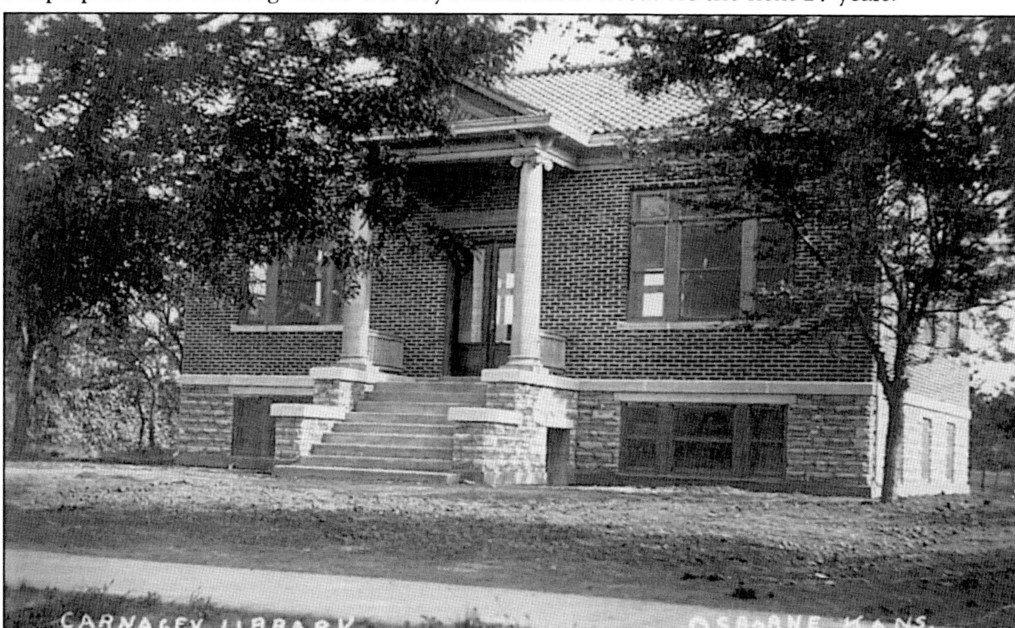

This is the Alton School as it appeared at the end of the 1910–11 school year. In 1910 additions were made to the building. The Alton High School was established in 1900 and it occupied the top floor of the schoolhouse, while the grade school was located on the ground floor. After 1925 the stone school housed only the lower grades. It was sold at auction in 1964 and razed in 1966.

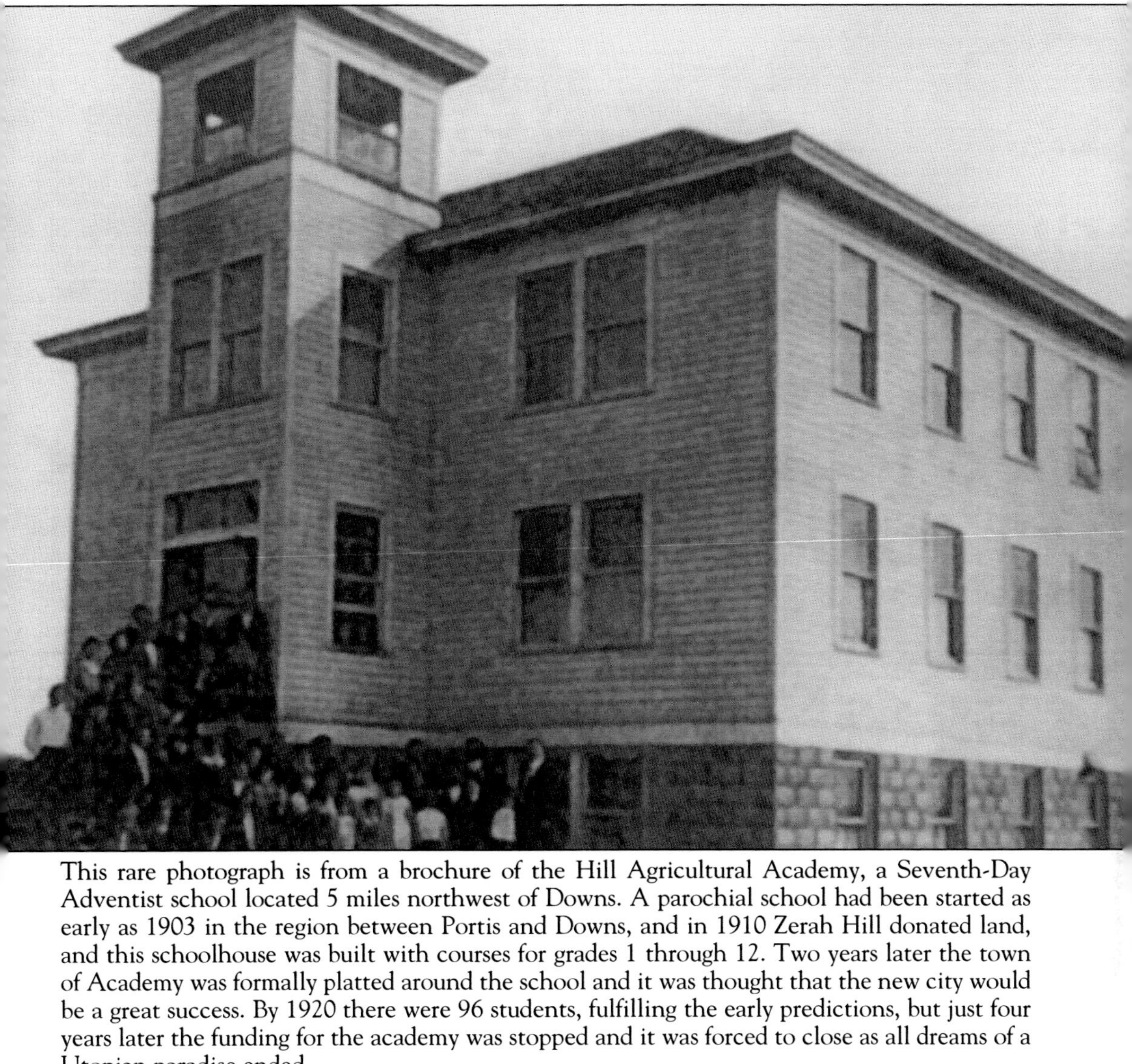

This rare photograph is from a brochure of the Hill Agricultural Academy, a Seventh-Day Adventist school located 5 miles northwest of Downs. A parochial school had been started as early as 1903 in the region between Portis and Downs, and in 1910 Zerah Hill donated land, and this schoolhouse was built with courses for grades 1 through 12. Two years later the town of Academy was formally platted around the school and it was thought that the new city would be a great success. By 1920 there were 96 students, fulfilling the early predictions, but just four years later the funding for the academy was stopped and it was forced to close as all dreams of a Utopian paradise ended.

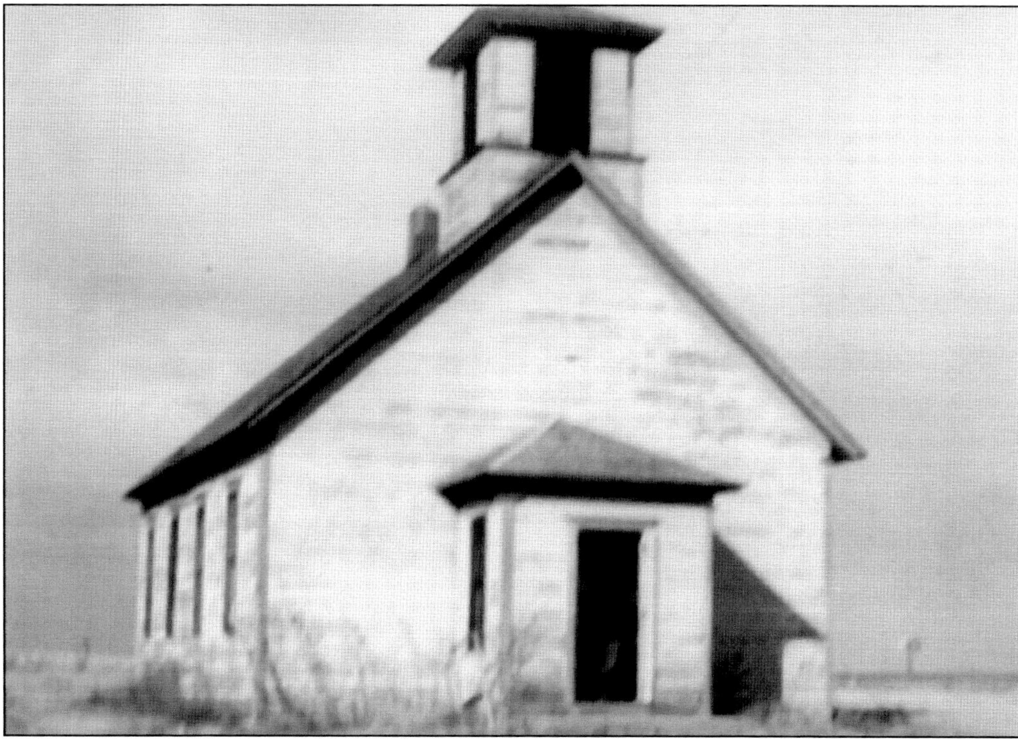

St. John's Catholic Church is pictured here as it was in the late 1930s. Located in eastern Osborne County at what was known as "Holy Corner," the church was built in the early 1900s and was one of two rural Catholic churches in the county. St. John's was affiliated with St. Boniface Church in Tipton, 4 miles to the northeast in Mitchell County, Kansas. It closed in the 1940s and was torn down.

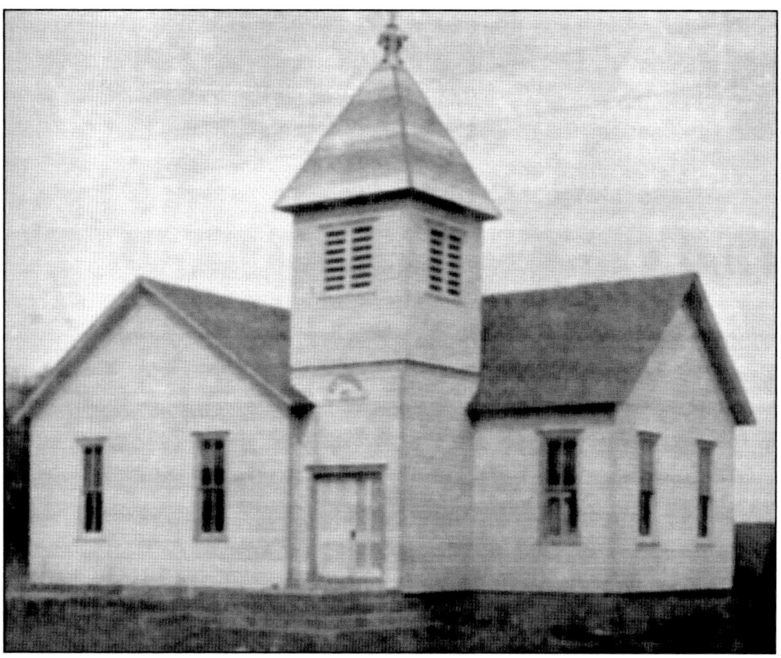

This photograph is of the second Covert Methodist Church building taken shortly after its completion in 1911. Located on North East Street, the new church was a welcome addition to the community. It was torn down in 1954 when the Covert Methodists merged with the rural Enterprise Methodist Church.

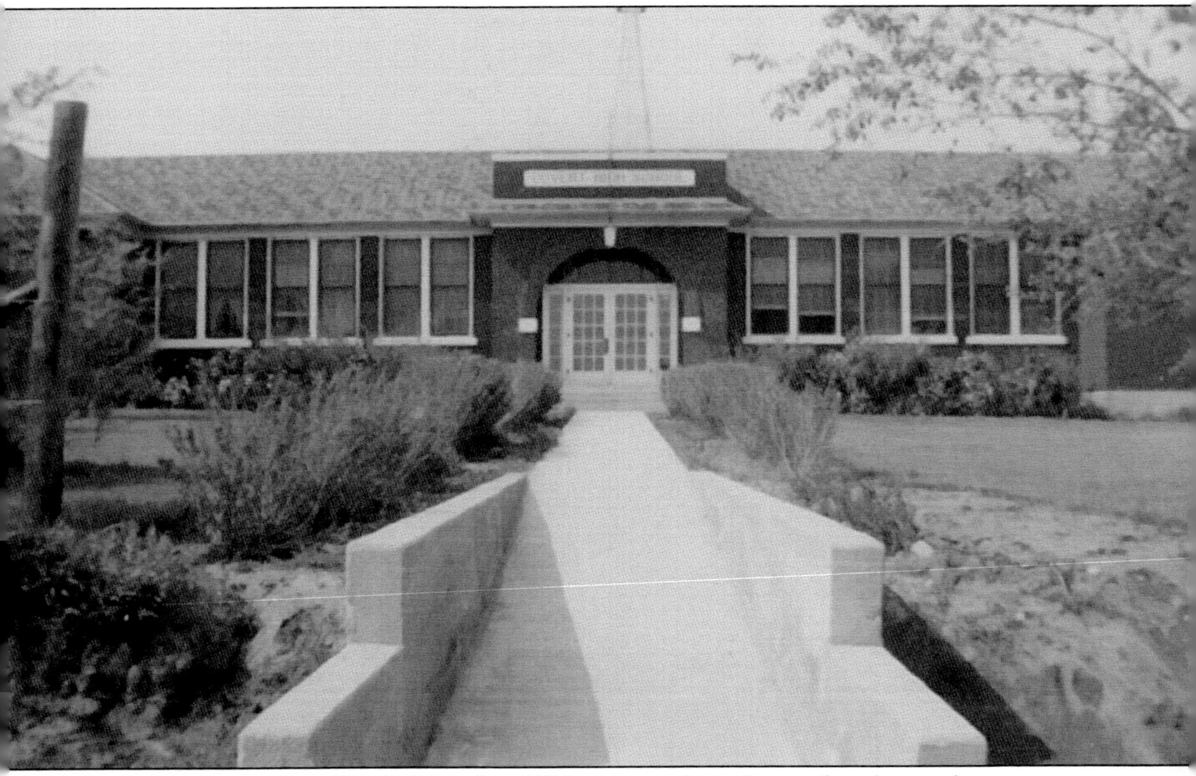

The second Covert Rural High School in 1937 is shown here. Located at the northwest corner of Liberty and Baker Streets, it was built in 1924 to replace the first schoolhouse, which was destroyed by fire. The first high school in Covert was organized in 1915 and for a number of years was the focal point of the town as its largest employer. In later years the high school was the principal reason for the community's existence at all. In athletics Covert's boys' and girls' high school basketball teams were consistent winners. It still holds the Kansas record for the smallest school to ever play in a state basketball tournament. This second schoolhouse also burned in 1951, and amid much sadness the high school was closed in 1952. By the 1960s Covert was a ghost town.

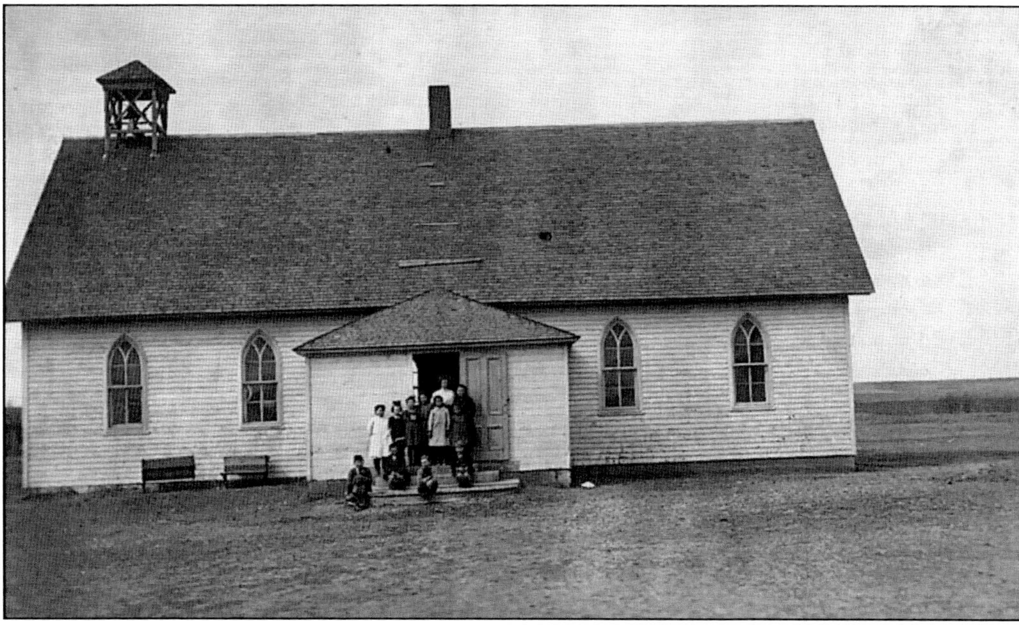

This photograph shows the second Bloomington School building in 1911. Originally the structure was built by the Antioch Church of Christ congregation and was erected in 1886. In 1888 the Bloomington school district bought the building. Eighty years later the school was closed and the building was sold to the Nelson Manufacturing Company. On March 19, 1981, a fire destroyed the old schoolhouse.

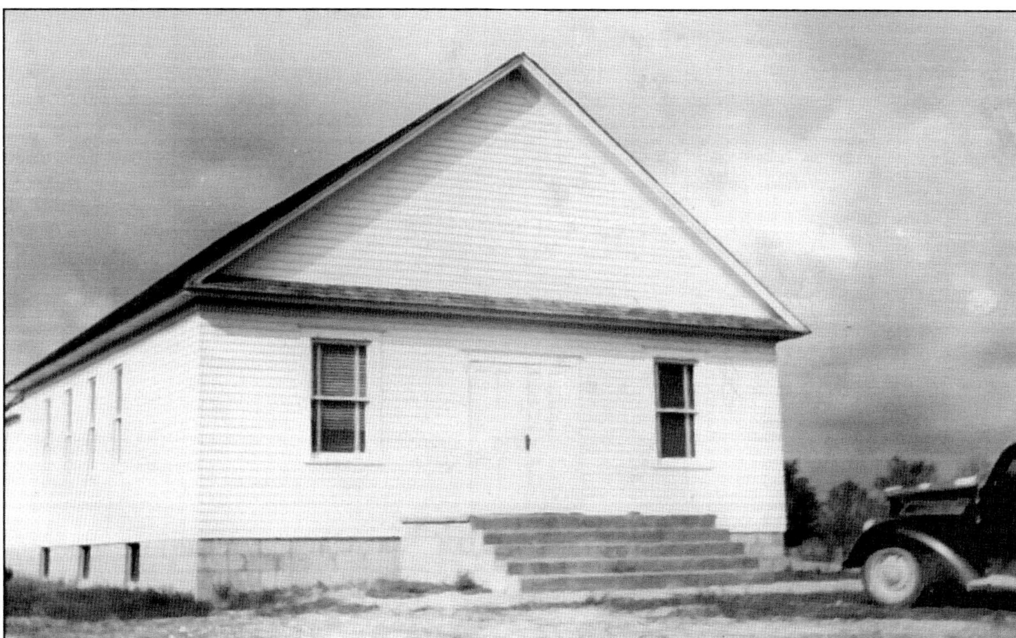

The Mount Ayr Friends Church was founded in 1874 and is located 7 miles south of Alton in western Osborne County. The previous church structure was ruined in a storm and when the Pleasant Valley schoolhouse became vacant it was moved to the site and dedicated as the new church building, shown here in the 1940s. Services continue to be held here.

Five

RURAL LIFE

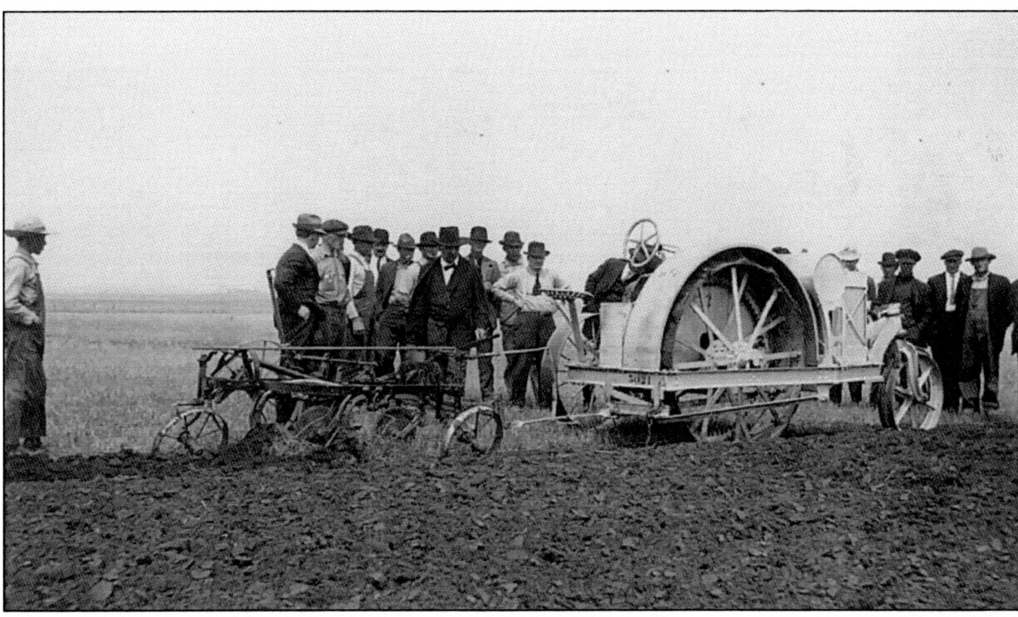

A group of interested farmers from the early 1900s is shown here inspecting one of the earliest tractors seen in the Bloomington area. This photograph signifies the change agriculture was undergoing at the time, from the horse to the mechanical beast.

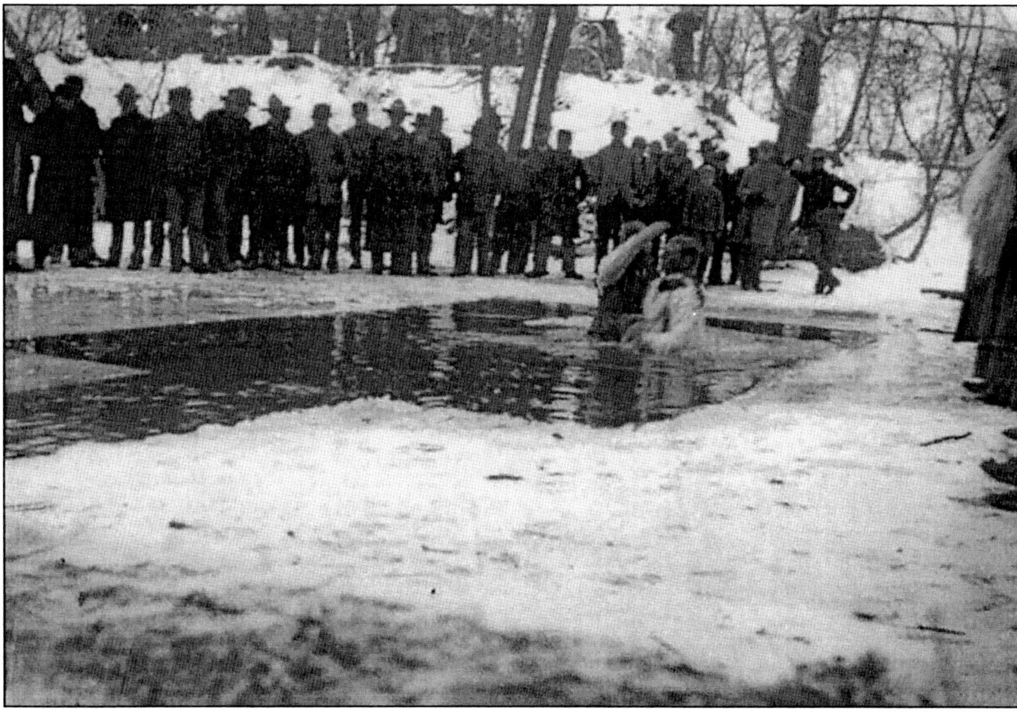

This unusual photograph is of a cold weather baptism in the South Fork Solomon River a mile south of Alton in the very early 1900s. It is unknown which religious faith is represented here. Note that the men are standing on the river ice while the women are above them on the riverbank in the background.

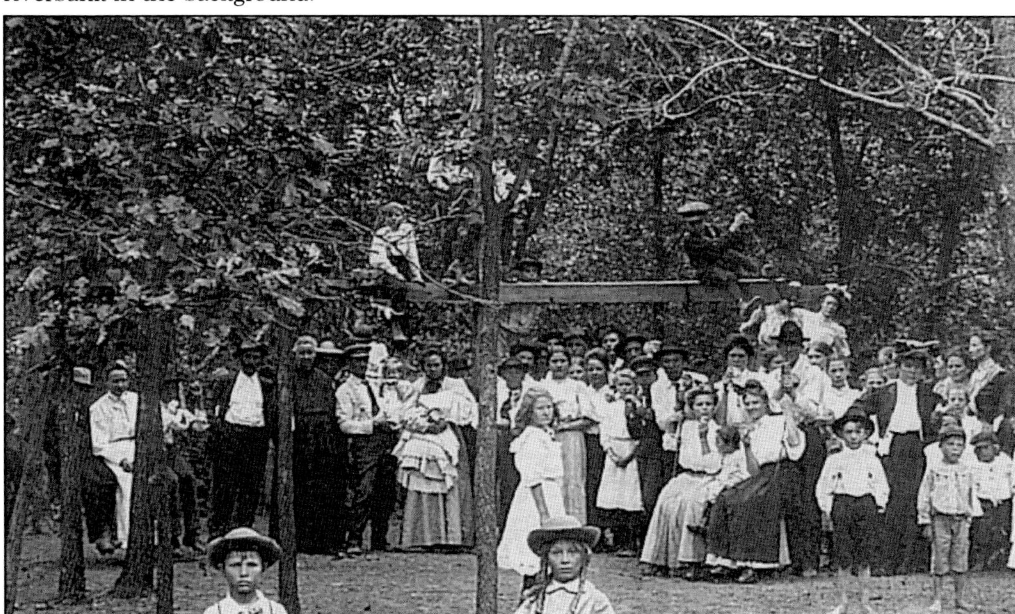

Pictured here is a Sunday school picnic on Kill Creek in west-central Osborne County that occurred shortly after 1910. Notice the clothing, with some children barefoot and some not. Also note the three children playing in the trees above two women riding in a swing.

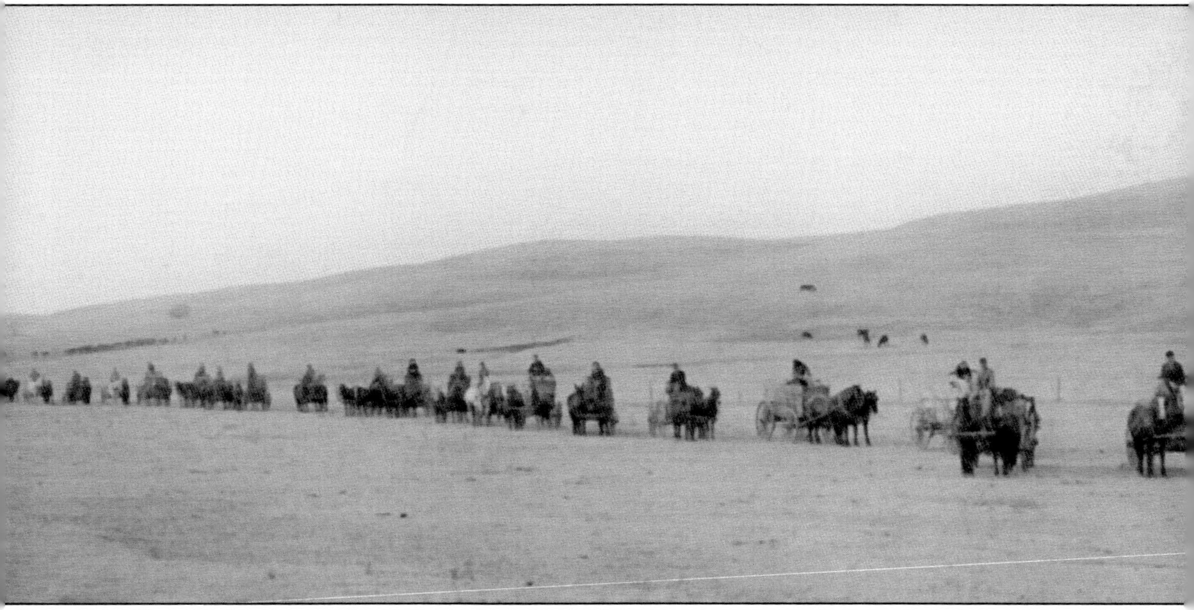

A large wagon train of neighbors can be seen here organizing to help the Milton Near family haul hogs from the family's farm on Kill Creek in west-central Osborne County to market in nearby Alton around 1900. It is most likely that the train followed the route of the old Russell-Bull City Freight Trail, which ran from 1871 to 1879 from Russell, Kansas, northwest to Bull City, now known as Alton, and passed through the Kill Creek community.

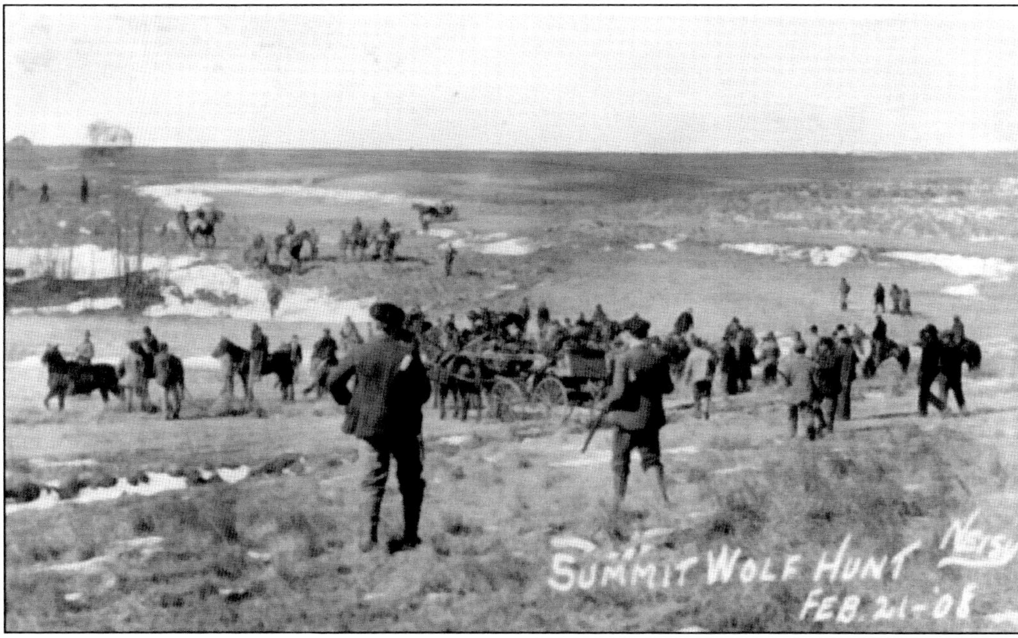

This view is of the gathered participants in the wolf hunt held in Summit School District, northern Osborne County on February 21, 1908. The county's farmers and ranchers periodically decided that wolves were a pest, but the actual aim of these hunts was reducing the numbers of coyotes and rabbits in the county.

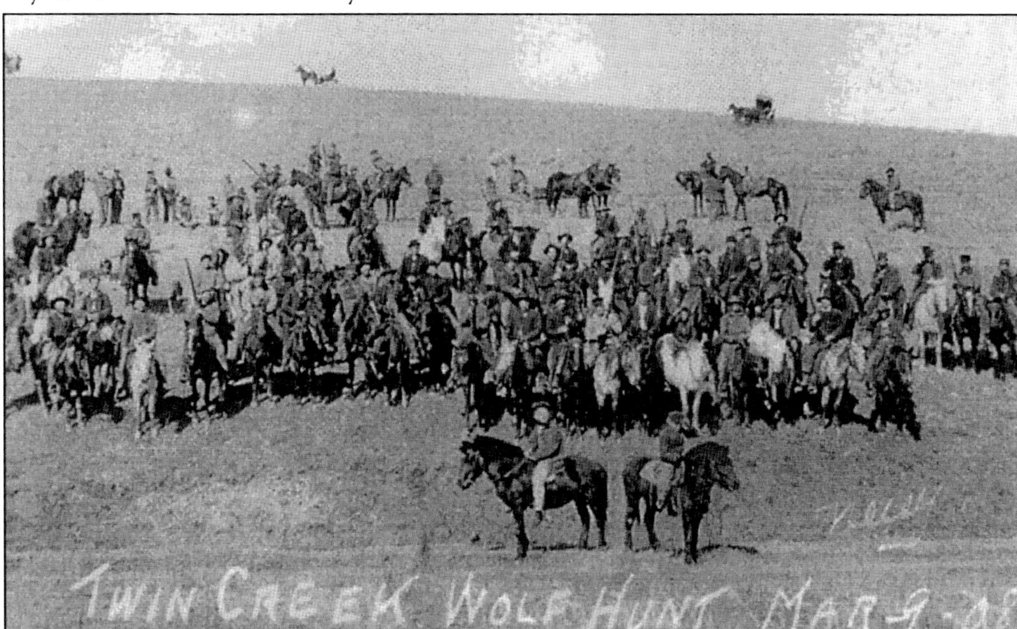

This is a look at the wolf hunt held along Twin Creek in south-central Osborne County on Monday, March 9, 1908. The hunt shown here covered 24 square miles of hills and creek valleys. At least ten of these wolf hunts were held throughout February and March with the largest involving over 1,200 men and boys. By World War I the wolf was largely extinct in Osborne County.

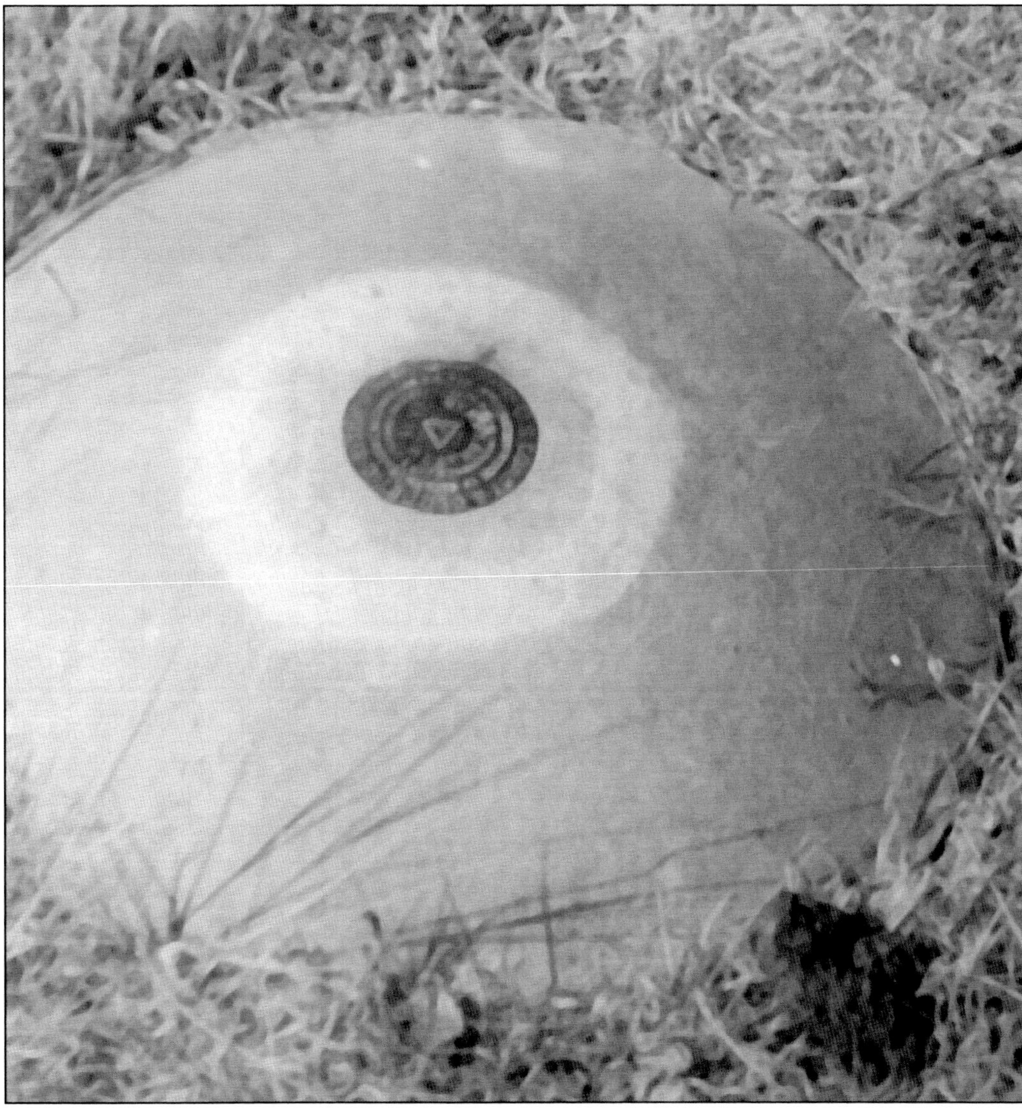

On the top of a hill in southeastern Osborne County this marker can be seen at one of the most unique sites to be found in the United States or anywhere, for that matter. This bronze disk marks the Geodetic Center of North America. On the disk is a tiny triangle, and inside the triangle is a dot that is being used by the United States Coast and Geodetic Survey to measure the size and shape of the earth. This dot is the controlling point of all land surveys in Canada, the United States, and Mexico. The Geodetic Center was first established in 1891 on what was then called Meade's Ranch. It became the North American Geodetic point of reference in 1927 and was placed on the National Register of Historic Places in 1973.

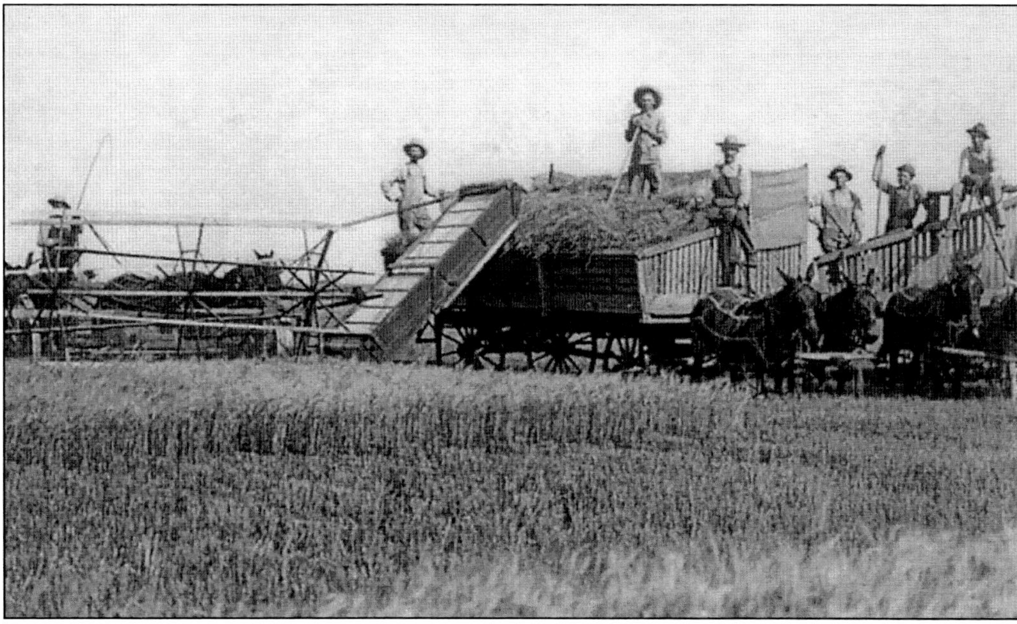

Pick's header crew pause here in a Bloomington area field long enough for a group photograph during the 1908 wheat harvest. The wagon being filled will then be taken to the threshing machine for the separation of the wheat from the chaff and straw.

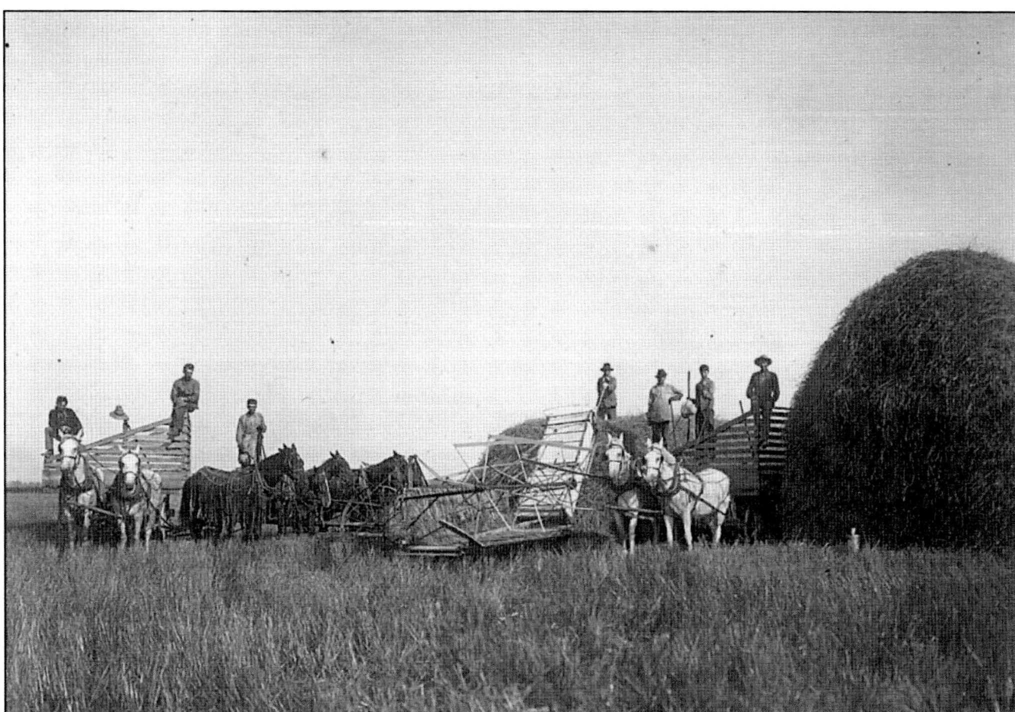

Shown here are a header crew taking time out to have their picture taken near Osborne in 1910. Notice the size of the haystack on the right compared to the water jug at its base.

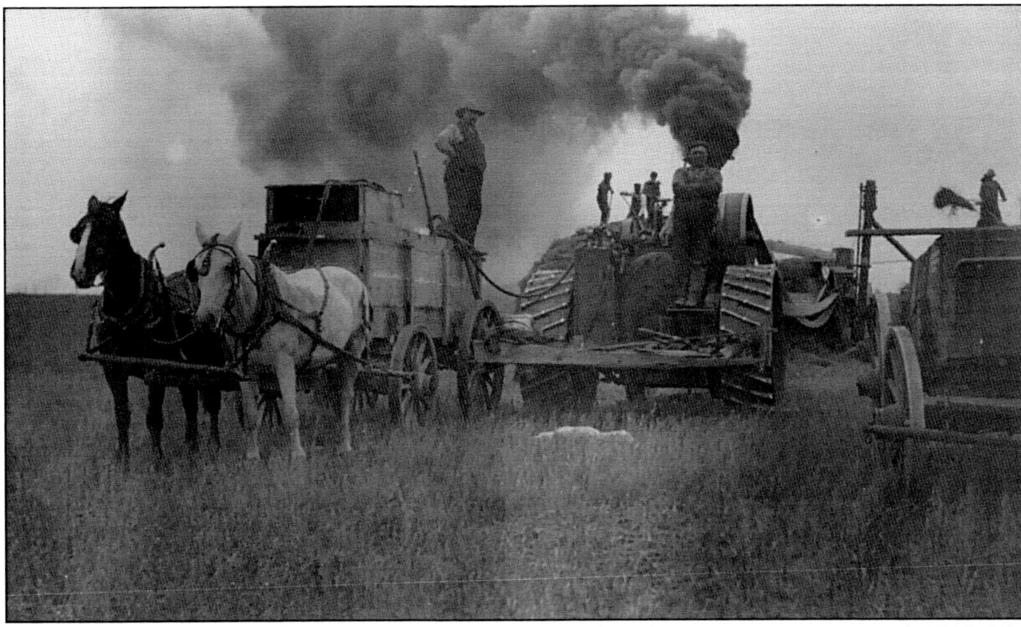

This picture is of a wheat threshing crew at work in the Bloomington area around 1910. The water wagon is on the left. Water was needed in large amounts for both the crew and running the steam-powered threshers.

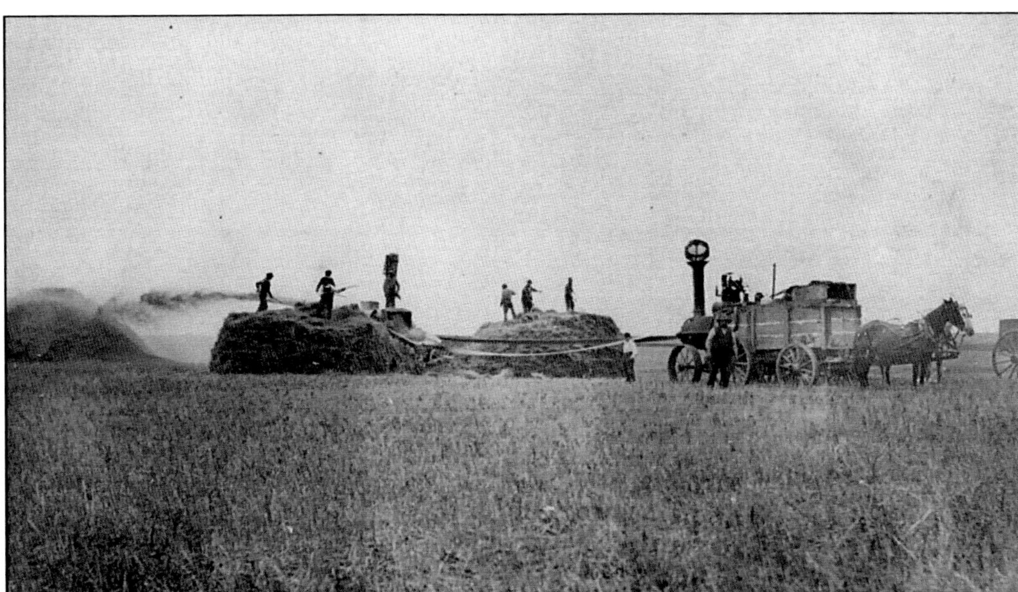

This is a good view of the wheat threshing crew at work in the Bloomington area, with the thresher seen ejecting the chaff and straw and thus creating a haystack.

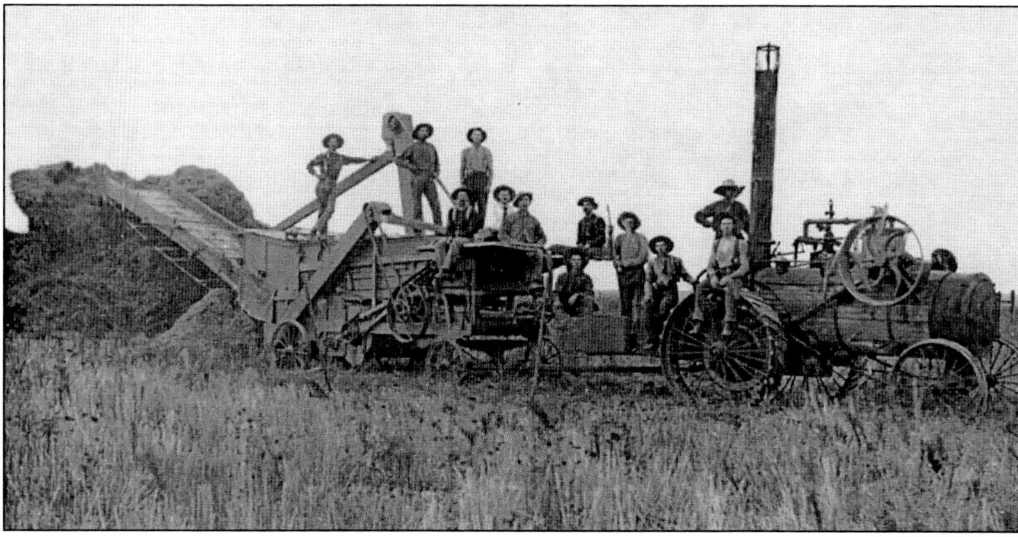

Shown here is an early threshing machine from the Alton area, taken in the latter 1890s. Within 15 years of this picture wooden parts on the early threshers gave way to all-metal components.

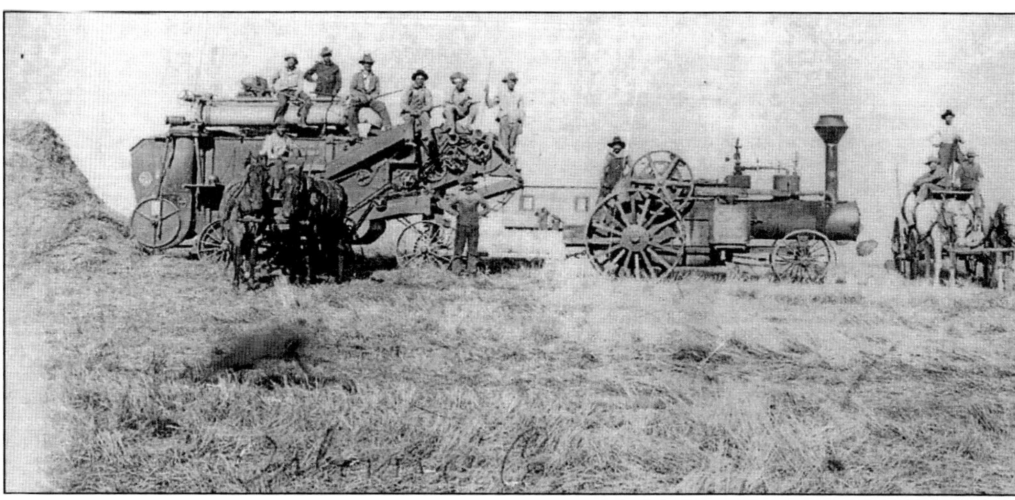

This Alton area threshing machine was owned by Sam Hibbs with Harry Guttery managing the threshing crew. Threshing machines were gradually replaced with the combine by the 1930s, and today only a few restored examples remain in museums.

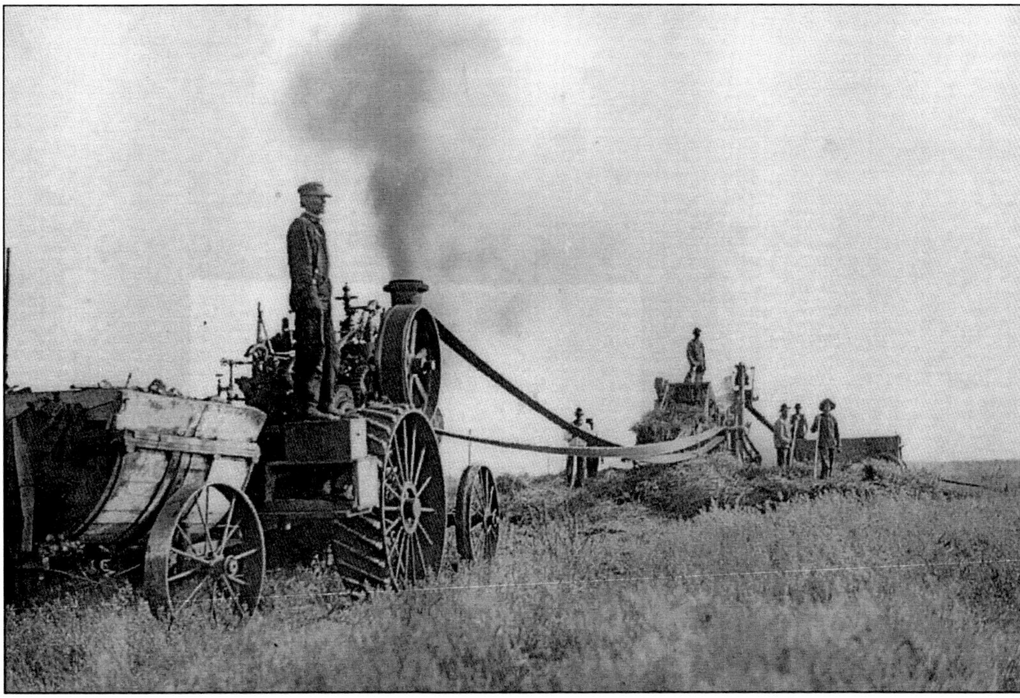

This is a good photograph of a horse-drawn threshing machine in actual operation near Alton in the latter 1890s. Belt-driven machines were a new sensation at the time and did much to enlarge both the machine's work capacity and its growing popularity.

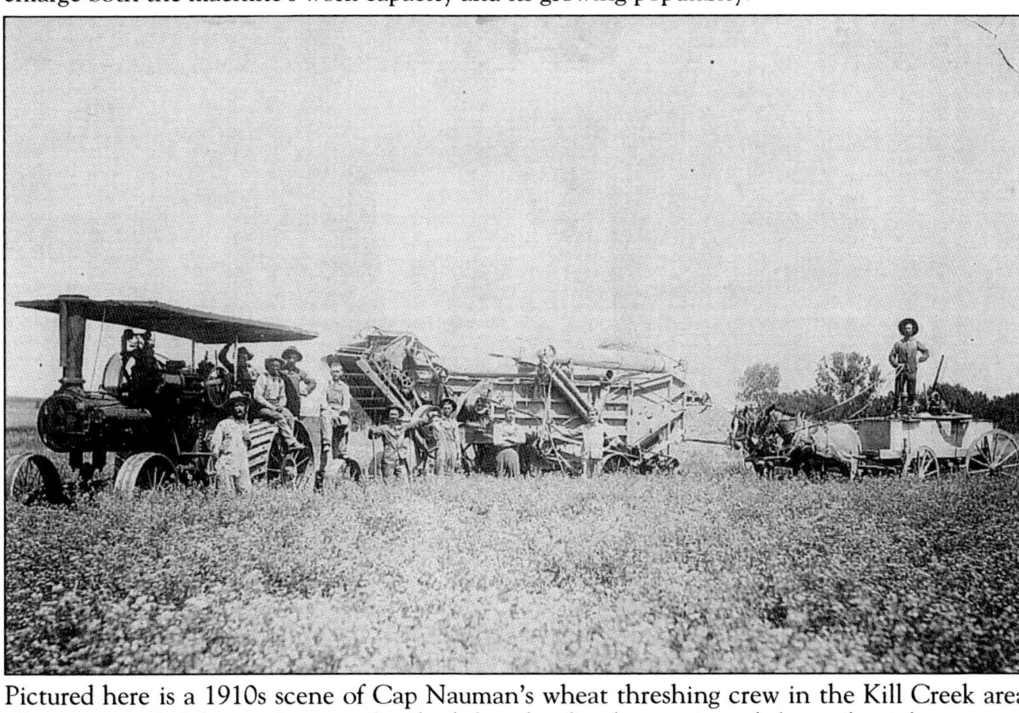

Pictured here is a 1910s scene of Cap Nauman's wheat threshing crew in the Kill Creek area of west-central Osborne County. On the left is the thresher engine while on the right is a man standing on the water wagon.

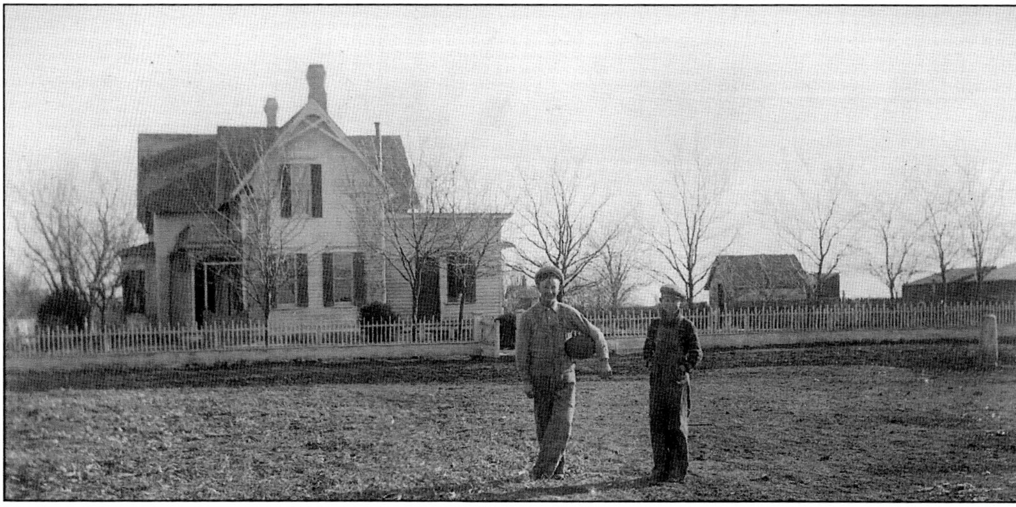

Herman and Frank Ise can be seen here at play on the west side of the Henry Ise farm home in 1895. Henry Ise homesteaded the farm in 1871 3 miles northwest of the present city of Downs. In 1873 he brought his new bride Rosa Haag there. The story of the family's struggle to make a living on the prairie is documented in son John Ise's 1936 classic novel *Sod and Stubble*.

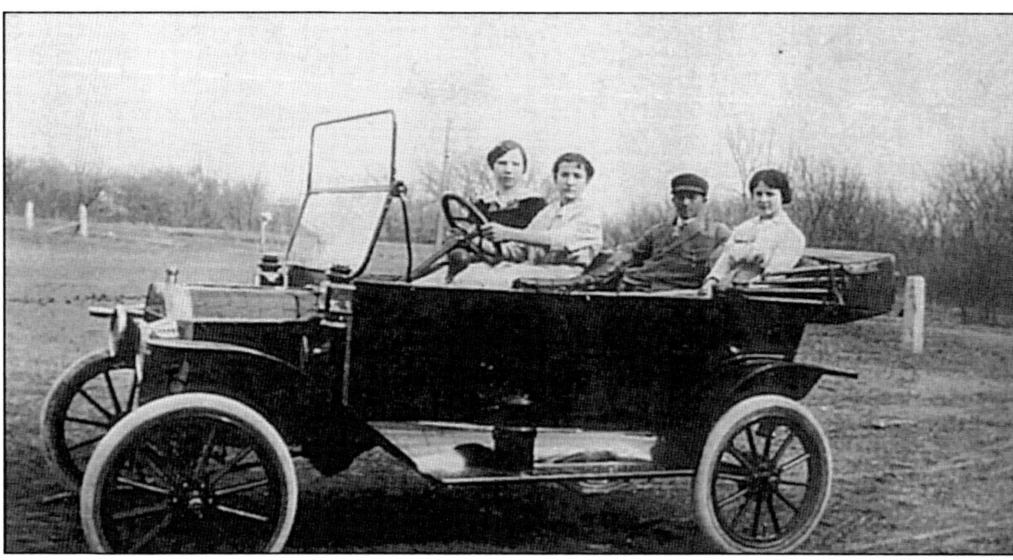

A group of young people are here trying out John Cooper's new 1916 Ford touring car near the Vincent community in southern Osborne County. At this time female drivers were rare and it was several years before they were seen as often as their male counterparts.

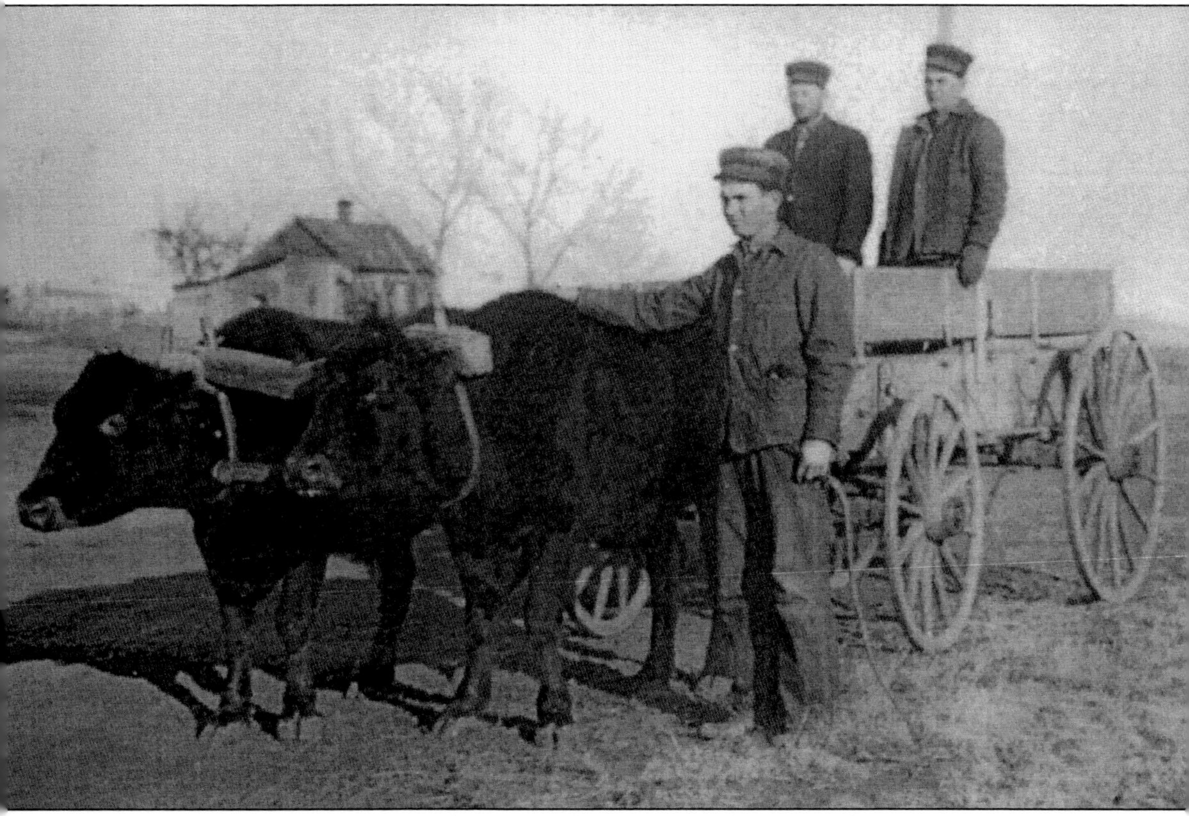

Taken in the 1890s, this photograph is of Hugh Stuart with his team of oxen. Oxen were the work animals of preference among the first white settlers in the county. However, they soon proved to be less dependable than the horse and mule, and within a short number of years only a few pairs were being kept on farms as nostalgic memories of those early days.

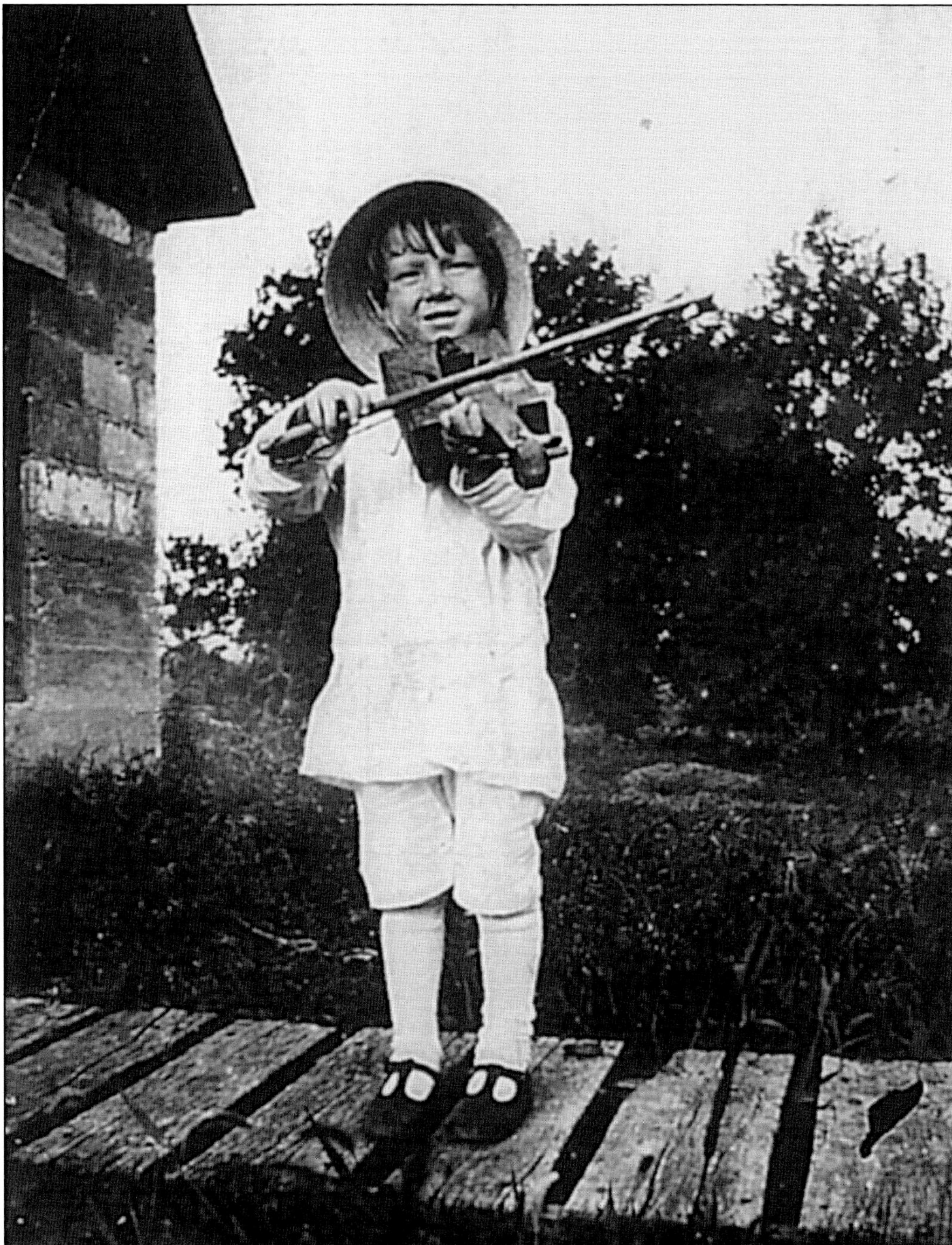

With the rollercoaster-ride that an agricultural-based economy dictates, the farmers of Osborne County have often had to "make do" with recycling whatever is available in order to provide food, shelter, and entertainment for their families. This photograph from southern Osborne County in 1919 is a good example. It features my four-year-old great-uncle Stacey Collicott playing a working fiddle made from a cigar box by his uncle Robert Irby. Stacey's father, grandfather, and aunt were all noted fiddle players.

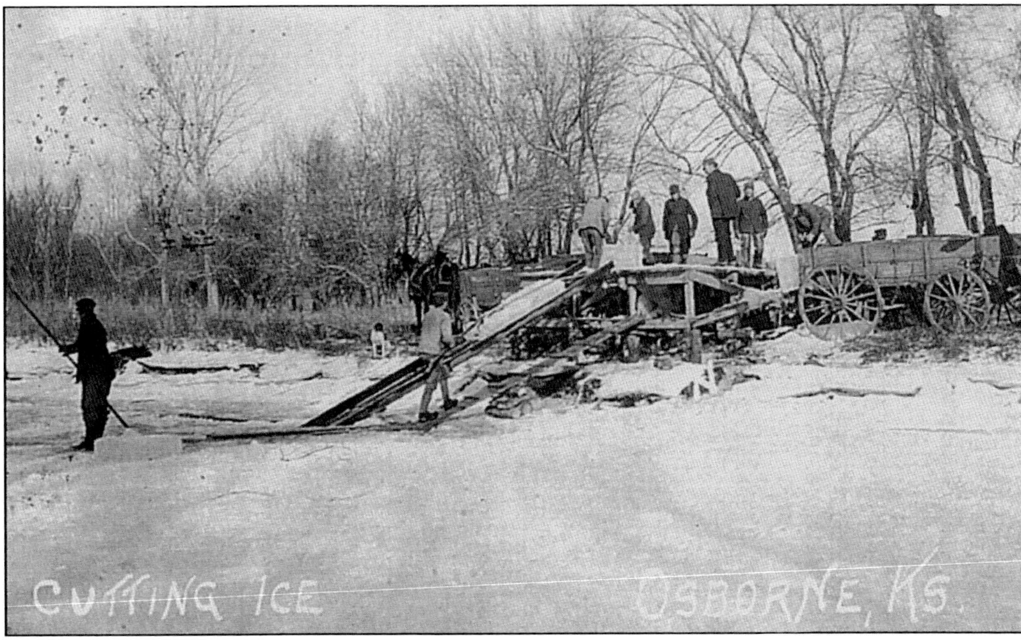

A crew is here shown hard at work in the winter of 1909 cutting ice from the South Fork Solomon River at Osborne. Among the workers is my great-uncle Elijah Collicott. The ice was 8 to 12 inches thick when cut. Then it was loaded into the wagons and packed with several feet of straw in ice houses, leaving a space around the walls. In this manner ice lasted well into the summer.

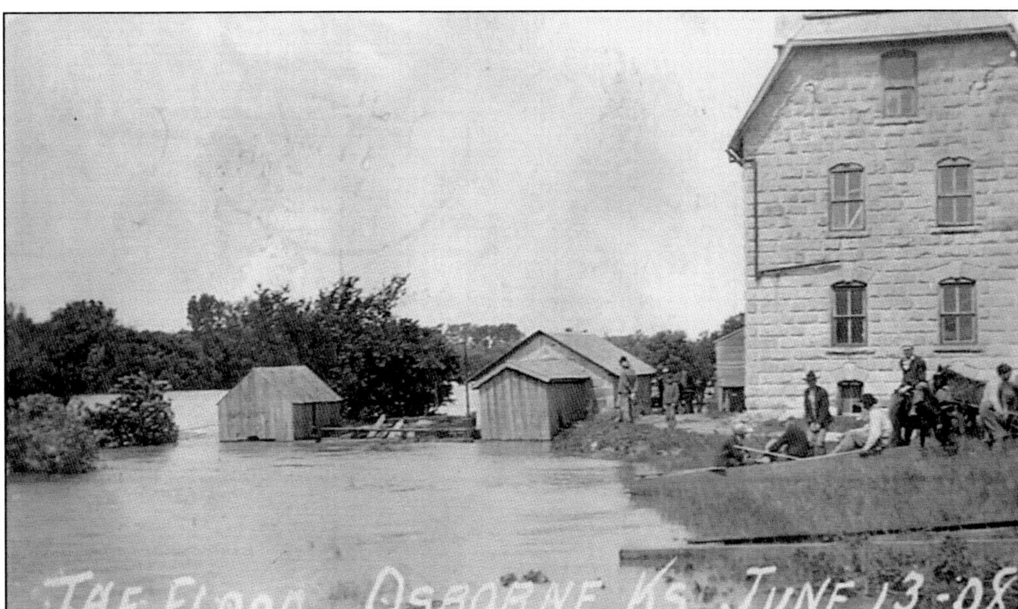

Flooding along the South Fork Solomon River at Osborne is shown in this postcard view dated June 13, 1908. In the right foreground are men with a boat who salvaged items from the flooded outbuildings of the Jackson Mill, seen on the right. Frequent floods occurred throughout Osborne County during the years of 1900 to 1920.

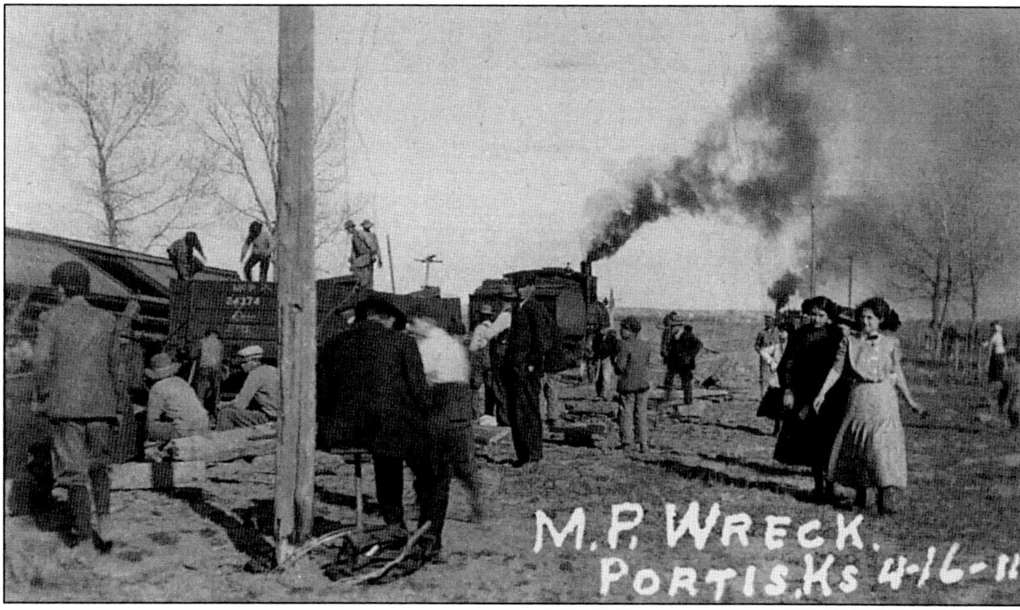

Pictured here are those cleaning up after the wreck of the Missouri Pacific Railroad's freight train No. 634, which occurred on Friday morning, April 16, 1911. Six empty cars and one loaded with wheat derailed 2 miles east of Portis, tearing up 200 feet of track in the process. Happily no one was injured, and 24 hours later the rail line returned to full service.

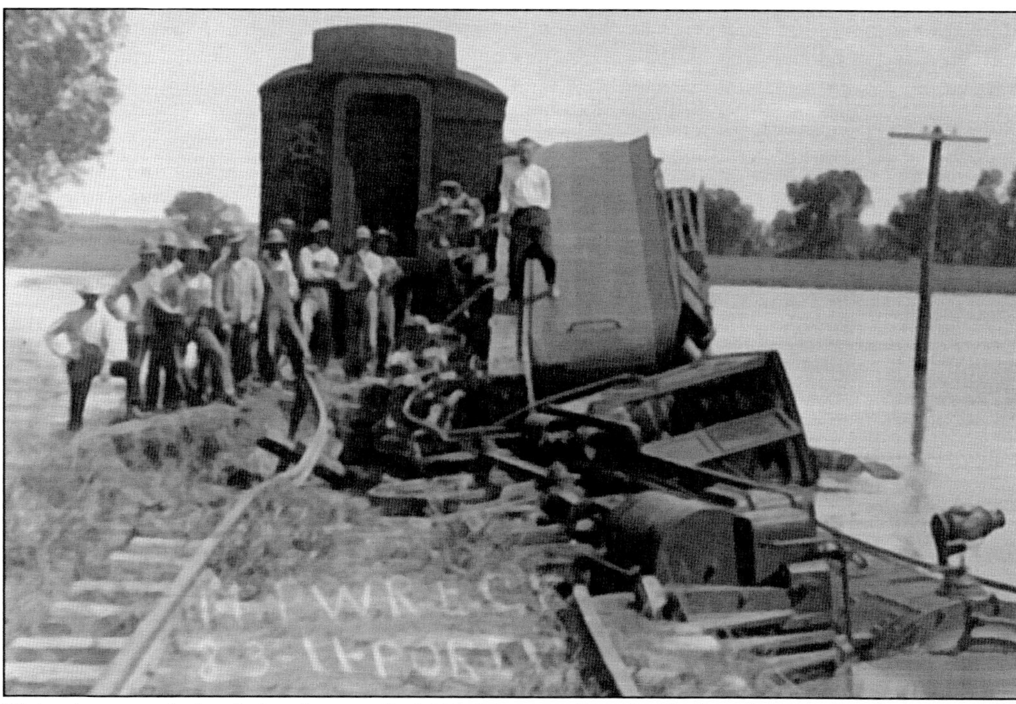

This photograph is of the August 3, 1911 Missouri Pacific Railroad train wreck a few miles east of Portis. High water washed out a portion of the tracks and compounded the railroad's problems with this second major accident within the previous four months.

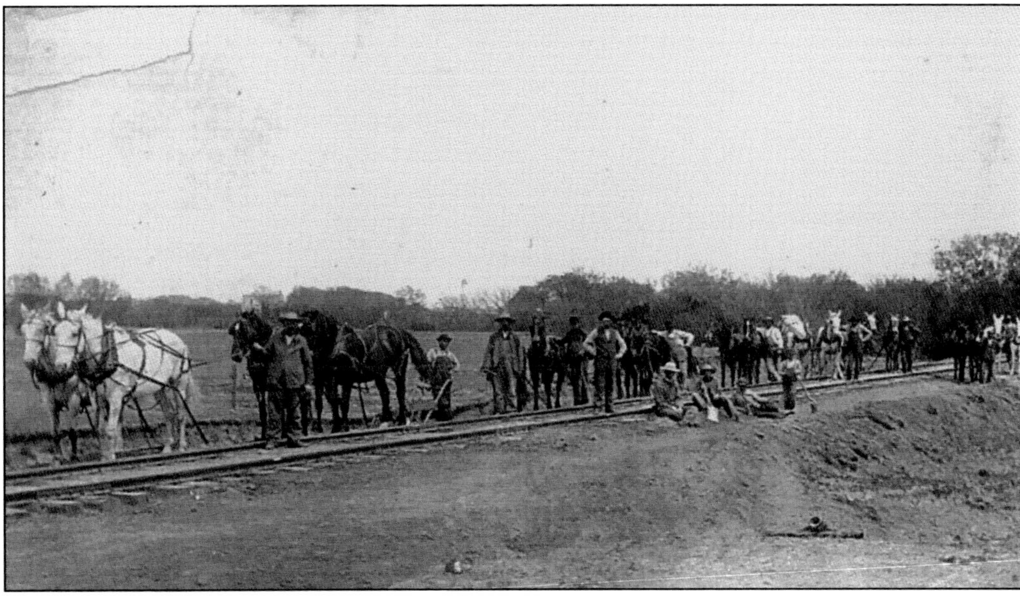

Missouri Pacific Railroad workers used teams of horses and mules to repair the railroad tracks west of Downs after the flood of 1911. Work on the railroad was hard and dirty and often dangerous, but the pay made it one of the better jobs to have in the area.

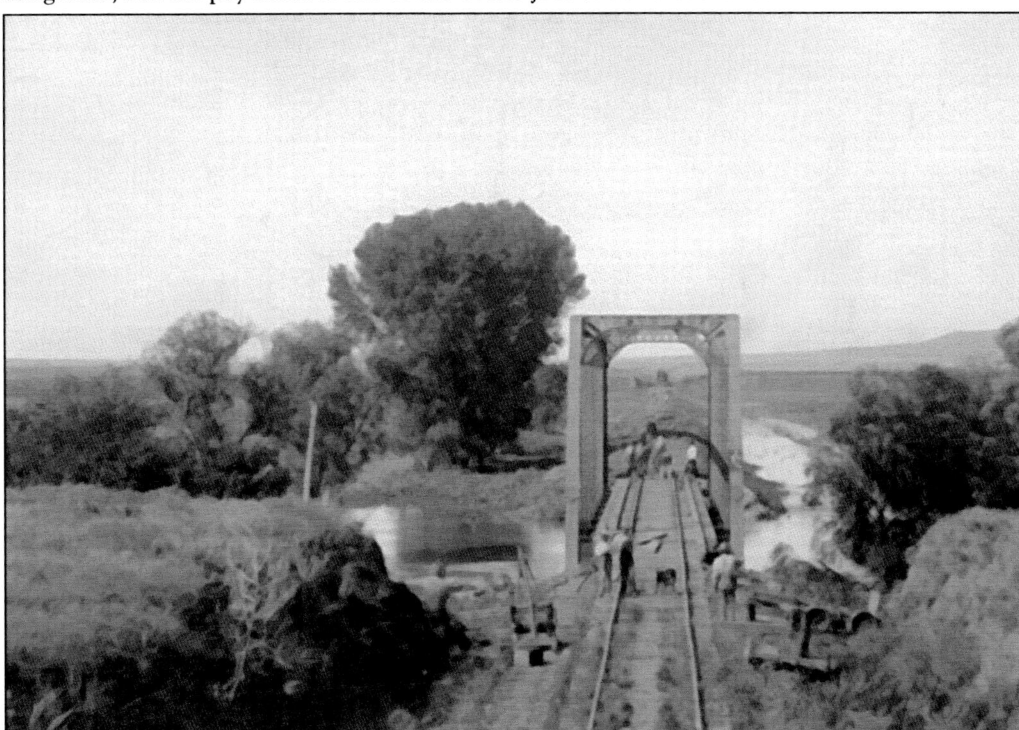

A crew is shown here repairing the Missouri Pacific Railroad bridge over the North Fork Solomon River just southwest of Downs after the flood of 1911. The view of the river valley is typical for the Blue Hills region in which Osborne County is located. Note the still high level of water in the river.

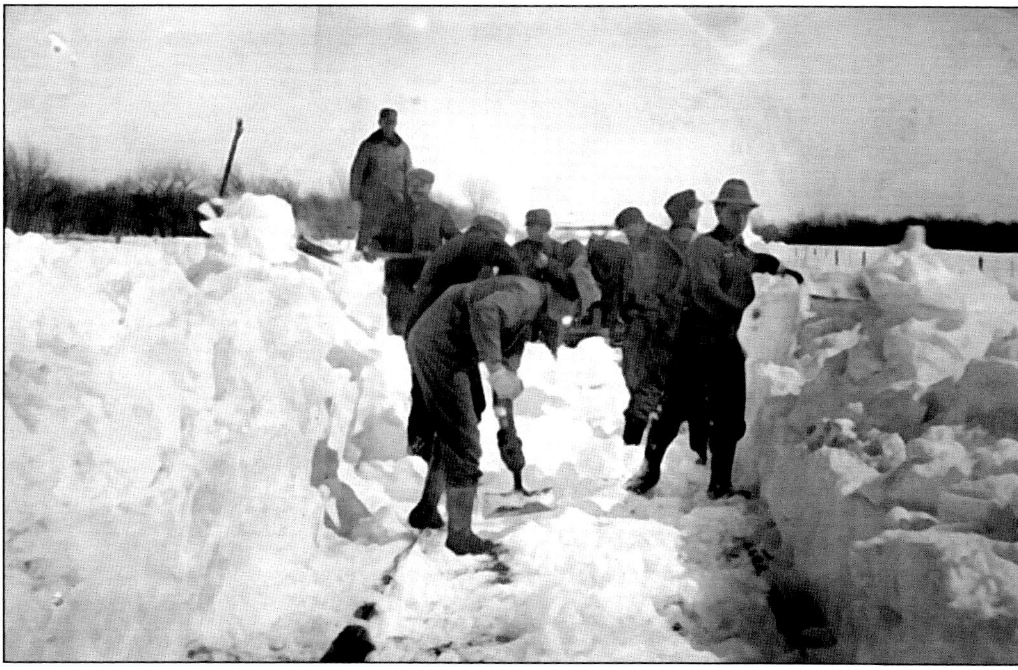

In this photograph a Union Pacific work gang clears the railroad tracks east of Natoma after the blizzard of March 1912. The wind had piled the snow so high that the trains could not penetrate the drifts and the railroad men were forced to do the job by hand.

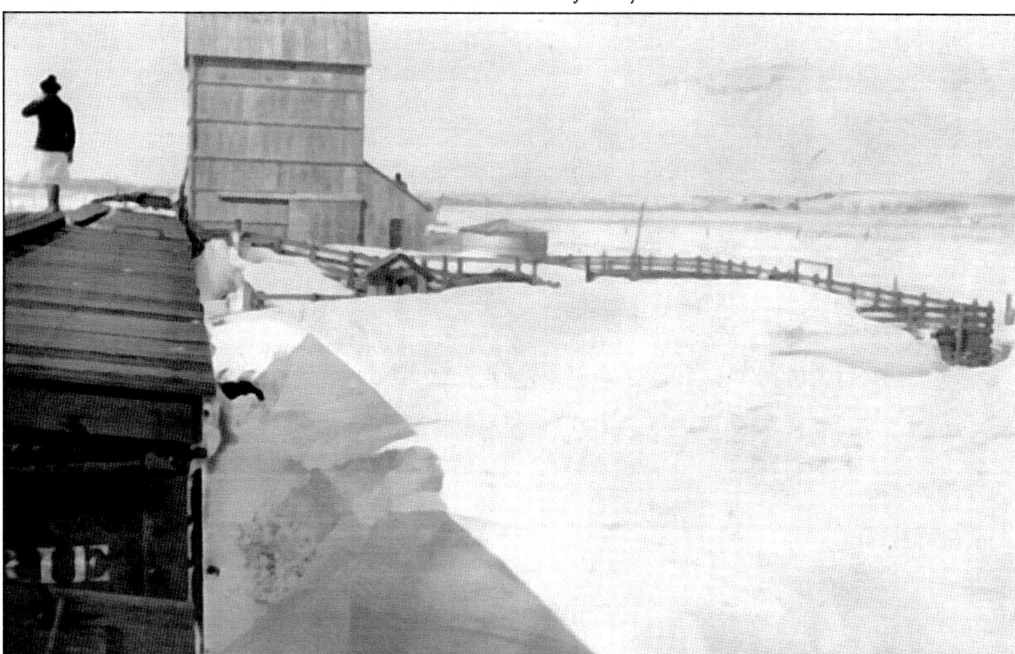

This view is looking down from atop a Missouri Pacific Railroad car at the snowbound Farmers Union Elevator and the railroad stockyards at Bloomington in March 1912. Heavy snows that fell during the last week of February and the first week of March paralyzed road and rail travel in the area for weeks.

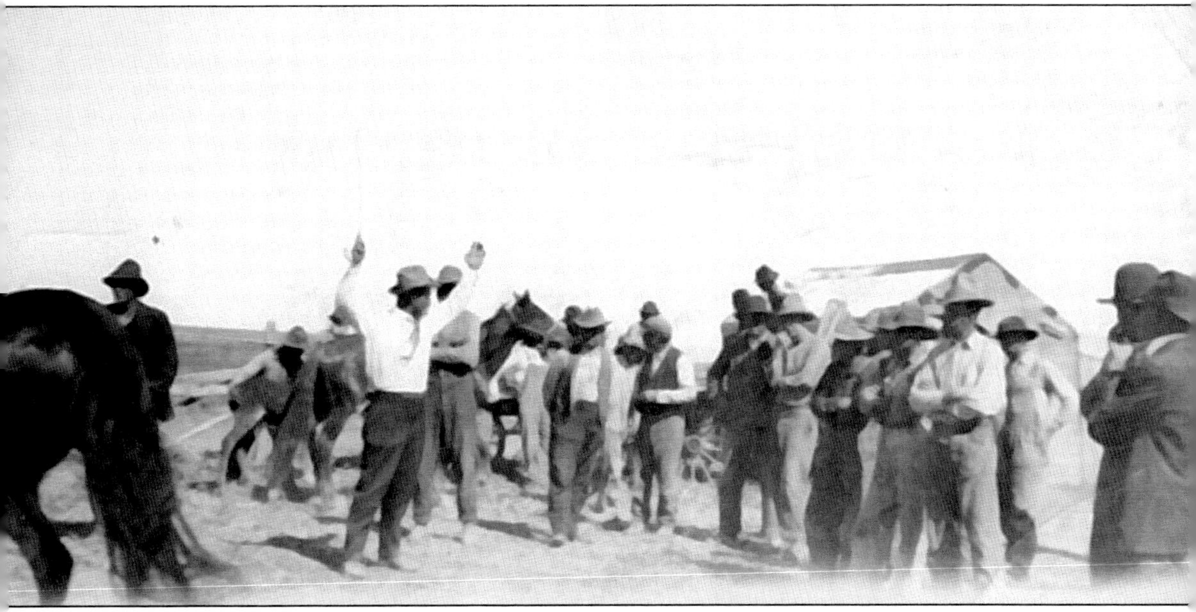

This is a rare photograph of a horse auction in progress in the Vincent area of southern Osborne County. The auctioneer has his hands raised high as he listens for the farmers and ranchers to shout out their bids. Country auctions such as this are still a common sight throughout the county.

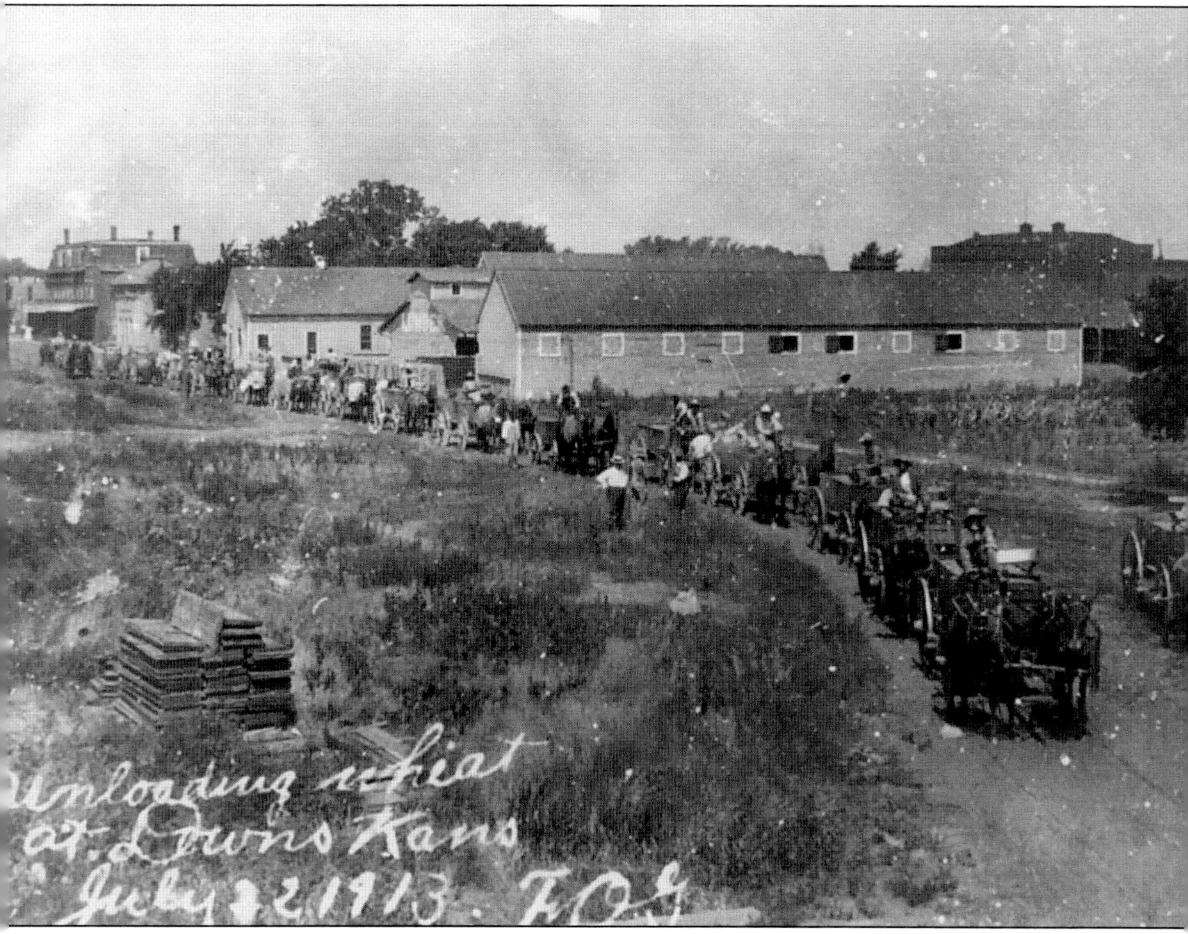

A long line of farmers is shown here patiently waiting to unload their wagonloads of wheat at the Nye and McMillen Grain Elevator along East Railroad Avenue in Downs on June 22, 1913. Notable structures of Downs' skyline can be seen in the background. In the upper left is the wooden tower of the Downs Fire Station and to its right is the roof of the Lipton Hotel. In the upper right is the top of the Wolfert Opera House. Centered behind the line of wagons are the buildings of the Rice and Johntz Lumber Company. By replacing the wagons with trucks, such a scene would appear little changed today, nearly 90 years later.

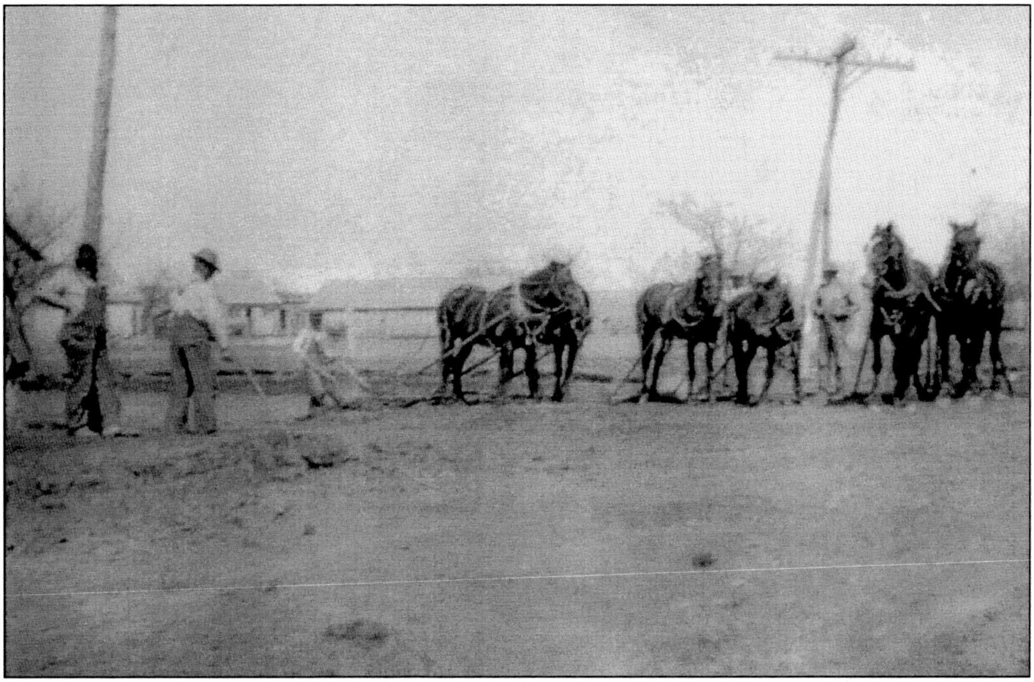

A group of workmen in the 1920s are shown grading Washington Street in Bloomington. They are preparing the street to become part of the newly designated U.S. Highway 40 North, now known as U.S. Highway 24.

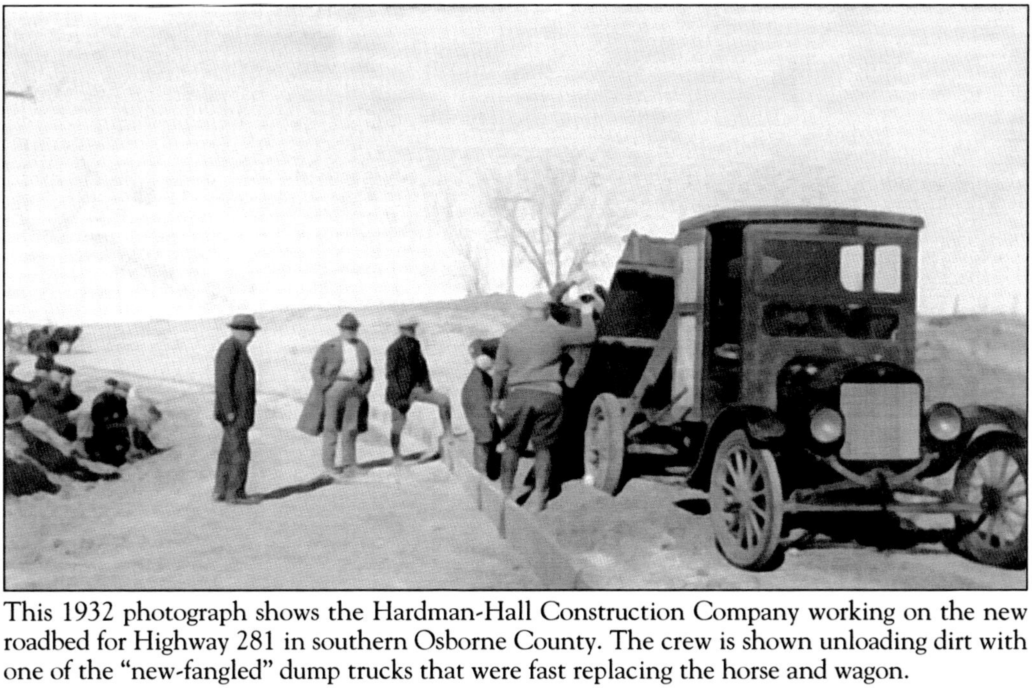

This 1932 photograph shows the Hardman-Hall Construction Company working on the new roadbed for Highway 281 in southern Osborne County. The crew is shown unloading dirt with one of the "new-fangled" dump trucks that were fast replacing the horse and wagon.

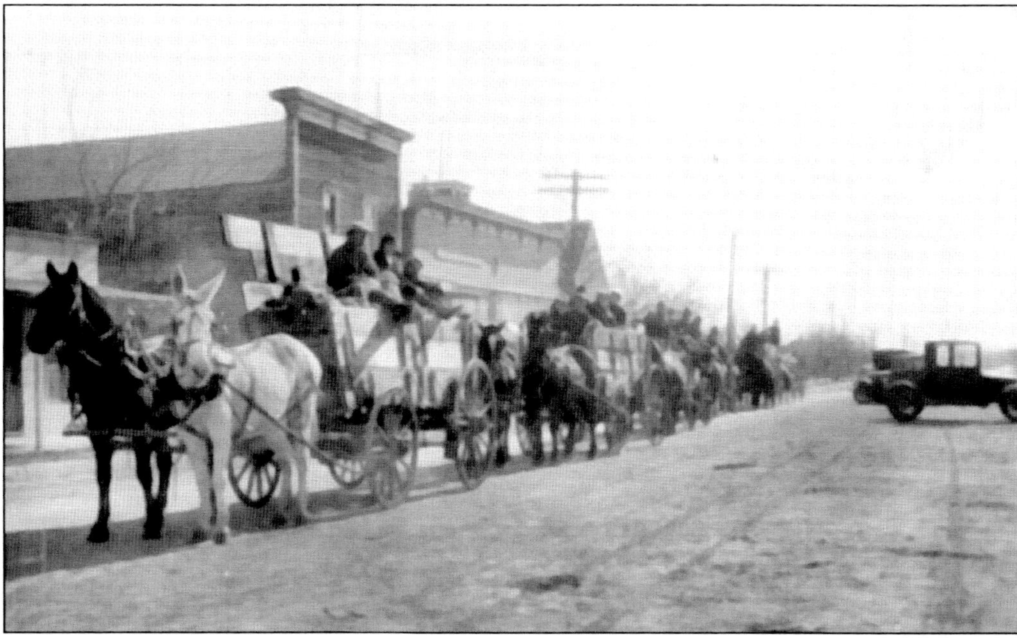

Pictured here are migrating workers on Market Street in Portis awaiting jobs husking corn during the harvest of 1915. The lids of the wagons were left up while husking so that the cobs could be tossed against them to fall down into the wagons. The tall buildings from left are the Portis Odd Fellows Lodge and the newspaper office. Behind them the roof of the Grace Brethren Church can be seen.

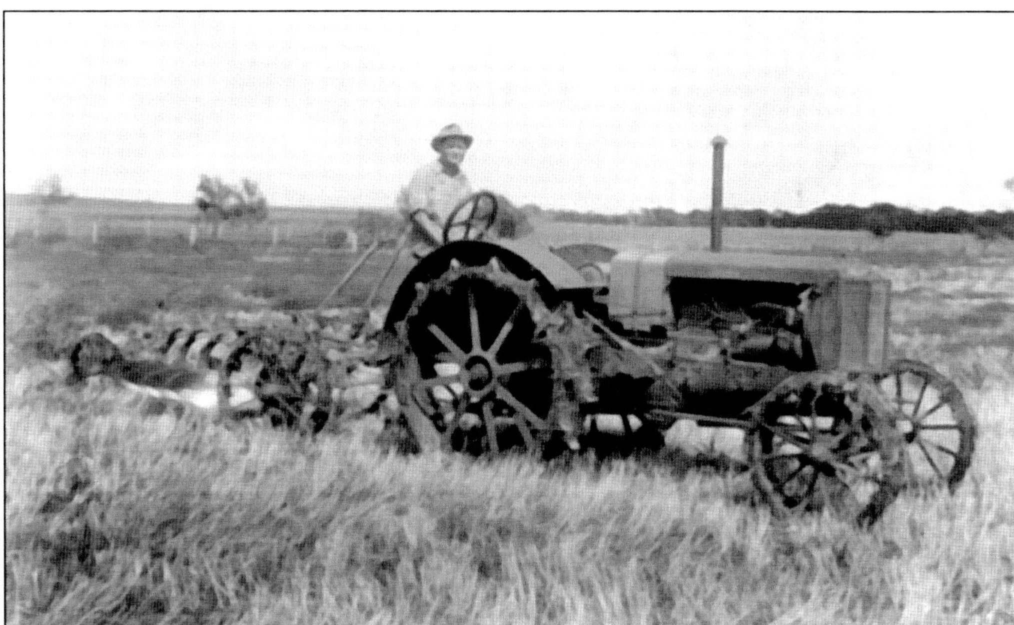

Taken in the 1930s, this is a fine photograph of a tractor and plow in central Osborne County. The old Wallis tractor was made in Racine, Wisconsin, and had seen plenty of work prior to this effort. By this time the tractor had replaced the horse to a great extent and the horse barns found on many of the county's farms became a thing of the past.

Six

Recreation and Bands

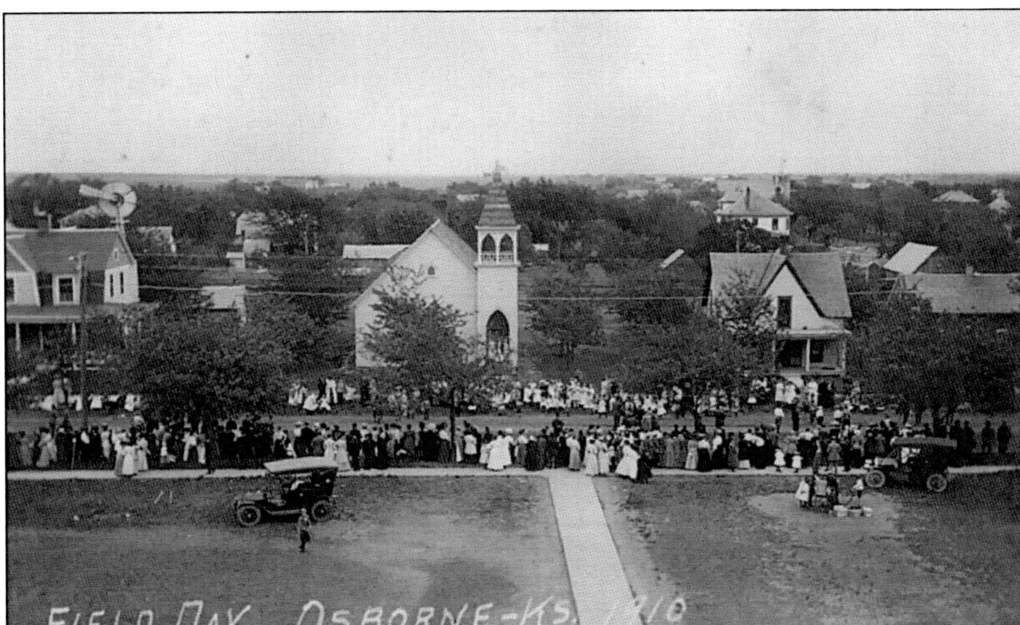

This postcard photograph shows the crowd watching the seventh annual Field Day exercises held on May 19, 1910, the last day of school in Osborne. Thirty student contests ranging from the crab race to the tin can and backward running races were held for prizes donated by local merchants. The photograph was taken from atop the high school looking east across North Second Street toward the Christian Church and parsonage.

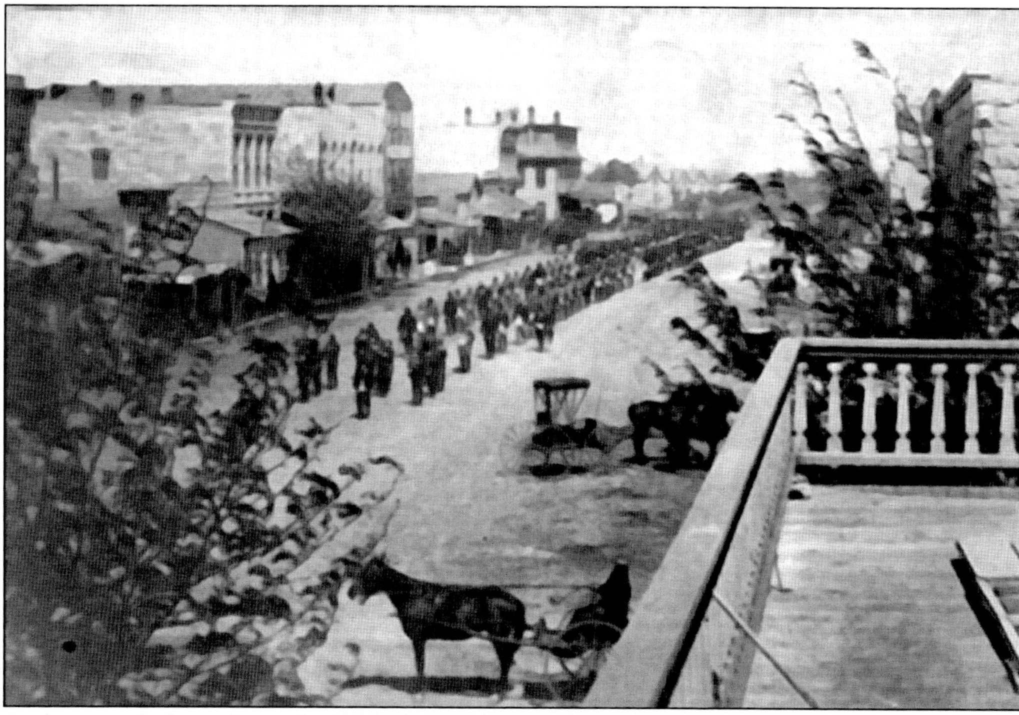

A photograph from the early 1900s shows the parade at the Downs Celebration. The view is from DeLay Street looking south along Morgan Avenue towards the Lipton Hotel. Note the band, the buggies, and the men standing on top of the building seeking a better view.

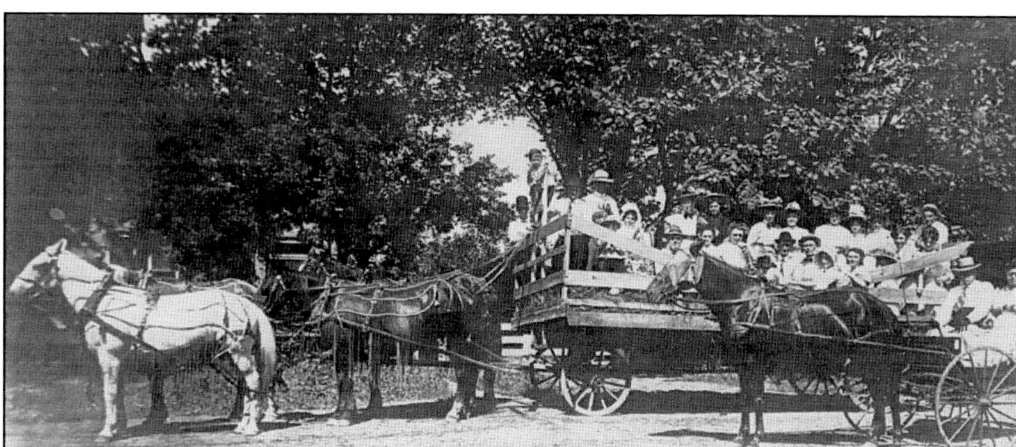

The Downs Celebration of 1904 featured a prize for the wagon bringing the largest group to the festivities. This photograph displays what we trust was one of the main contenders.

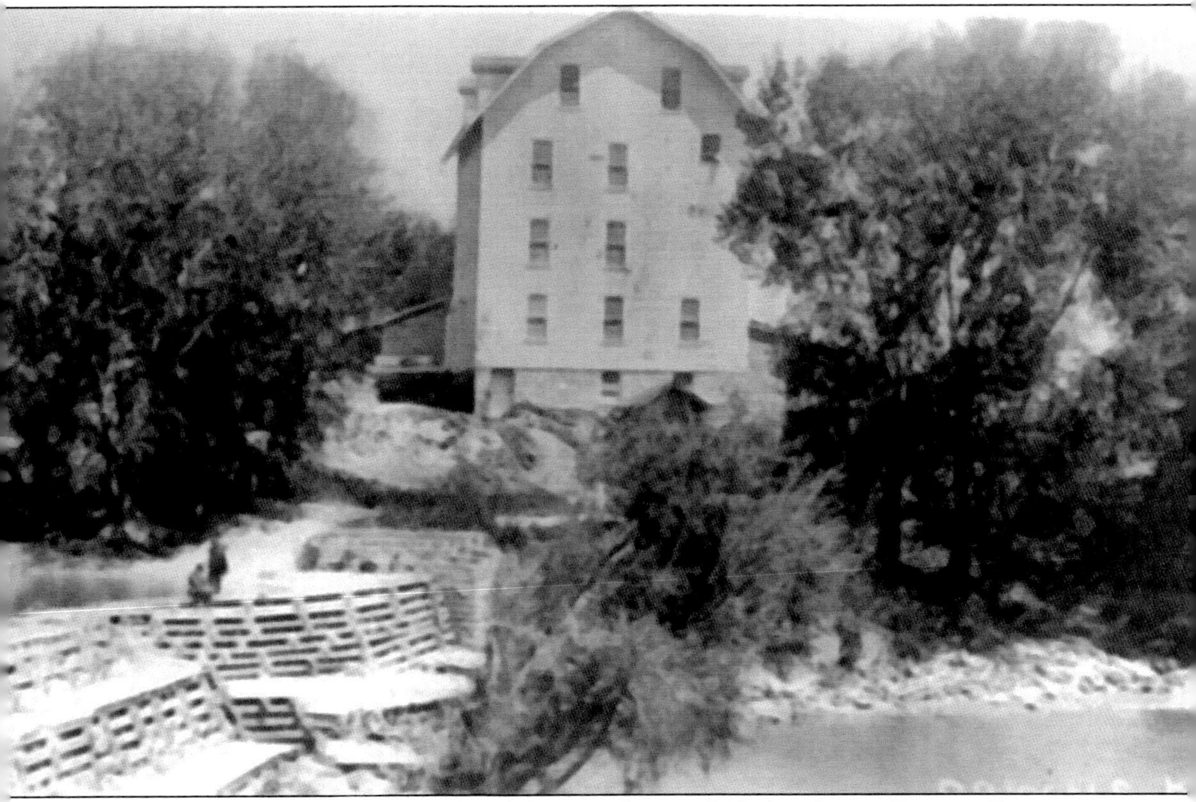

This view is of the Jackson Mill and mill dam on the North Fork Solomon River at Downs in the early 1900s. The wood-and-stone dam was a popular fishing and picnicking spot among the Downs citizenry for years. After the mill burned in the 1930s, the dam was allowed to deteriorate and eventually destroyed by the river waters.

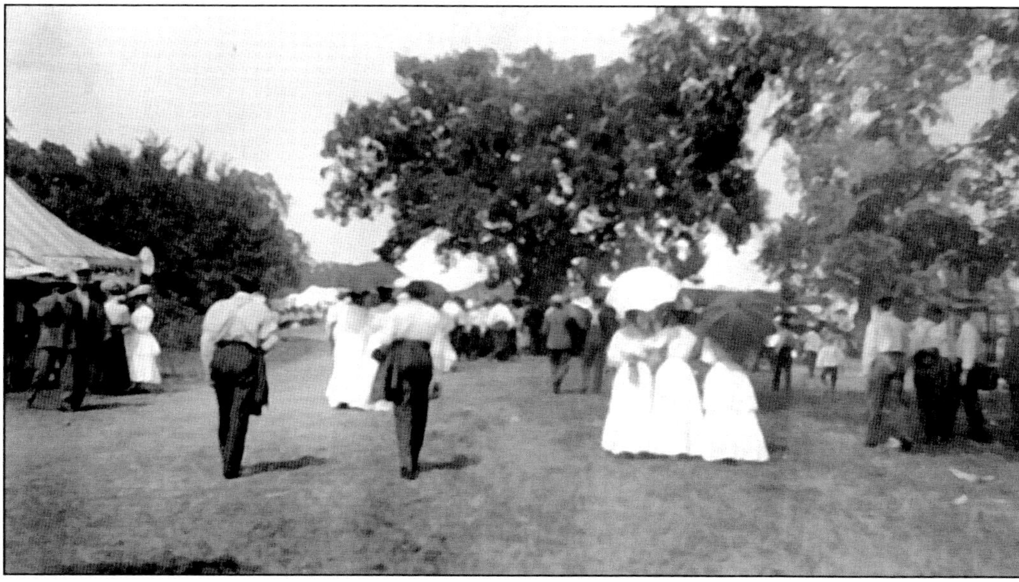

Leased in 1882 by W.C. Whitney as a 30-acre recreation site on Oak Creek 3 1/2 miles east of Downs in Mitchell County, Kansas, Lincoln Park grew in popularity until permanent annual camp meetings were established in 1896. In 1901 it became the Lincoln Park Chautauqua. Thousands came to hear educational and religious programs, as well as to hear speakers ranging from governors and presidents to popular entertainers of the day.

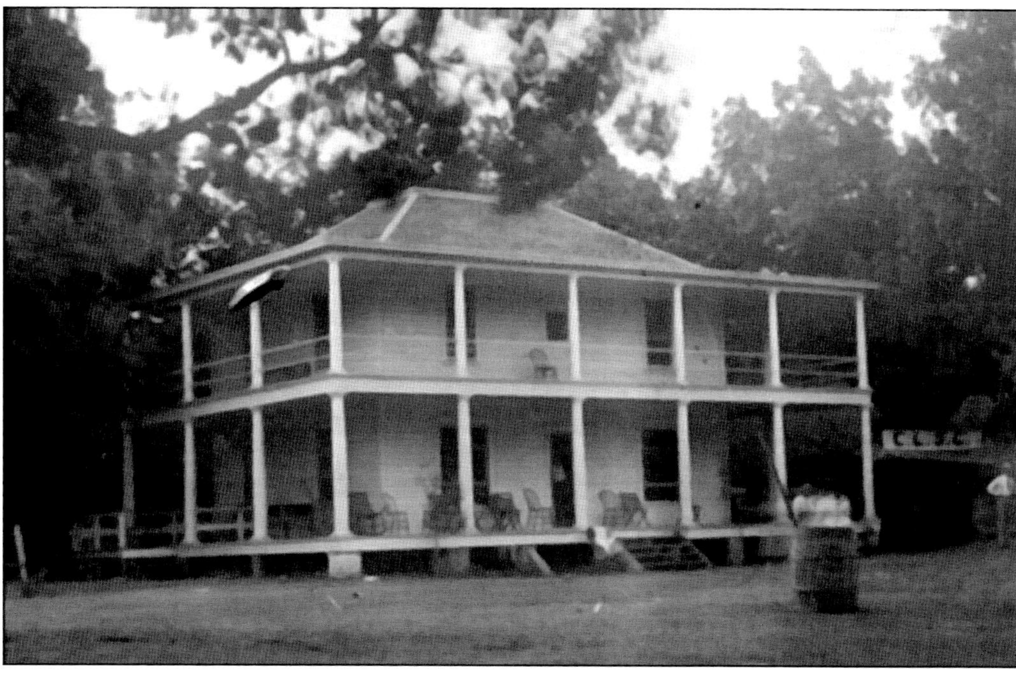

One of two permanent buildings built in Lincoln Park in 1906 was the Lillian Stevens Hall, which was funded by the WCTU. At its peak, the two-week Chautauqua was so popular that the Missouri Pacific Railroad ran special "Chautauqua trains" twice daily from Downs and Kansas City. Financial troubles, however, closed the park in 1913. During World War II the park's buildings were used as a German POW camp.

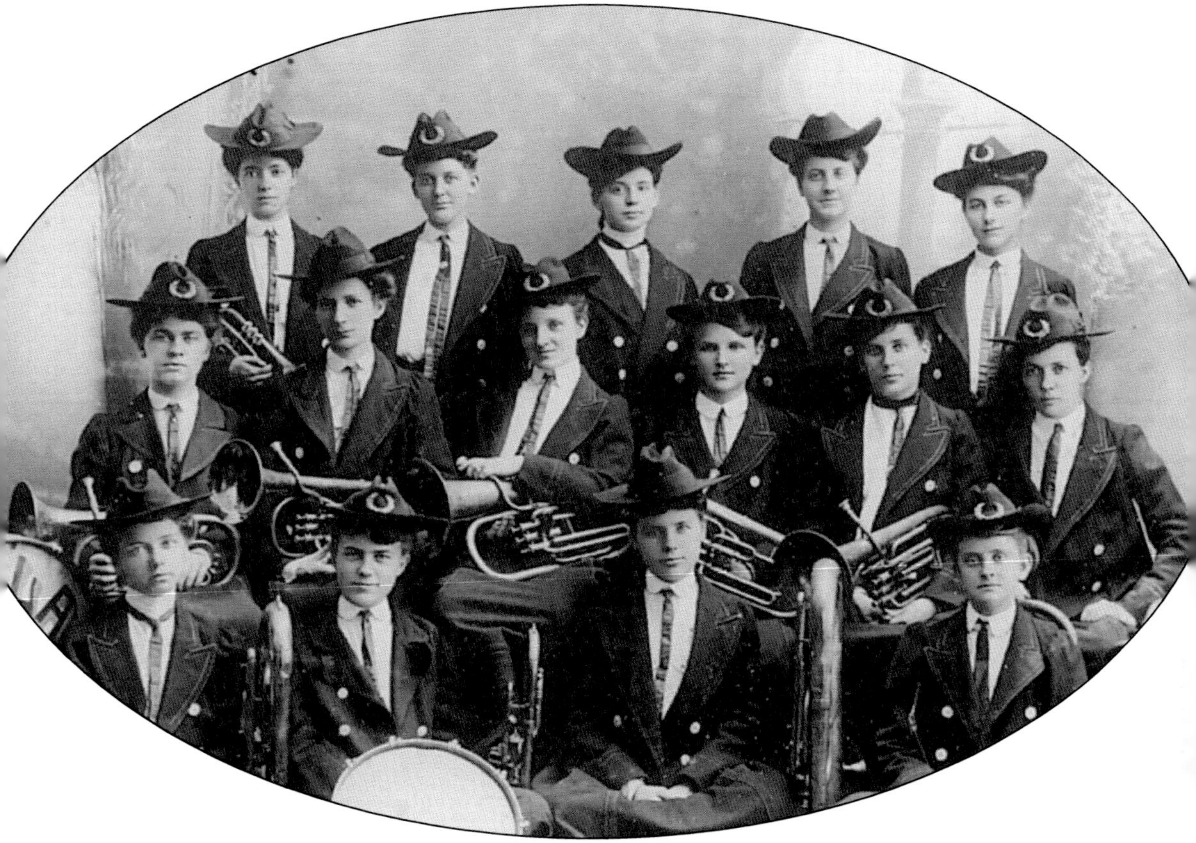

The Young Ladies Band of Downs was extremely popular during its brief years together. Clothed in uniforms of red suits, white waists, and red neckties, the Ladies came together in 1901 and embarked on a triumphant touring schedule across northern Kansas, much to the delight of young men everywhere. But sadly, all good things come to an end, and in August 1904 the Ladies organization disbanded.

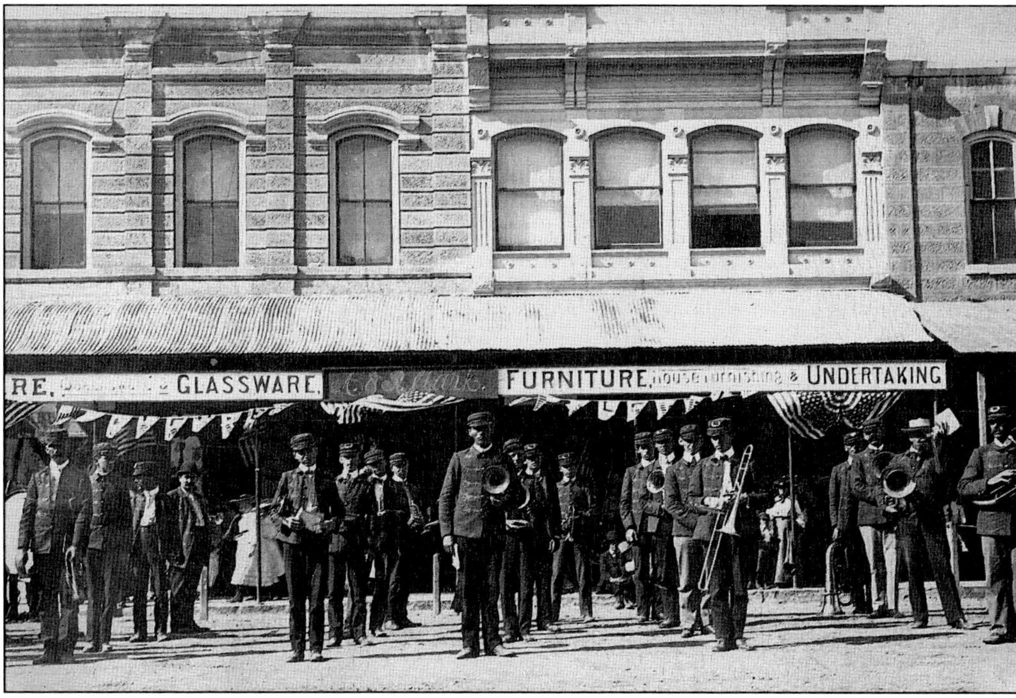

Pictured here is the 1903 Osborne Community Band in parade formation on West Main Street. Bands were a source of local pride for every city and town and Osborne was no exception. The city regularly provided funds for a band from the early 1880s until the 1930s, when backing for bands shifted to the school system's music department and their marching band, which carried on the tradition.

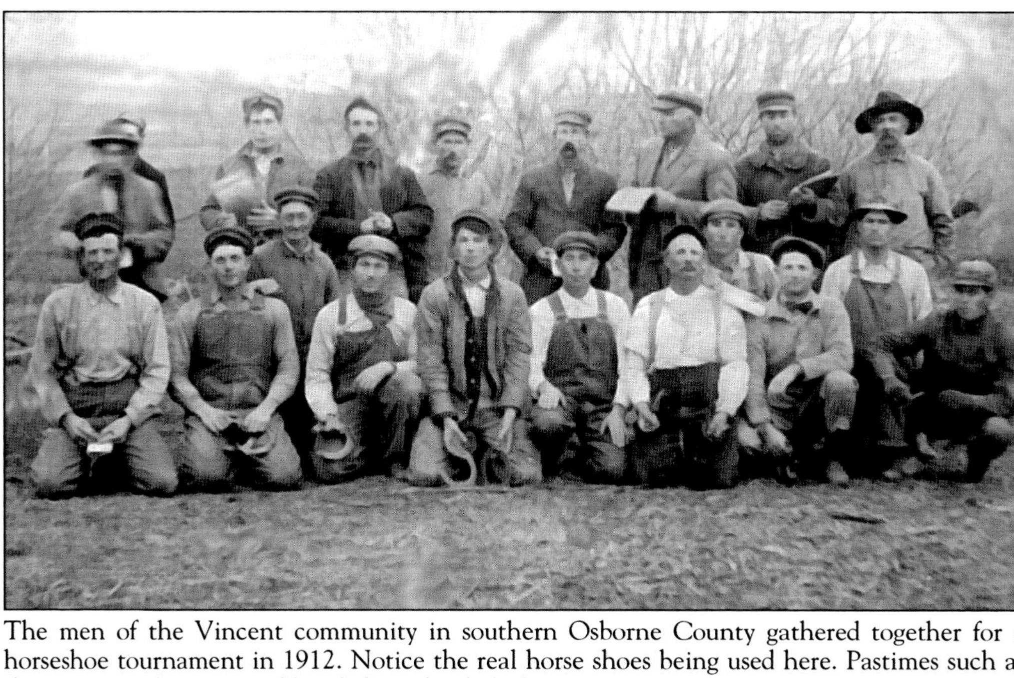

The men of the Vincent community in southern Osborne County gathered together for a horseshoe tournament in 1912. Notice the real horse shoes being used here. Pastimes such as this were a welcome social break from the daily farming routine.

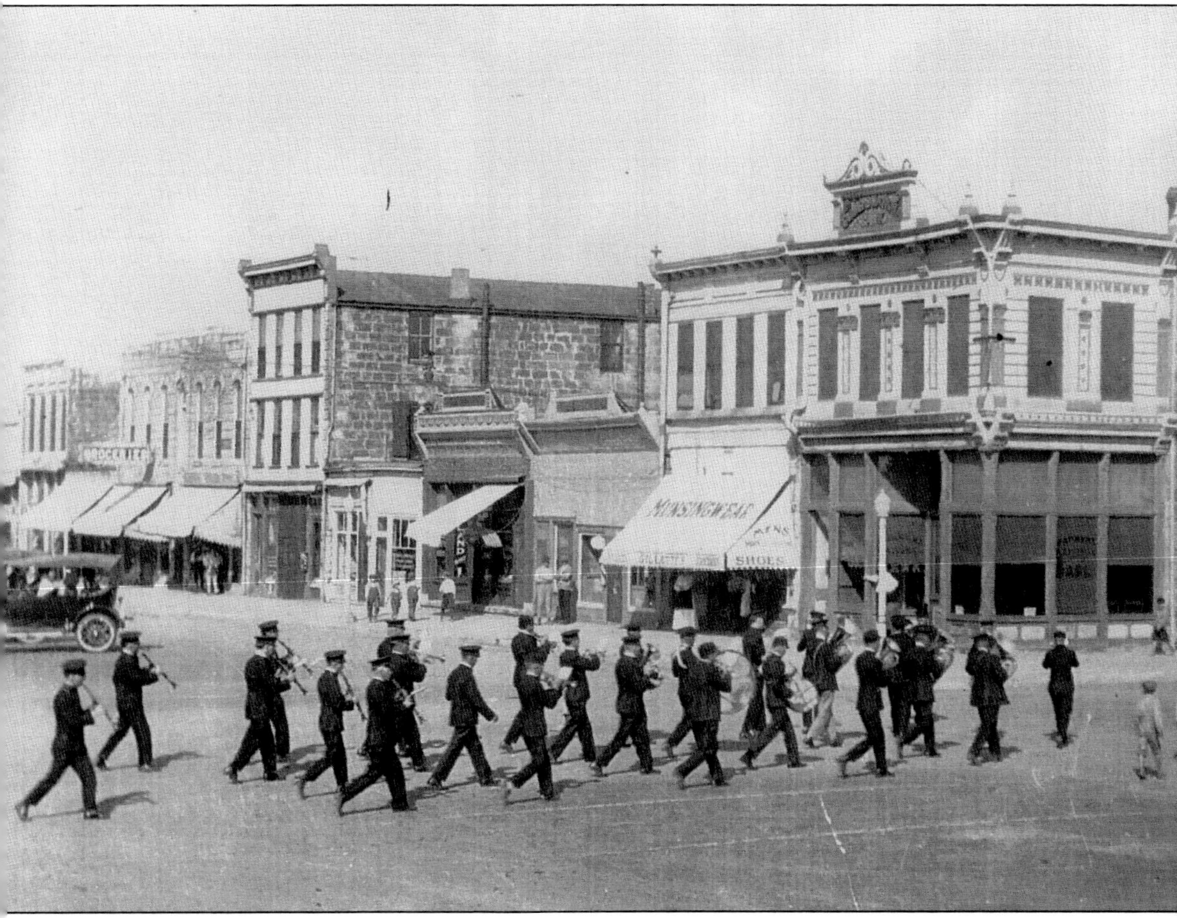

This is the Osborne Community Band turning off of South First Street onto West Main Street in the 1910s. The band remained a symbol of civic pride for decades. The picture shows a time when cars were allowed to park in the middle of Main Street. On the right can be seen the original front of the Farmer's National Bank, which began business in 1901.

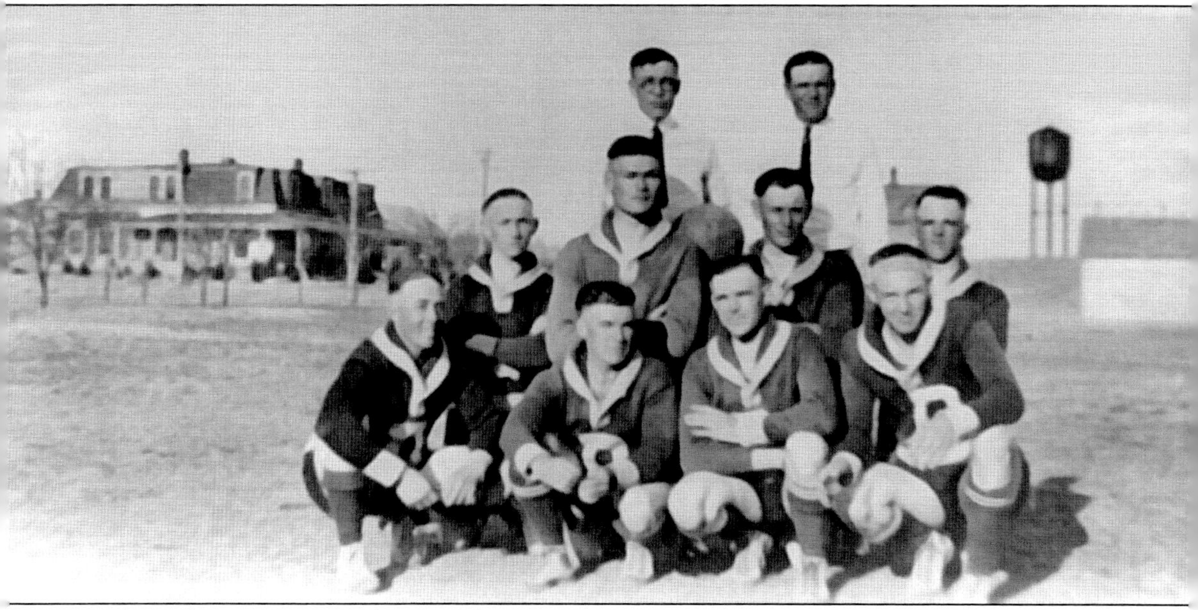

Shown here is a 1920s edition of the Portis Dynamos, Portis' much-feared town team, coached by their local newspaper editor Emmett Kissell. The Dynamos came together in 1913 and quickly became the scourge of Northwest Kansas as they routinely defeated opponents of every size and scope for 20 years. Even over 80 years later stories of the Dynamos continue to enliven their legendary status. Seen at left in the background of the picture is Dr. Claude Burtch's private hospital, which he ran in 1927–52. The Portis water tower is located in the right of the photograph.

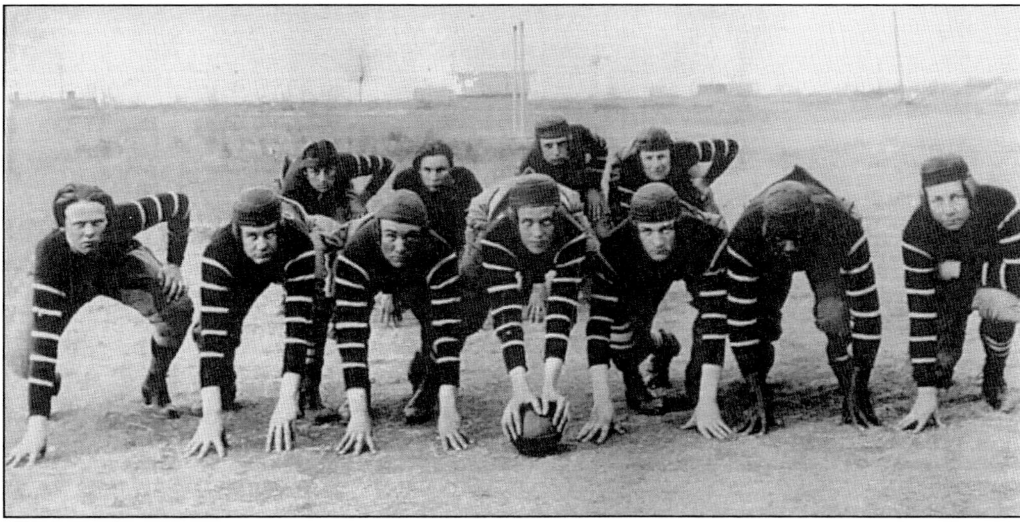

Captured in this photograph from 1921 is the high school football team scrimmage of the Downs Dragons. The almost no padding of the uniforms was the rule of the day.

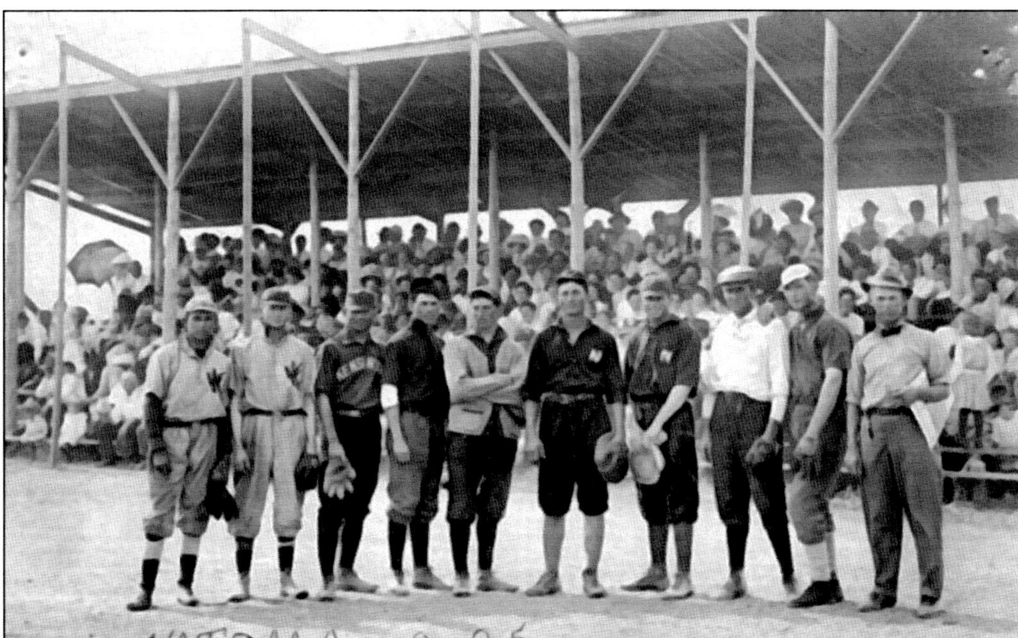

A meeting of the managers and captains before play begins at Natoma's baseball diamond on South Main Street in August 1925. It is believed that a tournament was in progress from the variety of uniforms. This was Natoma's first baseball team. The first baseball game played in Osborne County occurred in May 1871 at Osborne. In it the settlers used tree branches for bats and rock-hard soda biscuits for balls.

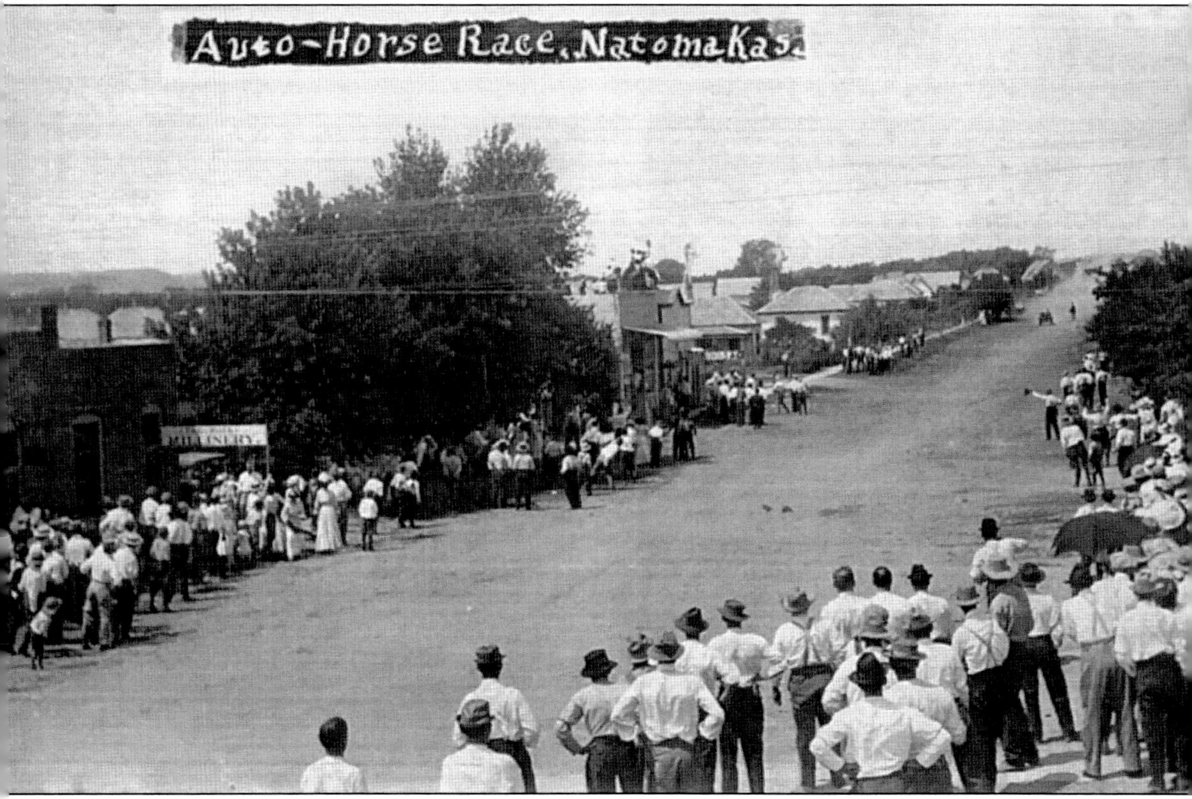

A large crowd gathered in Natoma to witness the highly publicized Auto Horse Race believed to be held about 1908. The race started a half mile north of town and came down a large sloping hill. The horse had the early lead and should have easily won, but horses tend to hold back running down a slope and this enabled the car to gain speed on the slope and eventually win the race.

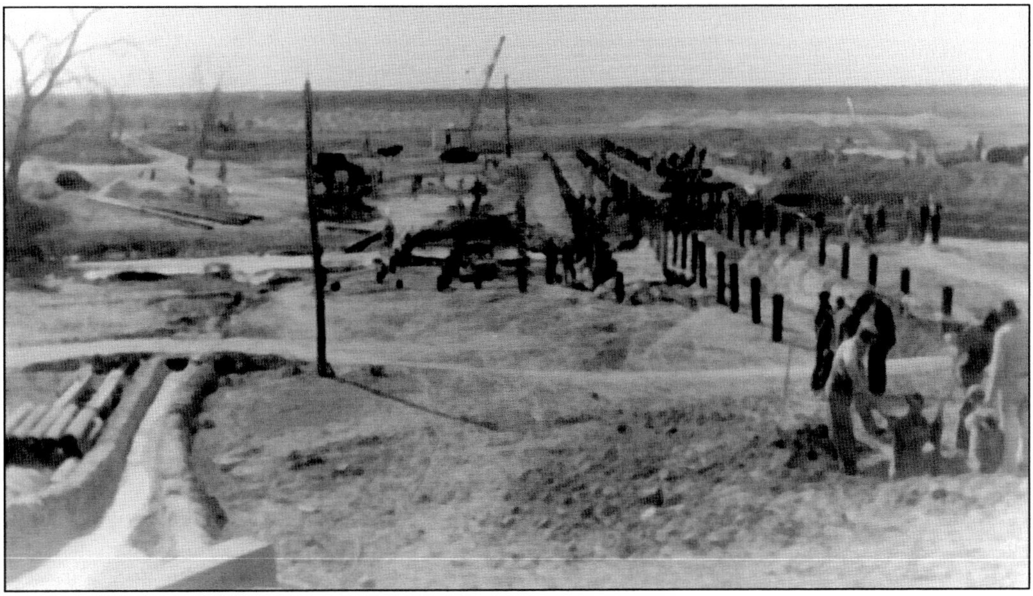

This photograph looks west at the construction site for the new dam being built on the South Fork Solomon River a mile west of Osborne in 1936. The large wooden posts were driven into the ground by a large steam shovel pile driver seen in the center background. The dam was a joint KERC and WPA project and was dedicated before a crowd of thousands in 1936.

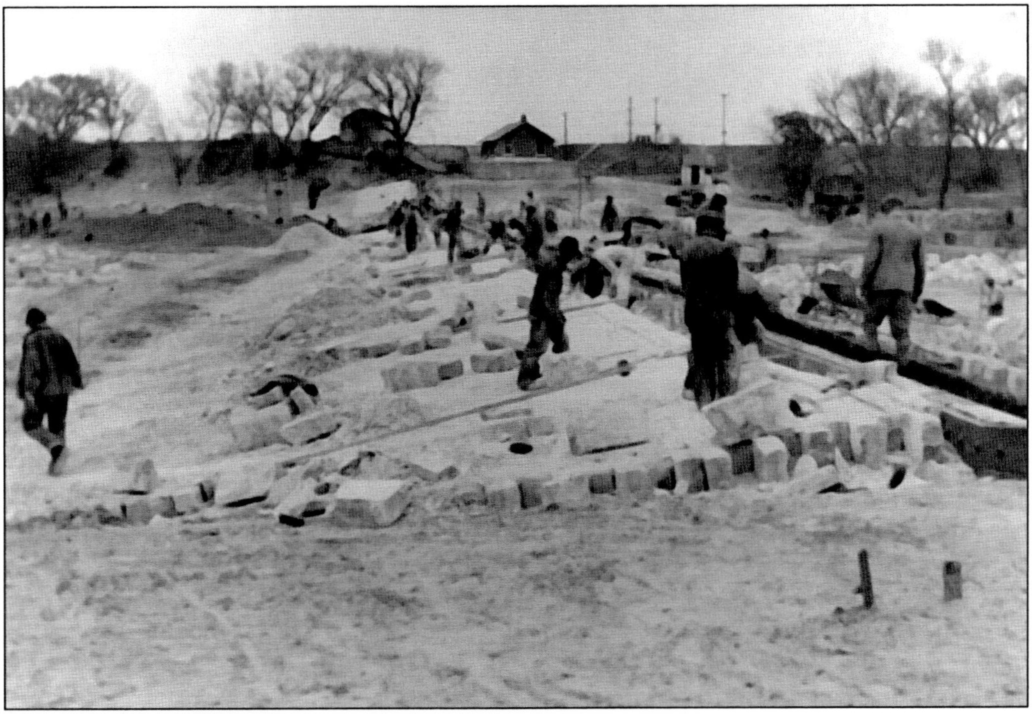

Viewed from the west, these workers are laying stone across the face of the new dam on the South Fork Solomon River west of Osborne in 1936. The impounded lake behind the dam was to both provide recreation and serve as a city water supply. But within a few months most of the new lake bed had silted in and the majority of the dam was left high and dry.

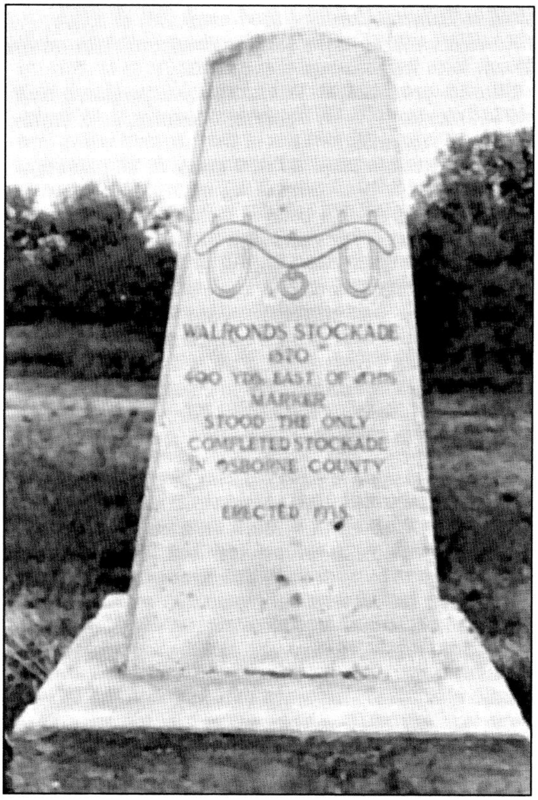

Taken in 1938, this photograph is of the newly placed Walrond Stockade historical marker located a mile south of Portis. By the late 1930s Osborne County was 65 years old, and with its formative years behind them the county's citizens now had time to view its history and to begin preserving it for future generations. In 1937 the county commissioners began this preservation by having four markers placed at the county's early stockades.

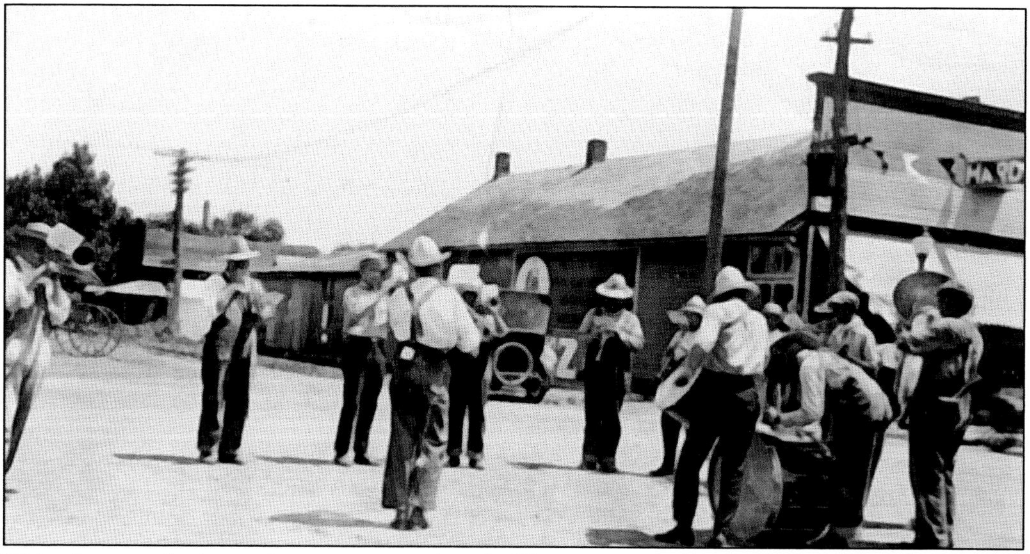

This photograph shows the community band of Luray at a practice session in the early 1930s. Luray is located just over the border from southern Osborne County in Russell County. While they may have practiced in overalls and farm hats as shown here, whenever a performance was at hand, the band's appearance in uniform evoked both pride and appreciation in their fellow citizens.